THE LAST
1000
YEARS

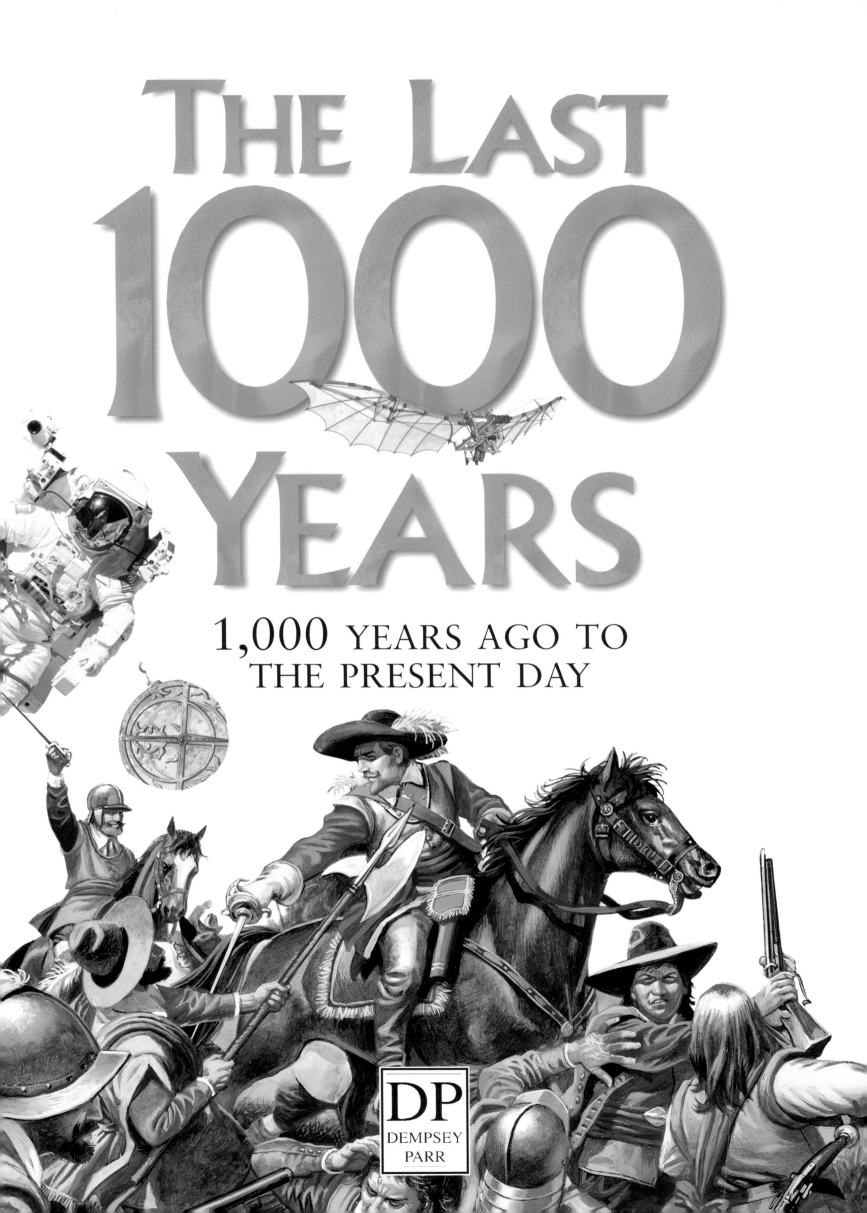

THE LAST
1000
YEARS

1,000 YEARS AGO TO
THE PRESENT DAY

DP

DEMPSEY
PARR

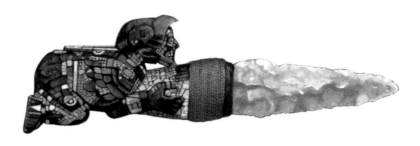

First published in 1999 by
Dempsey Parr
Dempsey Parr is an imprint of Parragon

Parragon
Queen Street House, 4 Queen Street, Bath BA1 1HE, UK

2 4 6 8 10 9 7 5 3 1

Copyright © Parragon 1999

Produced by Miles Kelly Publishing Ltd
11, Bardfield Centre, Great Bardfield, Essex CM7 4SL

ISBN 1 84084 507 4

Printed in Korea

AUTHORS
Anita Ganeri, Hazel Mary Martell, Brian Williams

GENERAL EDITOR
Charlotte Hurdman

DESIGN AND ART DIRECTION
Full Steam Ahead Ltd

SENIOR EDITOR
Rosie Alexander

ARTWORK COMMISSIONING
Branka Surla

PICTURE RESEARCH
Rosie Alexander, Kate Miles, Elaine Willis, Yannick Yago

EDITORIAL ASSISTANT
Lynne French

CONSULTANTS
Theodore Rowland-Entwistle, John Sherman

ADDITIONAL EDITORIAL HELP FROM
Suzanne Airey, Hilary Bird, Jenni Cozens, Pat Crisp, Paul Kilgour, Joanne Murray

EDITORIAL DIRECTOR
Jim Miles

Contents

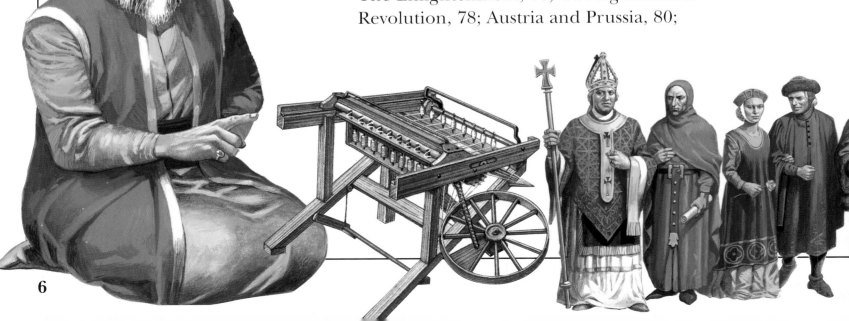

THE MODERN WORLD 112
Toward the Millennium 1900–1990s

REFERENCE PAGES 158

INDEX 170

Acknowledgments 176

The Last 1,000 Years

△ **The Domesday Book** was a nationwide survey of England (except the far north) made on the orders of William the conqueror in 1085. It was divided into two volumes, one covering the richest counties of Essex, Suffolk, and Norfolk, the other covering the remaining counties.

△ **Viking runes** carved on a stone. The letters of the Viking alphabet, called runes, were used to carve everyday messages on wood, metal, and stone. Some rune stones tell stories from Viking history recalling battles and heroic deeds.

One thousand years of history seems a vast amount of time, but humans and our ancestors have lived on Earth for at least two million years. The first civilizations appeared about 3500BC.

One of the first great civilizations grew up in Egypt. The Ancient Egyptians flourished along the River Nile in Africa in an empire that lasted for more than three thousand years. In Europe, the classical world of Ancient Greece and Rome, stretching across the thousand years from about 500BC to AD500, played a major role in shaping the modern world. Greek ideas in politics, philosophy, and science were spread by the Romans, who ruled over the most powerful empire the world had yet seen.

This book, however, concentrates on the last millennium, or one thousand years, of world history. The period from AD1000 to 2000 has seen our lives transformed. One thousand years ago the vast majority of people throughout the world lived off the land. Europe had just entered the Middle Ages, while China was far in advance of the rest of the world. This prosperous country already enjoyed the benefits of printing, paper money, and a postal system.

From the early 1400s, explorers from Europe set out to discover new routes to the great riches of the Far East. Sailors charted unknown waters and came across new lands and peoples. These contacts brought

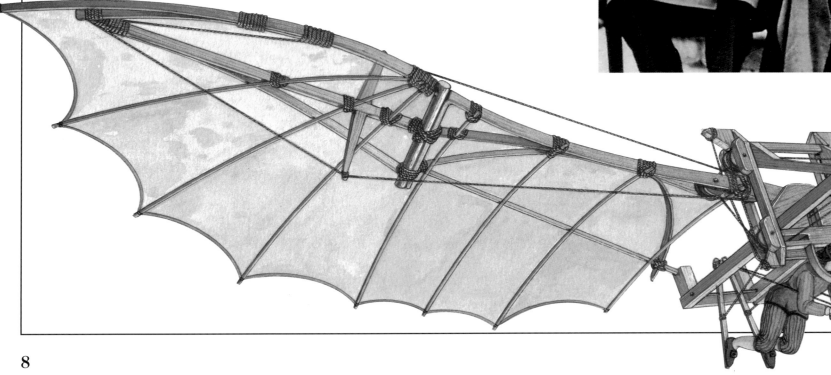

△ **Julius Caesar** (c. 101–44 BC) was a great general and dictator of the Roman empire. The culture, politics, and technology of the Romans still influence our lives today.

▽ **Churchill, Roosevelt, and Stalin** meet at the Yalta conference in February 1945. The years following World War II were shadowed by a bitter rivalry between the two superpowers, the United States and the former Soviet Union.

wealth and power to Europe, but disease and misery to many native populations.

Up until the 1700s, most countries were ruled by absolute monarchs. New ideas about personal freedom, however, began to challenge this power. Revolutions in America and France saw an end to the old order. Completely new methods of farming and industrialization helped Britain to become, by 1850, one of the most powerful countries in the world.

The 1900s has seen the world torn apart by two world wars and the development of weapons capable of vast destruction. It has also seen modern explorers leave the confines of our planet, a revolution in civil rights and equality between peoples. At the start of a new millennium, amazing advances in technology and communications have brought the peoples of the world much closer together.

▷ **Anne Frank's diary** is a vivid account of life for Jews living in Nazi occupied Europe during World War II.

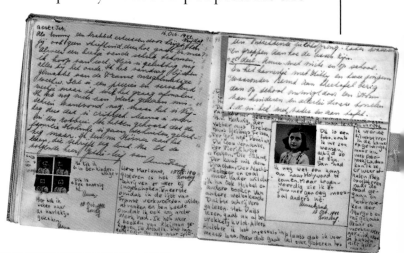

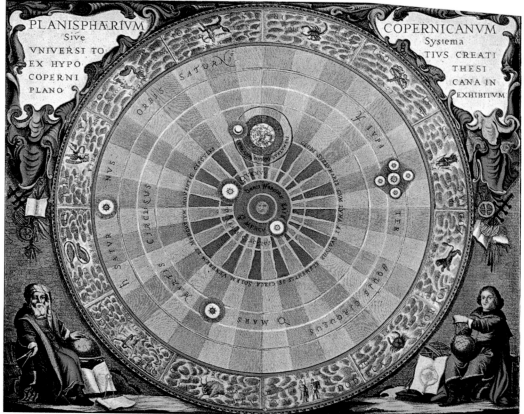

◁ **Leonardo da Vinci** (1452–1519) was a pioneer inventor and artist. This reconstruction of his flying machine was taken from detailed designs he made. His work, although ahead of its time, shows an explosion of interest in science.

△ **Nicolaus Copernicus** (1473–1543) was the first modern astronomer. He was the first person to prove that the Earth moved around the Sun at a time when everyone believed that the Earth was the center of the universe.

The Vikings

The Vikings set sail from their homelands in Scandinavia (Norway, Sweden, and Denmark) to raid the coasts and rivers of Europe, reaching to the Mediterranean and the Black seas. But not all the Vikings were raiders—many were peaceful farmers and traders who chose to settle in the new lands.

The Vikings' homelands in Scandinavia had mountains and forests, but little good farmland. Most Vikings lived close to the sea, tending small fields where they grew rye, barley, wheat, and oats, and vegetables such as turnips and carrots. They kept cattle and sheep, and caught fish in the rivers and fiords. Traders traveled on horseback or by boat to market towns like Kaupang in Norway or Hedeby in Denmark, to sell furs, reindeer antlers, and walrus ivory in exchange for weapons, jewels, and pottery.

Viking families lived in houses made of wood, stone, or turf. Smoke from the cooking fire found its way out through a hole in the roof, and in the smoky darkness people sat at wooden benches and tables to eat. Around the fire they played dice games and told stories. The Vikings loved telling stories, especially about their heroes and gods. The most important god was Odin the wise and one-eyed, but the most popular was Thor, the thunder god, whose symbol was a hammer.

THE VIKINGS

Late 700s The trading town of Hedeby in Denmark is founded.

841 Vikings found Dublin on east coast of Ireland.

850 Probable date of the Oseberg ship burial in Oslo Fiord, Norway; it is the richest Viking ship-burial so far found.

c. 860 Vikings begin to settle in the Baltic region. Vikings rule Novgorod in Russia.

c. 861 Ingolf is the first Viking to reach Iceland.

862 Vikings led by Rurik are invited by the Slavic and Finnish peoples of north Russia to rule them.

874 First Viking settlers reach Iceland.

900s Viking traders visit Constantinople, which they call Miklagaard.

960 King Harald Bluetooth of Denmark becomes a Christian.

982 Erik the Red reaches Greenland and founds settlement.

c. 1000 Erik's son, Leif Eriksson, lands in North America and calls the new land Vinland. But the Vikings never succeed in making a permanent settlement there.

1000 Jorvik is a prosperous town of about 10,000 people, the biggest Viking settlement in England.

1030 At the end of the reign of King Olaf the Holy, Norway is Christian.

1100s Swedish Vikings are the last to give up their old gods and convert to Christianity.

▷ *Many Vikings lived on small farms, often near rivers or the sea. They planted cereals and vegetables, and kept pigs, cows, goats, and sheep.*

Everyone worked hard. A Viking farmer often had thralls (slaves) to help with the work, but most men were karls (freemen). The leader of each community was the richest landowner or jarl, who was expected to share his wealth with his followers, by feasting and entertaining them in his great hall. The most powerful jarls in each country became King Viking leaders and tried to prevent quarrels becoming bitter blood-feuds between families. They also led bands of warriors on voyages.

The Vikings grew rich through trade and agriculture and as the population increased, farmland became increasingly scarce. From the late 700s, the Vikings began to venture from their homelands in search of better farmland and more riches.

Vikings were tough. They were used to hardship. They enjoyed huge meals, stirring tales of heroes, and physical sports such as wrestling, horse fights, and ice skating.

THE THING

The Viking law court was called the Thing. It was a meeting of local people held every year, and normally lasted for several days. Any freeman who had a complaint or an argument to settle could speak at the Thing. His neighbors would listen to his complaint or to both sides of a disagreement, and then give a judgment. A person refusing to obey the Thing's verdict became an outlaw— anyone could kill them.

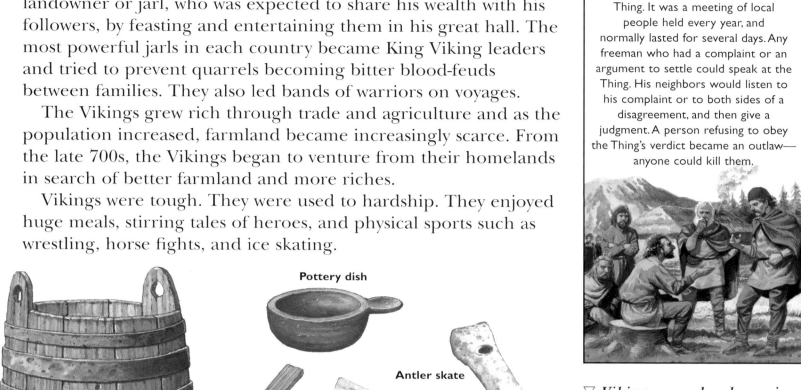

Pottery dish

Antler skate

Wooden bucket

Iron knife

Carved stone

Leather shoe

▽ *Vikings wore hard-wearing clothes* made from woolen or linen cloth. Women wore a linen dress with a wool tunic on top, fastened by brooches. Keys or combs hung from a chain, since the clothes had no pockets.

△ *Viking farmers made the most of their household items,* including tools, clothes, and furniture. They also made things to sell at market. Wood, ivory, deer antler, leather, pottery, bone, and iron were common materials.

The Vikings Abroad

When the Vikings sailed overseas in their longships, they were ready to kill and plunder. They went in search of trade and new lands in which to make their homes.

Viking longships were fast and strong enough to cross oceans. From the late 700s bands of Vikings set sail from Scandinavia to land on the coasts of western Europe. The sight of a Viking sail soon caused panic, for people knew the Vikings were fierce fighters with their favorite weapons—iron swords and axes. They raided monasteries and towns, carrying off slaves and booty.

The Vikings were also looking to seize land. Viking attacks on England began in 787, and from 865 Vikings from Denmark had begun to settle in eastern England. Vikings also settled in the Orkney and Shetland islands off the coast of Scotland, and the Isle of Man and Ireland. They attacked what is now France, but were bought off with the gift of Normandy in 911.

Sailing west into the Atlantic Ocean, Norwegian Vikings settled in Iceland (874) and Greenland (982), and landed in North America (c. 1000).

WEIGHING COINS

Vikings valued coins by weight, so many traders carried balance scales to check that a customer's money was good and to show another merchant that he wasn't being cheated. Small lead weights such as those below were used to check coins. Small scales for weighing silver have been found at Jorvik and other Viking settlements.

Lead weights

Silver penny

Scale

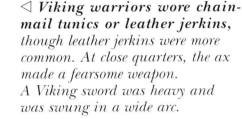

◁ **Viking warriors wore chain-mail tunics or leather jerkins,** *though leather jerkins were more common. At close quarters, the ax made a fearsome weapon. A Viking sword was heavy and was swung in a wide arc.*

▽ **Raiders rush from their longships** *during an attack on the English coast. The oared ships could be rowed up rivers and land on beaches, so Vikings often took their enemies by surprise.*

Swedish Vikings traveled as far east as the Black Sea, trading with Greeks and Arabs who called them the Rus—from which comes the name Russia. Vikings wandered in the markets of Baghdad and Constantinople, and goods from such exotic places found their way back to Viking towns such as Jorvik (York) in England and Dublin in Ireland.

Where Vikings settled, they often mingled with the local people. In England, King Alfred of Wessex led the fight against the invaders, but Viking settlements in eastern England (the Danelaw) left a permanent legacy in customs, laws, place names, and language. Viking words, for example, include knife and calf.

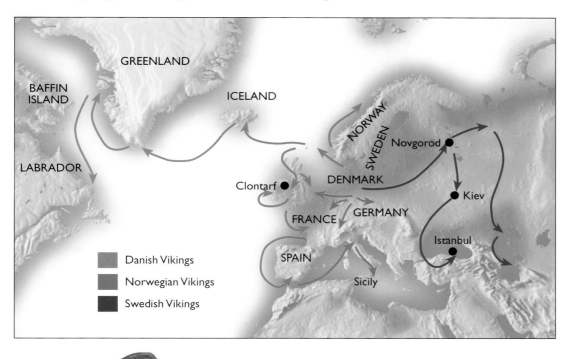

- Danish Vikings
- Norwegian Vikings
- Swedish Vikings

△ **Viking trade routes took** *them by sea and overland from Scandinavian market towns such as Hedeby (Denmark) to Jorvik (York), Dublin, Iceland, and the Baltic. Vikings traveled as far east as Novgorod (Russia), Baghdad, and Istanbul.*

THE VIKINGS ABROAD

787 First reported Viking raids on English coast.

795 Vikings begin attacks on Ireland.

834 Vikings raid Dorestad (in what is now the Netherlands).

865 Great army of Vikings lands in England.

866 The Vikings capture the city of York (Jorvik) in England.

878 English and Vikings agree to divide England between them after Vikings are defeated by King Alfred.

886 Viking siege of Paris is lifted after they are paid a huge treasure by King Charles II of France.

911 Vikings under Rollo are given Normandy to prevent further attacks on France.

1014 Irish victory at the battle of Clontarf means that the Viking dominance of Ireland is at an end.

1016–1035 Reign of Canute, Viking king of England, Denmark and Norway.

1066 Last big Viking attack on England, by Harold Hardrada of Norway. His army is defeated by King Harold at the battle of Stamford Bridge.

1066 William, Duke of Normandy, defeats King Harold at the battle of Hastings, England.

1072–1091 Norman armies conquer Sicily.

LIFE IN A CASTLE

500 Byzantines build strong stone castles and walled cities.

800s Arabs build castles in the Middle East and North Africa.

950 Earliest known French castle built at Doue-la-Fontaine, Anjou.

1000s Normans develop the motte (mound) and bailey (enclosure) castle. Normans wear chain mail armor.

1078 William I begins building the Tower of London, England.

1100s Stone keeps become the main castle stronghold.

1142 Crusaders take over Krak des Chevaliers in Syria.

1150–1250 Thousands of castles are built across what is now Germany.

1180s Castles with square-walled towers are built.

1200s The concentric or ring-wall castle is developed. Soldiers returning from the Crusades bring this improved design to Europe.

1205 Krak des Chevaliers is rebuilt by Knights.

▷ *Feasting in the great hall. The lord and lady sit on a raised dais, and knights and other members of the household at lower tables. Servants carry food from the kitchen outside, while dogs scavenge for scraps.*

Life in a Castle

Castles formed a mighty chain, linking together a conqueror's lands. Mighty stone fortresses dotted the landscape of Europe and the Middle East throughout the Middle Ages.

The earliest medieval castles were earth-mounds with a wooden stockade on top. Castles like these were built by the Norman invaders of England, often on the site of earlier Saxon and Roman forts. They were soon enlarged and strengthened, with water-filled ditches or moats, stone walls protected by towers, and a massive central stronghold called a keep. Castles were often built on hilltops, or to guard harbors, rivers, and vital roads.

Medieval castles were private fortresses for the king or lord who owned them. Safe inside, he ruled his lands and planned to make war on his enemies. A castle was also a family home, although early castles were cold and drafty, with no glass in the windows and only rushes on the stone floor. In the great hall, the lord and his followers feasted on food carried by servants from the kitchen. At night, everyone slept on the floor around the central fire, while the lord and his lady retired to their small private room, known as the solar. Before 1300, there were no bathrooms and lavatories emptied into the surrounding moat. For amusement, the lord and his friends hunted deer and boar in the forest or watched trained falcons bring down their prey.

The castle was patrolled and defended by foot-soldiers with spears and bows and by armored knights on horseback. Knights practiced with sword, lance, and ax, with their squires—young men training to be knights. When a castle was attacked, the defenders needed enough food and water to withstand a siege

◁ **Knights carried shields to ward off blows** and to identify themselves to friends. In the later Middle Ages, a shield displayed its owner's coat of arms (family symbol).

lasting weeks or even months. The castle walls had to be thick enough to stand firm against catapults, tunnels, and battering rams. The occupants often suffered from starvation or disease, and were forced to surrender. In due course, cannon and barrels of gunpowder placed in tunnels were far more effective at knocking down walls. This new technology brought the age of castles to an end by the 1500s.

△ **Jousting was combat on horseback** between two knights with blunt-tipped lances. It took place in a field, and was a social occasion with a large audience. A tournament was a bigger, rougher affair, in which groups of knights fought mock battles, sometimes with fatal mishaps. Safety measures, including blunt swords and padded armor, were only introduced in the 1300s.

The Feudal System

In western Europe, feudalism was a form of contract in the European upper classes whereby power was wielded across different castle-dominated districts.

In the Middle Ages, land was owned by a powerful lord (a king or a nobleman) or by the Church. The lord gave land to those who followed him and fought for him, who were called vassals. In return, a vassal promised to serve his lord by fighting for him and collecting taxes from the people who lived on his land. This was the key idea behind feudalism.

Feudalism developed among the Franks in the 700s (see pages 66–67). There had been many years of fighting and confusion following the collapse of the Roman empire in the late 400s. The Franks thought that a warrior-chief should look after his followers and reward them in return for their loyalty. Chiefs, or lords, held the land on which poor people (peasants) lived. Instead of owning or renting their own land, peasant-farmers were bound to serve their lord. In return, the lord protected them. This was not a bad system in troubled times.

▷ **"March", from a 15th-century manuscript** Les Tres Riches Heures de duc de Berry, *by the Limbourg brothers. It shows shepherds, peasants, and springtime farm tasks.*

DOMESDAY BOOK

The Domesday (Doomsday) Book was a survey of England made on the orders of William the Conqueror in 1085. Commissioners took details of who owned what land, and how many people lived in each village, collecting figures for 1085 and 1066. There are records for most old English villages and towns, but not for London.

▷ *In feudal society, the king held land and power. Next came the barons and bishops, and the mounted knights. In the middle were merchants and town craftworkers. Servants, foot-soldiers and peasants came at the bottom.*

16

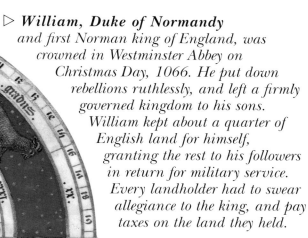

▷ **William, Duke of Normandy**
and first Norman king of England, was crowned in Westminster Abbey on Christmas Day, 1066. He put down rebellions ruthlessly, and left a firmly governed kingdom to his sons. William kept about a quarter of English land for himself, granting the rest to his followers in return for military service. Every landholder had to swear allegiance to the king, and pay taxes on the land they held.

Feudalism grew as kings granted more land to knights, the brave warriors on whose loyalty and fighting skills kings depended. It spread from France to England and Spain and was taken by the Crusaders to the East. Each lord governed his own lands, where his word was law. If there was war, he had to supply soldiers to the king's army. He acted as judge in disputes between his vassals, whether they were lesser nobles or humble peasants.

The feudal system began to fall apart in the 1200s. One reason was economic: people began to use money more, and preferred to pay rent for land rather than be bound by feudal service.

In the 1300s, new weapons such as crossbows, gunpowder, and cannon changed the way wars were fought. Cannons could smash castle walls and crossbows could pierce armor. Feudal lords and knights became less powerful.

THE FEUDAL SYSTEM

Late 400s Fall of the Roman empire leads to a breakdown in law and order across western Europe.

700s Feudal system starts among the Franks, based on arrangements for land-holding and defense. Threat of attack by Muslims from Spain encourages its spread.

700s Vassals have to supply soldiers to serve the lord on a certain number of days, usually 40 in every year.

1066 Normans bring the feudal system to England and strengthen it.

1100 It is now usual for a lord's oldest son to inherit his land holding or fief. (The word feudal comes from a Latin name for fief.)

1200s Feudalism becomes more complex, with layers of vassal-lord relationships from the king downward.

1215 King John signs the Magna Carta, limiting the powers of the King of England.

1265 Simon de Montfort, a baron, calls ordinary citizens to a meeting with barons and churchmen—the first real Parliament in England. This rebellion against King Henry III fails, but royal power in England is never the same again.

1300s Knights become less effective against bowmen and cannon. This speeds the end of feudalism.

Knight   **Merchant**   **Archer**   **Peasant**   **Beggar**

The Crusades

For European Christians, the Crusades were holy wars, with the promise of plunder in the service of the Church. For more than 200 years, Christian and Muslim armies fought for control of the Holy Land, the territory around Jerusalem in the Middle East.

Many Christian pilgrims visited Jerusalem, which was a holy city to Jews and Muslims, as well as to Christians. But Jerusalem was held by Muslim Turks and, in 1095, they banned Christian pilgrims from the city. This angered both the western Christian church based in Rome and the eastern Christian church based in Constantinople. From Rome, Pope Urban II called on Christians to free Jerusalem and so launched the First Crusade, or war of the cross. In 1096 a European force joined with a Byzantine army from Constantinople. Their leaders were inspired by religious faith and by a less spiritual desire to increase territory and wealth.

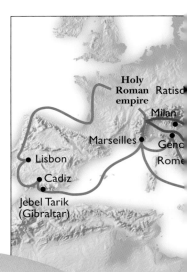

▽ *Krak des Chevaliers*, now in Syria, has sheer rock walls on three sides and a moat. The Muslims captured it by sending in a fake letter. Believing the message was a surrender order from their own leaders, the Crusaders inside opened the gates.

Holy Roman empire   Ratisd
Milan
Marseilles   Genc
Lisbon   Rome
Cadiz
Jebel Tarik (Gibraltar)

Impenetrable, steep ramparts

Catapults threw rocks and flaming tar

Battering rams broke down walls

Round towers gave defenders better angles for arrows

Boiling oil was poured on the attackers

▽ *Once Crusaders had conquered lands,* *they built strong castles to defend them. To capture a castle, soldiers had to break down massive gates, while arrows, boiling oil, and rocks were thrown on their heads. Castle defenders under siege faced starvation and bombardment by giant catapults which lobbed balls of flaming tar, the heads of prisoners, or diseased corpses over the walls.*

KEY

— *First Crusade*
— *Second Crusade*
— *Third Crusade*

▷ *Crusaders found the weather in the lands around Jerusalem incredibly hot. They soon learned from the Muslim soldiers and wore airy, loose robes over their armor and protected their heads from the Sun. They wore a red cross on their surcoat.*

◁ *The journey to the Holy Land was long and mostly done on foot. Crusaders had to be tough to endure sickness, hunger, thirst, and attack as they dragged their armor and supplies over rough, often desert, terrain.*

A Crusader knight

A Muslim warrior

In three years they captured Jerusalem and went on to set up Christian kingdoms in Palestine. But none of the seven later crusades matched this success.

The Crusades inspired many stories. There was bravery and honor on both sides. But the Crusades also had a less noble side. Before the First Crusade even set out, a People's Crusade wandered across Europe. This peasant army burned villages and was eventually massacred by the Turks. Then the Fourth Crusade of 1202 turned aside to loot the Christian city of Constantinople.

In the end, the Crusaders failed to win back the Holy Land. Europeans learned more about Eastern art and science, foods, and medicine. Contacts and trade between Europe and Asia grew during the Crusades.

△ *Transport ships were loaded with soldiers and equipment bound for the Crusades. Special groups of knights were founded to protect Christians on their journey. These included the Knights Hospitallers and the Knights Templars who became rich and powerful.*

THE CHILDREN'S CRUSADE OF 1212

was inspired by two boy preachers. Fifty thousand children in two groups, one from France and one from Germany, set off for the Holy Land. Some children died on the journey across Europe. Many more were taken to North Africa and sold as slaves. The Pied Piper legend may be based on the tragedy of these lost children.

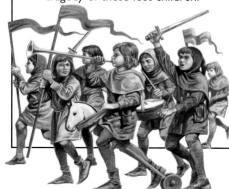

THE CRUSADES

1096 First Crusade is called by Pope Urban II. Peter the Hermit leads a peasant army across Europe.

1097 The main crusader army wins battle of Niceae (Turkey).

1099 The crusaders defeat the Turks and capture Jerusalem.

1147 Second Crusade sets out after Muslims capture the crusader kingdom of Edessa in 1144. German and French armies fail to cooperate and are beaten.

▷ *Saladin (1138–1193) was the greatest of the Muslim leaders who fought the Crusaders. He took Jerusalem, but in 1192 made peace with Richard I, allowing Christian pilgrims to enter the Holy City.*

1187 Saladin captures Jerusalem.

1189 Third Crusade is led by Frederick I Barbarossa of the Holy Roman empire, King Philip II of France, and King Richard I of England.

1191 Crusaders capture the port of Acre in Palestine.

1202 Fourth Crusade attacks Egypt instead of Palestine.

1204 Crusaders capture and bury Constantinople.

1212 Children's Crusade: few of 50,000 children return.

1221 Fifth Crusade: Crusaders fight the Sultan of Egypt.

1228 The Sixth Crusade ends when the Muslim sultan hands over Jerusalem.

1244 Muslims retake Jerusalem.

1249 Seventh Crusade is led by King Louis IX of France.

1270 Eighth Crusade also led by Louis. He and many of his men die of plague in Tunis.

1291 Acre, last crusader stronghold, is captured.

A Medieval Town

In the Middle Ages, towns in Europe were noisy and crowded by day, but quiet and dark at night, the silence broken only by cat and dog fights, late-night revelers, and watchmen calling out the hours. Churches, guilds, fairs, and markets all drew people into the towns.

If you walked through a medieval town, you took care where you stepped, because most people threw out their rubbish into the muddy streets. Open drains ran alongside and smelled awful. To fetch water, people went to the town well or bought it from the water seller, hoping it was clean. Pigs and chickens wandered in and out of small yards. Houses were built close together, with the top floors often jutting out over the street. Since most houses were made chiefly of wood, they caught fire easily. At night, the curfew bell warned people to cover or put out their kitchen fires.

Many houses were also shops and workplaces. Traders and craftworkers formed groups called guilds to organize their businesses and to set standards of work. Guilds also staged pageants, dramas, and religious processions, and set up training schools. Some towns were famous for their fairs and attracted foreign merchants from all over Europe, as well as entertainers such as jugglers, clowns, acrobats, minstrels, performing monkeys,

MONEY MAKES MONEY
European merchants usually carried silver coins, but Arabs preferred gold. As international trade increased, Italian merchants set up the first banks, using written bills of exchange to pay for goods instead of having to carry bags of heavy metal coins.

▽ *Market day in a medieval town. People brought in farm produce to sell, visited stalls and shops to spend their money, gossiped with their friends, and drank at the ale house. Strolling musicians, acrobats, or a dancing bear amused the crowds. Beggars and pickpockets did well too.*

Inn   Juggler   Merchants

and dancing bears. Fairs also attracted quack doctors and pickpockets ready to cheat innocent visitors from the countryside.

In towns, work was to be found building magnificent cathedrals and churches, as well as castles and defensive walls. Large trading cities in Europe, such as Hamburg, Antwerp, and London, grew rich from buying and selling wool and other goods carried across the sea in small wooden sailing ships. About 90 cities in northern Europe formed the Hanseatic League to fight pirates, win more trade and keep out rivals.

▷ **This medieval painting shows French tradesmen at work in their town shops.** *Tailors are stitching richly colored cloth (left), while a grocer sets out his wares (right). In the background a barber shaves a customer and a furrier lays out animal pelts.*

Entertainers

A MEDIEVAL TOWN
1136 Fire destroys many old, straw-thatched buildings in London.

1162 Work begins on the cathedral of Notre Dame in Paris, which by 1210 is a unified city with paved streets, walls and 24 gates.

1200s Many new towns are founded in Europe; city-states in Italy and Germany develop.

1209 New London Bridge built.

1260 The Hanseatic League is formed, first by the German towns of Lubeck and Hamburg.

1285 English merchants are banned from selling their goods in churchyards.

1300 The wool trade is at its peak in England; large churches are built in prosperous wool towns.

1344 First known use of the name Hanseatic League.

1348–1349 People flee towns during the Black Death.

1377 London by now has at least 50 guilds and a population of more than 35,000.

1400s Morality plays, in which actors stage tales of good against evil, are performed in churches or on open carts in the street.

1400s–1500s Renaissance architects begin to rebuild cities such as Florence in Italy.

△ **Stained-glass windows told stories in pictures.** *In church, people who could not read looked at the colorful illustrations of Bible stories in the church windows to learn more about the Christian faith.*

21

The Mongol Empire

"Inhuman and beastly, rather monsters than men..." is how the English historian Matthew Paris described the Mongols in the 1200s. Mongol armies sent a shockwave of fear around Asia and Europe, conquering a vast area of land that formed the largest empire in history.

The Mongols lived on the plains of central Asia, from the Ural mountains to the Gobi Desert. They were nomads, wandering with their herds and living in portable tent-homes called yurts. Their leaders were chiefs called khans. In 1206, Chief Temujin brought all the tribes under his rule and was proclaimed Genghis Khan, meaning lord of all. In a lifetime of conquest, he seized an empire that stretched from the Pacific Ocean to the River Danube.

The Mongols quickly conquered the Persian empire. They continued their attacks after Genghis Khan died and, in 1237, a Mongol army led by Batu Khan, one of Genghis' sons, invaded Russia. In the end western Europe was saved only when the Mongols turned homeward on the death of Genghis' son Ogadai Khan in 1241. News of the Mongols' advance created panic in Europe—some Church leaders claimed that the Mongols were sent by God to punish Christians for their sins.

MARE'S MILK

Mongols lived with and from horses. They drank mares' milk and fermented the milk in a skin bag hung from a wooden frame to make an intoxicating drink called kumiss. They drank to celebrate victories and sang to tunes played on fiddles with horsehair strings.

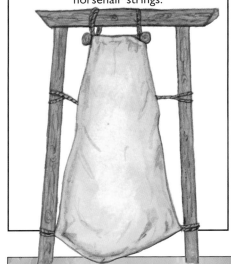

▽ *Mongols preferred to fight on horseback.* *Warriors controlled their horses with their feet, leaving their hands free to shoot bows and hurl spears. Mongol cavalry charges usually overwhelmed their enemies.*

△ **The nomadic Mongols** *roamed, seeking fresh grassland for their sheep, horses, and goats, carrying their felt houses (yurts) with them on ox carts.*

▽ **Genghis Khan's empire** *stretched from the River Danube in the west to the Pacific shores of Asia in the east. Later, Tamerlane carved out his own huge empire.*

Enemies feared the Mongols' speed and ferocity in battle. Mongol soldiers traveled with five horses each and were expert with bow and lance. They also learned how to use catapult artillery against cities. In victory, the Mongols were usually merciless, slaughtering cities full of people and carting away treasure. Yet they ruled their empire fairly if sternly. They demanded taxes but encouraged trade and tolerated all religions.

● Karakorum
MONGOLIA

Khanbalik (Beijing) ●

KATHAY   CIPANGU

MANGI

MONGOL EMPIRE

1206 Temujin is chosen to be khan of all the Mongols and takes the new name Genghis Khan.

1211 The Mongol army attacks China.

1215 Beijing, capital of China, is taken by the Mongols.

1217 All China and Korea are controlled by the Mongols who make their new capital on the steppes at Karakorum.

1219 The Mongols sweep west to attack the empire of Khwarezm (Persia and Turkey).

1224 Mongol armies invade Russia, and then Poland and Hungary.

1227 Genghis Khan dies. His son Ogodai is chosen as the new khan in 1229.

1237 Mongol generals Batu and Subotai invade northern Russia. Their army is known as the Golden Horde.

1241 Ogodai dies and his armies pull back from Europe.

◁ **Though ruthless in battle, Genghis Khan kept the peace in his empire. He wiped out whole cities, yet trade flourished.**

23

Kublai Khan and China

Genghis Khan's grandson was called Kublai Khan. When he became leader of the Mongols he moved from the windswept steppes of central Asia to rule the most splendid court in the world in China. At this time, China was the most sophisticated, technologically advanced country in the world.

Kublai Khan's armies overthrew the ruling Song dynasty in China. By 1279 he controlled most of this vast country, although his grip was less secure on the western parts of the empire. The new Mongol emperor moved his capital to Beijing, taking care to maintain many aspects of Chinese culture. China at this time had the world's biggest cities, including Kaifeng and Hangzhou (each with more than one million people). Chinese silks, porcelain, and other luxuries astonished travelers from Europe and Africa.

One famous visitor to Kublai Khan's court was Marco Polo, an Italian explorer. He later wrote in praise of Chinese cities, with their restaurants and baths, of China's fine postal system and its paper money – as yet unknown in Europe. The Chinese had discovered many technologies such as paper-making. Other inventions included the magnetic compass, printing with movable type, and, most amazing of all to startled foreigners, exploding gunpowder rockets.

MARCO POLO
In 1271 Marco Polo (1256–1323) traveled to China from Venice in Italy with his father and uncle, first by sea to Palestine and then by camel along the fabled Silk Road. This overland trade route linking China with the West had been made safe for travelers by Mongol rule. It was 24 years before the Polos returned to Italy. Marco Polo toured China in the service of Kublai Khan, calling him "the most powerful man since Adam."

▷ *The Chinese began making paper about 105,* when the imperial workshops announced the new technology. Paper-makers used hemp or mulberry tree bark for fibre. Later, they mashed rags or old rope into pulp. Pulp was spread on mesh trays to dry into sheets. Early paper was used for wrapping and clothes, not for writing on.

◁ *Merchants traveled in caravans for protection* against bandits. From China, strings of laden camels followed the Silk Road across mountains and deserts to the markets of the Middle East. They rested at caravanserai, or rest-stations. The Silk Road provided the only regular contact between Europe and China.

Cinnamon

Cloves

Ginger　　**Nutmeg**

△ *Spices for flavoring food* (and to disguise the taste of bad meat) were traded from the East Indies and India to China and the West.

Kublai Khan was a fair ruler as well as a brilliant general, and strengthened his empire by building long roads to connect far-flung territories. He organized charity for the sick and food supplies in case of famine. He also wanted to extend Mongol power and twice tried to invade Japan, but without success.

After the death of Kublai in 1294 the mighty Mongol empire began to decline and by the mid-1300s it had largely broken up. Then in 1369, Timur "Leng" (the lame), known as Tamerlane, made himself ruler of Samarkand in central Asia. He claimed descent from Genghis Khan and set out to re-create the Mongol empire. He conquered Persia, Iraq, Syria, Afghanistan, and part of Russia. In 1397 he invaded India and then died on the way to China in 1405.

△ *The Chinese developed a writing system* unlike any other. There were more than 40,000 characters, originally picture-signs, written with a fine brush. Calligraphy, the art of handwriting, is still admired today.

KUBLAI KHAN
1216 Kublai Khan is born.
1260 Kublai is elected Great Khan of the Mongols.
1271 Marco Polo sets out from Venice for China.
1274 Kublai Khan sends an army to invade Japan, but it is driven back by a storm.
1276 Mongols defeat the Song fleet near Guangzhou.
1279 Kublai Khan rules all China.
1281 A second Mongol attack on Japan is foiled by a typhoon, which the Japanese call kamikaze, the divine wind.
1294 Kublai Khan dies.
1325 Ibn Battuta begins a 24-year journey from his homeland Morocco through Persia, India, Indonesia, and on to China.

△ *The Muslim traveler Ibn Battuta (1304–1369)* covered more than 75,000 miles (120,000 km) on his wanderings and became a celebrity. He visited China in the 1340s, as an ambassador from the sultan of Sumatra.

1368 Mongols are driven from China by Ming forces.
1395 Tamerlane, a descendant of Genghis Khan, invades large parts of southern Russia.
1398 Tamerlane takes Delhi.
1402 Tamerlane defeats Ottoman Turks at Ankyra.
1405 Death of Tamerlane.

THE BLACK DEATH

1344 Bubonic plague breaks out in China and India.

1347 The plague reaches Genoa in Italy and spreads west across Europe.

1348 By the summer, the disease is killing people in southern England. By the winter, Londoners are dying.

1349 Black Death spreads to Ireland, Wales, and Scotland. Other regions affected include France, Spain, Germany, and Russia.

1350 The epidemic reaches Scandinavia.

1353 Black Death epidemic eases. As many as 20 million people in Europe are dead.

1358 Peasants' uprising in northern France. Rebellion is savagely put down.

1381 Peasants' Revolt in England, with rioting in Essex and Kent.

1400 Further outbreaks of the Black Death continue until this date.

▽ *Neither town governments nor local doctors could do much to fight the plague.* *Many people fled, leaving the sick to die, but some brave people stayed to care for the victims. Houses were marked with crosses to show where the disease had struck. The dead were carried away in carts for burial.*

The Black Death

The Black Death was the most horrific natural disaster of the Middle Ages. It was a devastating plague that killed many millions of people in Europe and Asia. One Italian historian wrote, "This is the end of the world."

The plague came to Europe from Asia in 1347. Disease ravaged a Mongol army fighting in the Crimea (southern Russia). The desperate Mongols catapulted diseased corpses over the walls of a fortress defended by Italians. When the Italians sailed home to Genoa, they carried the disease with them.

The disease was bubonic plague, passed to humans from infected rats through flea bites. The name "Black Death" came from the black spots that appeared on victims, who also developed swellings in their armpits and groin, or coughed up blood. Many people died the same day they fell ill. No medieval doctor knew why the Black Death struck or how to cure it. People killed cats and dogs believing they carried the disease, but not rats. To many Christians, the Black Death seemed a punishment from God, and religious fanatics took to the streets, whipping themselves as a penance for the sins of humanity.

The Black Death raged from China to Scandinavia. Sudden death struck daily and, as the epidemic spread, panic-stricken people fled from the towns.

They took the plague with them. So many died (perhaps a third of the people in Europe) that it is possible that villages were left deserted and fields overgrown with weeds. The Church lost many priests, the only educated men of the time.

The repeated plague attacks throughout the 14th and 15th centuries left Europe short of labor and pushed up wages. Unrest over wages and taxes led to an uprising in France in 1358 and to the Peasants' Revolt in England, led by Wat Tyler in 1381.

The monasteries were particularly badly affected, as half England's monks and nuns died. In some monasteries, only a few monks survived. Three archbishops of Canterbury died in one year. It was a huge blow to the Church. People who lived through the Black Death gave money to the Church for new buildings. Yet some church leaders also complained of the money-grubbing and loose-living of those lucky enough to still be alive.

BLACK DEATH
The black rat carried the fleas that transmitted the disease. The rats traveled on ships from port to port, and as they moved the Black Death spread at terrifying speed. There were rats and fleas in every medieval town and in most houses. Rubbish in the streets and poor sanitation made towns an ideal breeding ground for disease. Many towns lost half their populations. Some villages were abandoned, leaving only the graves of the dead.

◁ **This map shows how the Black Death spread.** As early as 1346 Europeans heard reports of a plague of terrible fury raging in China and India. The Black Death was about to hit them, like "the end of the world".

▽ **Estimates of how many people died vary.** This chart shows that the Black Death killed many more millions of people than World War I (1914–1918)—at least 25 million in Europe alone.

The Black Death killed 25 million people

World War I killed 10 million people

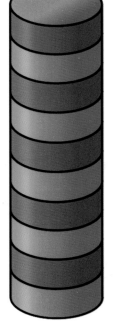
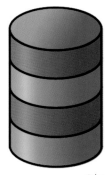

27

African Kingdoms

AFRICAN KINGDOMS

750 By this date most of North Africa has been overrun by Arab armies. Muslim faith spreads rapidly westward.

770 In West Africa, Soninke people begin to build the kingdom of Ghana, led by King Maghan Sisse.

800 Ife kingdom in Nigeria and Kanem-Bornu (north of Lake Chad) become prominent.

800s Arabs and Persians set up trading posts at Malindi, Mombasa, Kilwa, and Mogadishu in East Africa.

900s Ghana controls gold and salt trade and also buys cloth from Europe.

969 Fatimid dynasty conquers Egypt. They build a new capital at Cairo and found one of the first universities.

999 Baganda is first king of Kano in western Nigeria.

1043 Mandingo empire of Jenne founded in West Africa.

1054 Abdallah ben Yassim begins Muslim conquest of West Africa.

1062 Muslim Berbers called Almoravids build their capital of Marrakech.

1070 Ghana is conquered by the Almoravids.

1100 All Muslim Spain now part of Almoravid empire.

1163 Almohads overthrow Almoravids and rule northeast Africa and Spain.

1173 Saladin declares himself sultan of Egypt.

1190 Lalibela is emperor of Ethiopia (to 1225).

1200s Founding of Benin kingdom under the first oba, Eweka.

1240 Ghana becomes part of the new Mali empire when it is conquered by King Sundiata Keita.

1250 Mamelukes rule in Egypt.

1307 Mali empire at its height under Mansa Musa, with its capital at Timbuktu.

1332 Probable year of Mansa Musa's death.

1440–1480 Reign of the most famous oba of Benin, Ewuare the Great.

In this period, the riches of the mightiest kingdoms in Africa impressed Muslim and European visitors who came to their courts. Much of this wealth came from trade in gold, salt, and slaves.

Many northern African kingdoms were Muslim and, from there, preachers took Islam to West Africa. In the kingdom of Ghana (modern-day Gambia, Guinea, Mali, and Senegal), Muslim traders marveled at warriors with gold-mounted swords and shields guarding the king in his capital of Koumbi Saleh. Even the guard dogs around the royal pavilion wore gold collars. Ghana reached the peak of its power in the 10th century, when it controlled both the gold and salt trade.

In the 1300s, Muslim camel caravans crossed the Sahara Desert to the city of Timbuktu. They carried cloth and luxury items to exchange for slaves, leather goods, and kola nuts (used as a drug). Timbuktu was the capital of Mali, an Islamic kingdom which replaced Ghana as the most powerful empire in West Africa. Mali's most famous ruler, Mansa Musa, made a pilgrimage to Mecca in 1324, with an entourage of 60,000 followers, giving away vast quantities of gold as he went. His fame spread as far as Europe, where his kingdom was shown on maps as a land glittering with gold. Spanish craftsmen decorated his palace. The emperor

◁ *Mansa Musa on his pilgrimage to Mecca riding at the head of a large army, with camels, horses, and foot soldiers. His fame spread as far as Europe.*

▷ *The empires of medieval Africa included Ghana and later Mali and, in the west, the kingdoms of Kenam-Bornu, Ife, and Benin. Timbuktu in the Sahara was a city famed for its wealth, when Mali was at the height of its power in the 14th century. It was later overshadowed by Jenne.*

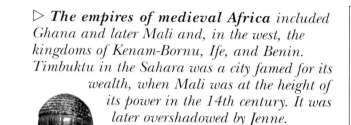

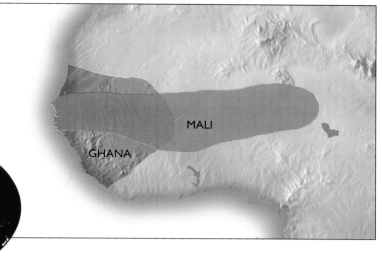

MALI

GHANA

rode at the head of an army of armored cavalry and a baggage-train of gold-laden camels. Farther south were kingdoms just as splendid, such as Ife and Benin, where trade made powerful rulers rich. The craftworkers of Benin made cast bronze figures, the finest metal sculptures in Africa. Benin's ruler, the oba, lived in a walled city where he relaxed with his 100 or so wives. The people of Benin traded with the Portuguese, when their ships began sailing along the West African coast in the 1400s.

In eastern Africa, people living in what are now Somalia, Kenya, and Tanzania practiced farming and herding, and also made iron tools. They traded in ivory, animal skins, and slaves with cities on the coast, which were visited by ships from Arabia and India. These trading cities, such as Kilwa in Tanzania, even sent ambassadors to China, and their rulers decorated their palaces with carpets from Persia and Chinese ceramics. The people of the east coast became Muslims in the 1100s, but people inland maintained traditional beliefs. The east-coast prosperity lasted until almost 1500, when the Portuguese took control of trade in the region and the trading cities were destroyed.

△ *The craftsmen of Africa were skilled in metalworking. This bronze hand altar shows a Benin king with his wives, servants, and soldiers. The lost-wax process was used to make bronzes of superb quality.*

△ *Trade was carried on without money. People used cowrie shells, like these strung on a cord, as currency. They also bartered, exchanging goods of equal value. Peoples of different cultures were able to trade without speaking, by "silent trading" or exchange of goods.*

Japan's Warlords

Medieval Japan was a land without strong emperors. Power instead lay with warlords and they maintained control using their armies of fearsome samurai warriors.

The emperors of Japan were dominated by powerful military families. From these soldier clans came the shoguns, or overlords, who really ruled the country, such as the powerful Minamoto Yoritomo (1147–1199).

The shoguns drove off attacks from Mongol China with their fiercely loyal samurai warriors. A samurai held land, like a knight in Europe, but left farming to the peasants while he hunted or trained with sword and bow. The samurai eventually came to form an elite warrior class that practiced Zen Buddhism, a philosophy which had been brought to Japan from China in 582.

From the 1300s, Japan was torn by violent civil wars between lords known as daimyos who built castles to guard their lands. The daimyos led armies of samurai warriors. In 1338 a samurai named Ashikaga Tokauji became the emperor's shogun.

THE DIVINE WIND

The Japanese felt the gods protected them from invasion. In 1274 and 1281, Kublai Khan sent Chinese fleets to conquer Japan. The first fleet withdrew, in the face of a storm. The second invasion fleet was scattered and sunk by a typhoon, which the Japanese called kamikaze, "the divine wind," and it was the subject of paintings like this one.

The Hundred Years War

Edward III became king of England in 1327. He believed he also had a claim to the French throne so, in 1337, he declared war on France. War between England and France lasted on and off until 1453.

His forces won a sea battle at Sluys and two great land victories at Crécy and Poitiers, but were driven back by the French king Charles V and his commander Bertrand du Guesclin. In 1360 Edward gave up his claim to the French throne in return for land.

Years of truce followed until the English king Henry V renewed his claim to the throne in 1414. He led his troops to France where, in 1415, they defeated a much larger French army at Agincourt. To make peace Henry then married the French king's daughter, but he died in 1422 before his baby

◁ *The death of Joan of Arc.*
The English hoped her death would end French resistance, but in fact it was they who lost ground. The French were inspired to victory. By 1453 only Calais was left in English hands, and Joan's dreams for France had come true.

His family thus became the governing family.

The most powerful daimyo was Hideyoshi Toyotomi (1537–1598), a peasant who rose to become a samurai warlord. He seized control of all Japan and tried but failed to conquer Korea. Hideyoshi controlled Japan from 1585 until his death. One of Hideyoshi's lieutenants, Ieyasu, became shogun in 1603, and founded the Tokugawa dynasty.

◁ *A Samurai warrior wore a steel horned helmet* and body armor made in pieces from leather or lacquered iron strips, so it was fully flexible. He fought with bow, sword, and lance. Modern martial arts have their origins in samurai training.

son could become king of France. The fighting continued as the French were inspired by a peasant girl named Joan of Arc (1412–1431) who claimed to hear voices from God. She fought until the English caught her and burned her at the stake as a witch. Under the weak rule of Henry VI, the divided English lost ground. But English fortunes changed decisively when the Duke of Burgundy changed sides, and the English lost first Paris, then Rouen.

By 1453, they had lost all French territory except Calais.

▽ *Soldiers fought with halberd* (far left), longbow, primitive cannon, and crossbow. Only knights, such as England's Black Prince, wore full armor. If knocked from his horse, a knight hoped to be ransomed.

JAPAN'S WARLORDS

582 Buddhism reaches Japan.

939 Start of civil wars in Japan.

995 Literary and artistic achievements under rule of Fujiwara Michinaga (to 1028).

1192 Minamoto Yoritomo sets up military government or shogunate.

1219 Hojo clan rules Japan (to 1333).

1274 Mongols try to invade Japan, and again in 1281, but are driven back by storms and the "divine wind."

1333 Emperor Daigo II overthrows the Hojo shoguns and rules to 1336.

1336 Revolution followed by exile of Daigo II. Ashikaga family rule as shoguns until 1573.

1400s Long period of civil wars.

100 YEARS WAR

1337 Edward III goes to war with France, claiming the throne.

1340 Sea battle of Sluys (off Belgium) won by the English.

1356 Poitiers is a victory for the English led by Edward III's son, the Black Prince.

1380 Death of Charles V of France who was succeeded by the mad Charles VI.

1415 Victory at Agincourt gives Henry V control of France.

1420 Henry V marries Catherine, daughter of Charles VI.

1422 Henry V dies.

1431 Joan of Arc is burned to death.

1453 End of the Hundred Years War.

31

The Age of Discovery

Explorers and empires 1400–1700

The 1400s mark the end of the Middle Ages. In Europe, the new ideas of the Renaissance and Reformation transformed the way people thought about themselves and the world, and the way they lived. Three events are often picked out as marking the end of the medieval period and the start of the modern age. They are the fall of Constantinople in 1453, which ended the last traces of the old Roman empire; the development of printing in the 1450s, which made books available to anyone who could read; and the first voyage of Christopher Columbus to the Americas in 1492.

This period marks a time when the peoples of the world came into increasing contact with each other. People in America, Africa, and Asia had greater contact with Europe. Europeans increased their power in the world through trade, through

the use of new technology such as cannons and muskets, and through a restless search for new lands and wealth that sent explorers and adventurers across the oceans. By the 1600s, several European countries had established permanent colonies overseas.

This period also saw many new ideas and challenges to old beliefs. Religious quarrels led to bitter wars. There were power struggles between kings and parliaments, as democratic government slowly developed. From the 1500s, there were startling advances in science, with inventions such as the telescope and microscope revealing new wonders, and prompting new questions. Great scientists such as Copernicus, Galileo, and Newton challenged the old ideas, and a new freedom of thought began to shake the foundations of society.

THE AGE OF DISCOVERY

1464 Rise of Songhai empire in Africa.

1488 Portuguese explorers reach the southern tip of Africa.

1492 Columbus sails from Spain to America.

1497 Portuguese explorers sail across the Indian Ocean to India.

1500 Renaissance at its height in Italy.

1501 Start of Safavid dynasty in Persia.

1517 Martin Luther begins the Reformation in Europe.

1520 Suleiman rules the Ottoman empire.

1522 First around-the-world voyage by Magellan's expedition.

1526 Babur founds the Mughal empire in India.

1535 Spain completes conquest of the Aztec and Inca empires.

1543 Copernicus puts forward the revolutionary idea that the Sun, not the Earth, is the centre of the Solar System.

1568 War of liberation in the Spanish Netherlands begins.

1571 Battle of Lepanto is a victory for European Christians against the Muslim Ottoman Turks.

1588 Spanish Armada fails to invade England.

1590 Japan is united by Hideyoshi.

1606 First known European landing in Australia.

1609 Galileo uses a telescope to study the stars and planets.

1618 30 Years War begins.

1620 Mayflower pilgrims from England land in America.

1642 English Civil War begins.

1643 Louis XIV becomes king of France.

1665 Isaac Newton demonstrates the nature of light.

The Renaissance

The Renaissance was a rebirth of interest in the art and learning of ancient Greece and Rome and many historians say that it marked the end of the Middle Ages and the beginning of our modern world. It began in northern Italy in the 14th century and spread throughout Europe, changing the way Europeans saw themselves and how they thought about the world.

The Renaissance began in the universities and monasteries of Italy, where people rediscovered old manuscripts in Latin and Greek on science, art and literature. Some of these manuscripts were brought to Italy by Greek scholars fleeing Constantinople after that city's fall to the Ottoman Turks in 1453. Scholars tried to understand Greek and Roman beliefs, which placed more emphasis on the significance of human life on Earth rather than on an afterlife. In literature, great Italian poets such as Petrarch began to explore human emotion. By the early 1500s, three painters of genius—Leonardo da Vinci, Michelangelo, and Raphael—were at the height of their powers, bringing a new energy and realism to art while architects designed new and elegant buildings that echoed the classical styles of ancient Greece and Rome.

The Renaissance was fueled by new technology. Printing with movable type, developed by Johannes Gutenberg in Germany, made books cheaper and more plentiful, so new ideas could be read by more people.

▷ *The great dome of Florence Cathedral in Italy, designed by Filippo Brunelleschi, the first major architect of the Italian Renaissance. Work on the dome, inspired by his study of Rome's ancient buildings, began in 1420. It took 14 years to complete.*

▽ *A flying machine drawn, but never built, by the Italian Leonardo da Vinci. This sketch shows a kind of ornithopter, a machine that would flap its wings, like a bird. As well as being an artistic genius, Leonardo was a visionary, devising several futuristic machines.*

▷ *The new universe, as conceived by the Polish astronomer Copernicus in his revolutionary new theory of 1543. He put the Sun, not the Earth, at the center of the universe. This challenged the established theory of the 2nd-century Greek astronomer Ptolemy.*

PLANISPHÆRIVM Sive VNIVERSI TO EX HYPO COPERNI PLANO

Some new ideas were astounding, such as the revolutionary suggestion by a Polish scientist, Nicolas Copernicus, that the Sun and not the Earth was the center of the Solar System.

The Renaissance changed the Western world forever.

▷ **Dante Alighieri whose poem The Divine Comedy** *explores love, death, and faith. Dante wrote in his own language, Italian, and not Latin, the language of scholars.*

▽ **A print workshop in Denmark, about 1600.** *The technology of printing with a screw press and metal type spread throughout Europe. Books were printed cheaply in many languages, and read by more people, eager for information.*

THE RENAISSANCE

1306 Italian artist Giotto di Bondone paints frescoes (wall-paintings) that are more lifelike than typical medieval paintings.

1308 Dante Alighieri begins writing *The Divine Comedy*, in his native Italian not Latin.

1387 Geoffrey Chaucer begins *The Canterbury Tales*, written in English. Florence University appoints its first professor of Greek.

1416 Italian sculptor, Donatello, breaks new ground with free-standing figures, including his nude David.

1453 Constantinople is captured by the Turks; many of its scholars flee to Italy.

1454 Johannes Gutenberg perfects printing with movable type. By 1476 William Caxton is printing in London.

1466–1536 Life of Desiderius Erasmus, a Dutch scholar, philosopher and writer. He published studies of the Old and New Testaments.

1478 Lorenzo de Medici makes Florence a center of art and learning. Sandro Botticelli finishes his painting *Primavera* (spring).

1503 The rebuilding of St. Peter's in Rome begins. Leonardo da Vinci paints the *Mona Lisa*.

1508 Michelangelo paints the ceiling of the Sistine Chapel in the Vatican, Rome.

1513 Niccolo Machiavelli, an Italian political writer, writes *The Prince* on the theory of government.

1516 Sir Thomas More publishes *Utopia*.

1532 Hans Holbein, Flemish artist, is at work in England.

1543 Nicolas Copernicus puts forward his ideas about the Solar System.

1590 William Shakespeare is writing plays in England.

The Aztecs

The Aztecs were fierce warriors who conquered a huge empire that eventually reached all the way across Mexico and was at its height in the early 1500s. But in 1521, Aztec rule came to a sudden end when they lost their empire to a small band of Spanish treasure-seekers.

The Aztecs came to dominate other Native Americans in Central America by fighting constant wars with their neighbors. Their capital, Tenochtitlan, was founded in 1325 on an island in the middle of Lake Texcoco, which is now the site of modern-day Mexico City. Tenochtitlan was a walled city of 100,000 people. It had stone temples and a network of canals along which people paddled canoes. Roads on top of raised causeways linked the island to the mainland and Aztec farmers

THE AZTECS

c. **1200** Aztecs settle in the Valley of Mexico.

1325 The traditional date for the founding of Tenochtitlan.

1400s Aztecs control the surrounding region, in alliance with the neighbouring city-states of Texcoco and Tlacopan.

1440–1469 Reign of Montezuma I. The empire is extended.

1500 The empire is at its height. The Aztecs rule more than 10 million people, most of whom belong to other tribes.

1502 Montezuma II becomes emperor.

1519 Spaniards led by Hernando Cortés march on Tenochtitlan. They are aided by tribes hostile to the Aztecs, and are welcomed by Montezuma, who believes Cortés is the god Quetzalcoatl.

1520 The Aztecs rise up against the Spanish invaders. Montezuma is wounded and dies.

1521 Cortés and his men attack and capture Tenochtitlan. End of the Aztec empire.

▷ **The heart of the Aztec empire was the Valley of Mexico,** *but it extended far east into what is now Guatemala. Most major cities were built in the fertile central Valley of Mexico. Each was a busy market center.*

● Tenochtitlan

▷ **Like the Maya, the Aztecs built pyramid-temples.** *This Mayan pyramid at Uxmal gives some idea of what the Aztec Great Temple at Tenochtitlan may have looked like before the Spanish reduced it to rubble.*

◁ *The great Calendar Stone* bears in its center the face of the Sun-god Tonatiuh. The stone measures 4 yards (3.7 m) across and weighs about 25 tons. It was unearthed in Mexico City in 1790.

▽ *Aztec warrior chiefs wore feather headdresses.* Throughout their empire, there was a profitable trade in bird feathers and other animal products, such as jaguar skins. Poor people wore simple clothes made from plant fiber. They grew corn and vegetables to feed the rulers in the city.

grew vegetables on artificial islands built in the lake.

The Aztecs were very skilled in sculpture, poetry, music, and engineering. They worshiped the Sun as the giver of all life, and each year priests sacrificed thousands of victims to the Sun-god, cutting out their hearts as offerings. Other sacrificial victims were drowned or beheaded. These deaths, the Aztecs believed, were needed to bring good harvests and prosperity.

Aztec farmers grew corn, beans, and tomatoes, and Aztec merchants traded throughout the empire. The ruling class were warriors, wearing jaguar skins and headdresses made from the tail feathers of the quetzal, a sacred bird. All warriors had to capture at least one enemy for sacrifice, and conquered peoples were forced to pay taxes to the Aztec emperor.

In 1519 Spanish treasure-seekers led by Hernando Cortés attacked the Aztecs. The Aztecs believed Cortés was a god, and their emperor Montezuma II was taken prisoner. Aztec spears and clubs were no match for Spanish guns and by 1521 the Aztec empire was finished.

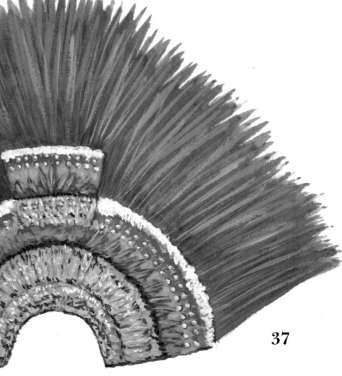

The Incas

From the mountains of Peru, the god-emperor of the Incas ruled a highly organized empire. Civil war and Spanish invasion finally caused the empire to fall.

The Incas took over from the Chimu as rulers of the Andes mountains of South America. Their civilization reached its peak in the 1400s under the ruler Pachacuti who defeated an invading army from a neighboring state. Pachacuti went on to reform the government of the Inca kingdom, appointing officials to run the country and a central administration to control the building of towns and the efficient working of farms and workshops. From the capital city Cuzco, Pachacuti and his successors greatly increased the Inca empire to include parts of Chile, Bolivia, and Ecuador. The Incas built stone cities and fine roads for trade—by barter since they used no money. Farmers terraced the mountain slopes to grow corn, cotton, and potatoes. In 1525 the Inca empire was at its greatest extent. In 1527 Huayna Capac died and the empire was split between his two sons.

In the 1530s a Spanish expedition led by Francisco Pizarro arrived to seek gold in South America. The Europeans were impressed by the

▽ **The Spanish were vastly outnumbered in their battles with the Incas.** *But they had horses, armor, and guns. Many Incas fought gallantly, but with their king murdered, they were quickly defeated.*

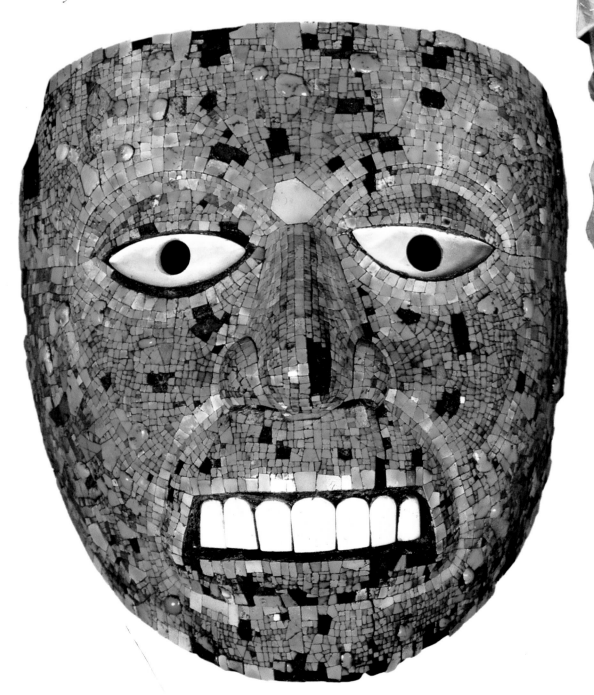

Inca capital city of Cuzco—its palaces and temples, sanitation and water supply, and the fortress of Sacsahuaman with huge stones which fitted together perfectly without using mortar. Although they had neither writing nor wheeled vehicles, the Incas' many skills included music, bridge-building, and medicine. Some scientists believe that all Incas shared the same blood group and that it is possible that they were able to practice blood transfusion.

△ *A gold raft depicting El Dorado, a legendary ruler whose body was said to be dusted with gold every year. Such tales aroused the greed of European invaders.*

▽ *A mosaic mask made from mussel shells. Masks of gods' faces were worn by Inca priests for ceremonies, and were often richly decorated.*

Though few in number, the Spaniards had horses and guns, both new to the Incas. The Incas were weakened by seven years of civil war. In 1532, Pizarro captured the Inca ruler Atahualpa and demanded for his ransom a room full of gold and two rooms full of silver. It was paid but Atahualpa was killed by the Spaniards anyway. The leaderless Inca armies were swiftly defeated, although resistance to Spanish rule continued from scattered mountain forts, such as Machu Picchu, until 1572.

△ *The Incas had a swift communication system, using fast runners carrying messages in the form of quipus (knotted cords). A message could be sent more than 120 miles (200 km) in a day along a system of paved roads.*

39

Voyages of Discovery

In the late 1400s and 1500s, Europeans set out to explore the oceans. Building stronger ships capable of longer voyages, they went in search of trade, new lands, and treasure.

When the Byzantine empire fell to the Ottoman Turks in 1453, the old trade links by land between Europe and Asia were cut. How would Europeans get the spices from Asia that were essential to flavor their food? To find new routes to the spice-producing islands and out of curiosity and the spirit of adventure, Europeans set sail.

The Portuguese were the first to go exploring. A Portuguese prince, Henry the Navigator, took a keen interest in shipbuilding and navigation. He directed Portuguese sailors west into the Atlantic and south to explore the west coast of Africa, where they set up forts and traded in gold and ivory. Spanish, French, Dutch, and English sailors followed. Instead of sailing east, some sailed west hoping to find a route to India. One famous voyage was made by Christopher Columbus, the first 15th century explorer to cross the Atlantic and return. Portugal and Spain began to settle and plunder the Americas, dividing it between them by treaty. By 1517 the Portuguese had reached China and nearly 30 years later they arrived in Japan.

△ *Philip II became king of Spain in 1556 and ruled until 1598.* A devout Catholic, he encouraged his sailors and soldiers to explore and plunder, and convert to Christianity the "heathen" peoples they conquered. During his reign, overseas trade and conquests brought fabulous wealth to Spain. He worked incredibly hard, alone in an office in his huge palace El Escorial (built 1563–1584).

▽ **Navigators used the cross-staff and astrolabe to fix their ships' position by the sun and stars.** *The magnetic compass pointed North, but was not always reliable.*

Cross-staff

Astrolabe

Compass

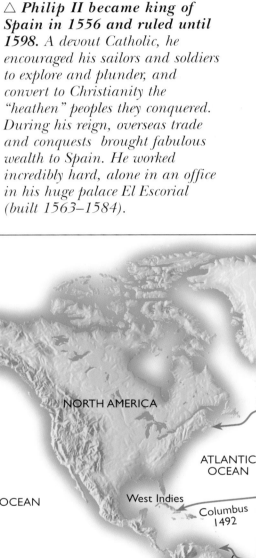

NORTH AMERICA

ATLANTIC OCEAN

PACIFIC OCEAN

West Indies

Columbus 1492

Vespucci 1499–1500

SOUTH AMERI

Magellan 1519–2

Cape Horn

Strait of Magellan

The ships used by the explorers were small, but more seaworthy than the clumsy vessels of the Middle Ages. They used a mixture of square and lateen (triangular) sails for easier steering and greater maneuverability. Sailors had only crude maps and simple instruments to guide them on voyages lasting many months. In 1519 a Portuguese captain, Ferdinand Magellan, set out from Spain with five ships. They sailed around South America, across the Pacific Ocean to the Philippines (where Magellan was killed in a fight with local people) and across the Indian Ocean to Africa. Only one ship found its way home to Spain, becoming the first ship to sail completely around the world.

NEW WORLD FOODS

As well as gold and silver treasures, European explorers brought back new foods from the Americas. Potatoes, tomatoes, and peppers, plants native to America, were all unknown in Europe before 1500. Potatoes were at first a luxury, served only to rich people at banquets. Chocolate, from the cacao tree, was first brought to Spain from Mexico in 1520. Also from the New World came tobacco, turkeys, and corn.

Potatoes

Tomatoes

Peppers

VOYAGES OF DISCOVERY

1419 Portuguese sail to the Madeira Islands.

1431 Portuguese reach the Azores.

1488 Bartolomeu Dias of Portugal explores west coast of Africa as far south as Cape of Good Hope.

1492 Christopher Columbus, an Italian sailing for Spain, makes his first voyage to America with three ships.

1494 Spain and Portugal divide the Americas between them by the Treaty of Tordesillas.

1497 John Cabot, an Italian in the service of England, sails to Canada. The Portuguese explorer Vasco Da Gama sails around Africa to India.

1500 Pedro Alvares Cabral from Portugal sails to Brazil in South America.

1501 Italian Amerigo Vespucci sails to South America. A map published in 1507 names the continent America after him.

1509 Spain begins settlement of the Americas.

1513 Spanish explorer Vasco Nuñez de Balboa is the first European to see the Pacific.

1517 Portuguese traders reach China.

1522 First round-the-world voyage is completed by Ferdinand Magellan's Spanish crew.

1524 Italian Giovanni da Verrazano searches for a northwest passage from Europe to Asia.

◁ *The voyages of Magellan, Columbus and Da Gama revealed to Europeans that the world was larger than ancient geographers had believed. They sailed across oceans and landed on continents unknown to earlier Europeans.*

Cabot 1497

EUROPE

ASIA

● Constantinople

CHINA

INDIA

PACIFIC OCEAN

Philippines

AFRICA

● Calicut

East Indies

Da Gama 1497–99

The Moluccas

Janszoon 1605

Dias 1487–88

INDIAN OCEAN

Del Cano 1519–22

Cape of Good Hope

Spain and Portugal

Spain became the superpower of Europe in the 1500s. Spanish and Portuguese explorers led the way in the European voyages of discovery, to the Americas and to Asia.

Medieval Spain was divided between Christian and Muslim kingdoms. After wars of reconquest, the two Christian monarchs who ended Muslim rule in Spain were Ferdinand of Aragon and Isabella of Castile. In 1469 Ferdinand and Isabella were married, uniting Spain's two strongest Christian kingdoms. By 1492 their forces had captured Granada, the last Muslim outpost in Spain. The new rulers were intolerant of other religions and set up the Spanish Inquisition to search out heretics – both Christians who held different beliefs from the established Church and people of other faiths, such as Jews.

In the 16th century, Spain became Europe's strongest nation. Its power was based on a strong army, which fought wars in Europe (against the Dutch, for example) and on a large navy,

▽ *In the 1400s, Spain was not yet one kingdom.* Aragon and Castile were the strongest Christian kingdoms, while Granada was ruled by Muslim emirs, who had once held southern Spain.

▷ **Columbus leaves the court of Spain,** *having won the support of King Ferdinand and Queen Isabella for his westward voyage. Columbus set sail on August 3, 1492. He was convinced that the Atlantic was a narrow ocean.*

HENRY THE NAVIGATOR
Prince Henry of Portugal (1394–1460) dreamed of exploration overseas, and brought together seamen, shipbuilders, and mapmakers to plan voyages. With Henry's encouragement he Portuguese built new, stronger ships called caravels. They sailed west to reach the Canary Islands and the Azores, and south to explore the coast of Africa. Each voyage took the explorers further into the unknown.

which controlled the profitable trade in gold and silver from Spain's newly conquered empire in the Americas. Spanish power reached its peak during the reign of Charles I (1516–1556) who also became Holy Roman emperor in 1519 and so controlled lands in Germany, Austria, and the Netherlands, as well as parts of France and Italy. On his death, his lands were divided between his son Philip II (who ruled Spain, the Netherlands, and Spanish colonies in the Americas) and his brother Ferdinand (who became Holy Roman emperor).

By 1580, the Spanish empire included Portugal. With its long Atlantic coastline and shipbuilding skills, Portugal had led the way in European exploration of the oceans. Its sailors had opened up new trade routes to Asia. The Portuguese already controlled an overseas empire that included large stretches of coastline in East and West Africa, Brazil and India, as well as trading posts such as Goa in India, Macao in China and many islands in Southeast Asia.

▷ *Arabic script on Spanish stonework. Muslim craftworkers left a brilliant legacy in southern Spain, especially in the architecture of cities such as Granada and Cordoba.*

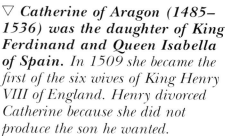

▽ *Catherine of Aragon (1485–1536) was the daughter of King Ferdinand and Queen Isabella of Spain. In 1509 she became the first of the six wives of King Henry VIII of England. Henry divorced Catherine because she did not produce the son he wanted.*

SPAIN AND PORTUGAL

711 Muslims invade southern Spain (which includes what later becomes Portugal).

Early 1000s Muslim central rule of Spain collapses in civil war. Many small Moorish states and cities are set up. Christian states begin the reconquest of Spain.

1043–1099 El Cid (Rodrigo Diaz de Vivar), warrior hero of medieval Spain, fights for Christian Castile.

1143 Portugal gains independence from Castile.

Late 1200s Granada is the only Moorish kingdom in Spain.

1385 John I of Portugal fights Spain and makes an alliance with England. His son, Henry the Navigator, begins Portugal's rise as a sea power.

1479 Aragon and Castile become one kingdom.

1492 Moors are forced out of Granada. Jews are expelled from Spain. Columbus sails to America.

1512 Ferdinand seizes Navarre to complete unification of Spain.

1521 Spain conquers Aztec empire in Mexico.

1535 Spain conquers Inca empire of Peru.

1556 Philip II becomes king of Spain: Spanish empire is at its height.

1565 Spain colonizes the Philippines.

1568 War in the Spanish Netherlands begins.

1571 Battle of Lepanto: warships of Spain and Austria defeat a Turkish fleet in the Mediterranean.

1580 Spain conquers Portugal and holds it until 1640.

1588 Spanish Armada sails to invade England, but fails.

43

AFRICAN EMPIRES

1300s European rulers try to contact the legendary Prester John. Great Zimbabwe is the heart of a powerful Bantu kingdom, one of a chain from the Indian Ocean coast north to the Congo River.

1335 The Songhai ruling dynasty is founded.

1341 Suleiman is king of Mali to 1360.

1430s Portuguese begin exploring the west coast of Africa.

1460s Portuguese explorers reach Sierra Leone and buy ivory, pepper, palm oil, and slaves from the kingdom of Benin.

1464 Songhai breaks away from Mali's control.

1468 Sonni Ali captures Timbuktu.

1481 Portuguese traders set up a fortress at Elmina in the Gulf of Guinea. The Portuguese use such forts as bases to trade with African rulers.

1488 Portuguese explorer Bartolomeu Dias rounds the Cape of Good Hope.

1493 Askia Muhammad I heads new ruling dynasty in Songhai, now at its peak, and takes over Mandingo empire.

1506 The African kingdom of Kongo has its first Christian king, Afonso I.

1511 A Portuguese explorer reaches Great Zimbabwe, by now in decline.

1520 A Portuguese mission travels to Ethiopia (lasts until 1526).

c. 1530 The transatlantic slave trade from Africa to the Americas begins.

1571–1603 Idris Alawma rules the empire of Kanem-Bornu in the Sudan region.

1591 Songhai empire is defeated by Moroccans, aided by Spanish and Portuguese soldiers.

African Empires

Africa in 1500 was a continent with many kingdoms and empires. The richest African rulers commanded trade in gold, ivory, and slaves—goods that attracted European traders.

Portuguese traders sailing the coasts of West Africa heard tales of wondrous kingdoms in the heart of the continent. The strongest was Songhai, a Muslim kingdom that controlled trade across the Sahara Desert. In 1464 King Sonni Ali freed Songhai from the control of the Mali empire and went on to overrun the empire, expanding Songhai and its capital, Gao. A new dynasty was founded in 1493 by Askia Muhammad I, who gained great wealth from the trading cities of Jenne and Timbuktu. He commanded a large army and ruled from a splendid court through a sophisticated system of government departments. Songhai rule lasted until 1591, when it was overthrown by Moroccans armed with guns.

Another Muslim empire stretched through parts of modern-day Chad, Cameroon, Nigeria, Niger, and Libya. This was Kanem-Bornu, an empire that thrived on trade between northern and southern Africa and reached its peak under Idris Alawma from

▷ **Traders gather to do business in Timbuktu.** *The city at the southern edge of the Sahara Desert was the center of the gold and salt trade. Its Muslim scholars acted as counsellors to the ruler of the Songhai empire, Askia Muhammad I. Merchants came from as far as Morocco to sell cloth and horses there.*

▽ **Ethiopia was a mostly Christian kingdom.** *Ethiopian Christians built churches like this one, cut from solid rock. Fifteen rock churches survive at Lalibela (then called Roha), the capital in the 1200s. The cross-shaped church is actually hollowed out of the rock.*

PRESTER JOHN

Travelers told tales of Prester ("priest") John, a fabulously rich ruler. He was first said to be a Christian king in Asia, and later to be the ruler of Ethiopia in Africa. One story claimed he had a magic mirror in which he saw everything going on throughout his empire. Another story tells that, in one of Prester John's kingdoms, great ants dug up gold for his treasury.

about 1570. In northeast Africa was Ethiopia, a Christian empire in the heart of Muslim Africa. Europeans heard tantalizing tales of its legendary Christian ruler, Prester John. Here, and to the south, Africans lived by farming and cattle-herding.

By 1450 a settlement at Great Zimbabwe in central Africa was at its greatest extent. Built over a period of about 400 years, Great Zimbabwe was probably a royal residence surrounded by massive walls and a high tower. Used by rulers as their stronghold and administrative center, the site was a major religious, political, and trading center. The people of this prosperous African kingdom used copper and iron, and traded in gold with Sofala on the east coast (present-day Mozambique). By 1500 the civilization that built Zimbabwe was in decline.

▷ *The ruins of Great Zimbabwe. The walled citadel was once surrounded by village houses, fields and grazing cattle. The stone walls were built for defense and to show the power of the ruler.*

▽ *This map shows the most important kingdoms of Africa at this time—Songhai in the western sub-Sahara region, Kanem-Bornu farther east, Ethiopia in the mountainous northwest, and Great Zimbabwe in central-southern Africa.*

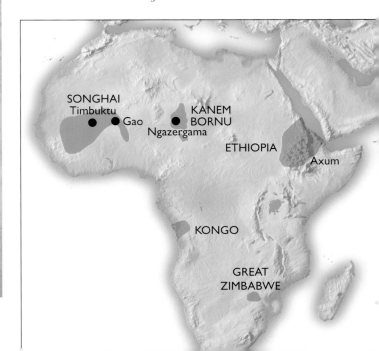

SONGHAI
Timbuktu
Gao
KANEM
BORNU
Ngazergama
ETHIOPIA
Axum
KONGO
GREAT
ZIMBABWE

The Reformation

The Renaissance aimed to restore church practice closer to the Old and New Testaments. These changes in thinking led to the Reformation—a challenge to the established Christian church in western Europe.

The Renaissance led to writers from the time before Christ (mainly those of ancient Greece and Rome) being read again, and their ideas inspired a new philosophy known as humanism—the belief that humans were in control of their own destinies. Humanism arose at a time of growing discontent in the western Christian church over the way the church was run. In 1517 Martin Luther, a German monk, protested publicly at what he saw as the church's theological corruption and called for reform. His campaign began what is known as the Reformation and led to the formation of the Protestant church as his ideas

◁ *John Calvin, religious reformer, was born in France.* *He believed that only people chosen by God would be saved from damnation. His reforms became known as "Calvinism."*

THE REFORMATION

1498 Savonarola, an Italian friar who preached church reform, is burned at the stake in Florence.

1517 Start of the Reformation. Martin Luther nails 95 theses against the sale of indulgences (pardons for sins) on a church door in Wittenberg, Germany.

1519 Ulrich Zwingli starts the Reformation in Switzerland.

1521 The Diet (assembly) of Worms is convened. Luther is excommunicated.

1529 Henry VIII breaks with Rome so that he can divorce Catherine of Aragon. In 1534 he is made head of the Church of England.

1532 John Calvin starts Protestant movement in France.

1534 Ignatius Loyola founds the Society of Jesus, or Jesuits.

1536 Dissolution of the monasteries in England.

1541 John Knox takes the Reformation to Scotland.

1549 A new prayer book, the Book of Common Prayer, is introduced in England.

1555 England returns to Catholicism under Mary I. Archbishop Cranmer is burned at the stake.

1558–1603 Elizabeth I, a Protestant, rules England.

1562 Religious wars in France between Catholics and Huguenots (Protestants).

1568 Protestant Dutch revolt against Spanish rule starts.

1572 St. Bartholomew's Day Massacre: many Huguenots in France are killed.

1581 Protestant Netherlands declare independence from Spain (not recognized by Spain until 1648).

1588 Defeat of the Spanish Armada.

1598 Edict of Nantes gives Protestants and Catholics in France equal rights.

were taken up and spread by rebels in other countries such as Ulrich Zwingli in Switzerland and John Calvin in France.

The new technology of printing spread these new ideas. The Bible, which previously had been available only in Latin, the language of scholars, was translated into local languages for all to read. Some rulers used discontent with the church to further their own affairs. Henry VIII of England, for example, wanted his marriage to Catherine of Aragon dissolved. He asked the Pope for a divorce, but when the Pope refused, Henry broke with the church in Rome as a means to get his own way.

From 1545 the Catholic church fought back with a movement known as the Counter Reformation, sending out Jesuit priests to campaign against the spread of Protestantism and convert the peoples of the Spanish empire. The split between Christians in western Europe led to wars as countries struggled with new religious alliances. Catholics and Protestants persecuted one another, often in the cruellest ways. As religious disputes in Europe continued into the 1600s, some people left Europe and sought religious freedom in the new world of America.

◁ Martin Luther believed that people were saved by faith alone, that the Bible was central to that faith, and that church services should be in everyday languages, not in Latin.

▽ The Spanish sent the Armada against England in 1588 to restore Catholic rule. An English fireship attack off Calais helped fight off the planned invasion, and the great fleet was eventually wrecked and scattered by storms around the coasts of northern Britain.

◁ King Henry VIII made himself head of the Church of England to gain a divorce. He was not, in fact, a supporter of Protestant beliefs.

Ottomans and Safavids

The Ottoman capture of Constantinople in 1453 marked the beginning of a Turkish golden age. They controlled the eastern Mediterranean and the Near East, and their armies moved west to threaten Europe. They fought many wars against their Muslim rivals in Persia, the Safavids.

After the fall of Constantinople, the Ottoman Turks renamed the city Istanbul and it became the center of a Muslim empire that, at its peak, stretched from Algeria to Arabia and from Egypt to Hungary. Most of these conquests were made during the rule of Suleiman I (1520–1566), who was known as the Law-Giver to his own subjects and as the Magnificent to Europeans. The Turks invaded Persia (modern-day Iran), captured Baghdad, took control of the island of Rhodes, and crossed the river Danube

▽ *A map showing the Ottoman and Safavid empires.* Lawyers, poets, architects, and scholars came to the royal courts of their rulers from all over the Islamic world.

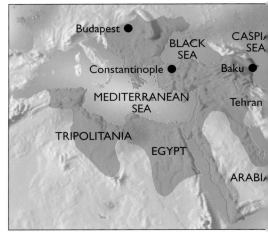

▽ **The Ottoman sultan Suleiman I** *made the Ottoman empire a power to be respected and feared, not just in the Middle East but in Europe as well. He was called Suleiman the Magnificent.*

into Hungary, where they won the battle of Mohacs in 1526.

By 1529 the Turkish army was outside the city walls of Vienna and looked likely to burst into western Europe. However, the siege of Vienna was lifted and Europe relaxed. Ottoman fleets of galleys (oared warships) controlled the Mediterranean Sea and Turkish pirates, such as the fearsome Barbarossa (Khayr ad-Din Pasha), raided ports, captured merchant ships, and carried off Christians to be slaves. Ottoman sea power, too, was checked, when in 1571 a combined Christian fleet defeated the Turkish fleet at the naval battle of Lepanto in the Gulf of Corinth in Greece. This battle ended Turkish threats to Europe by sea.

Suleiman also tried three times to conquer Persia, which from 1501 was under the rule of the Safavid dynasty founded by Shah Ismail I. Here the people were Shiites, not Sunni Muslims as in the Ottoman empire. Safavid rivalry with the Ottomans continued under Shah Abbas I (1557–1628). From his capital of Isfahan with its beautiful tiled mosques, Shah Abbas I ruled not only Persia but also most of Mesopotamia (modern-day Iraq). Wars between the two empires continued throughout the 16th century and helped to stop the Ottoman empire advancing into Europe.

OTTOMANS AND SAFAVIDS

1288 Osman becomes ruler of the Ottoman Turks. Defeats Byzantine army in 1301.

1402 Tamerlane rules most of Ottoman empire (until he dies in 1405).

1453 Ottomans capture the city of Constantinople, which is renamed Istanbul.

1463 Ottoman Turks conquer Bosnia, having already captured Serbia (1459).

1501 Foundation of the Safavid dynasty in Persia, by Shah Ismail I.

1517 Ottoman Turks conquer Egypt, defeating Mamelukes.

1520 Suleiman I becomes sultan of the Ottoman empire.

1522 Turks capture Rhodes.

1526 Battle of Mohacs in Hungary is won by the Turks.

1529 At the siege of Vienna, capital of Austria, the Turks fail to capture the city.

1534 Turks capture Tunis, Baghdad, and Mesopotamia.

1565 Turks attack Malta, but are fought off by the Knights of St. John.

1571 Battle of Lepanto. Don John of Austria destroys the Ottoman fleet led by Ali Pasha.

1587 Shah Abbas I comes to the throne of Persia.

1590 Turks and Persians make peace.

c. **1600** The Ottoman empire begins to decline.

▽ *A Persian carpet of the 1500s. Spinners and weavers made these famous carpets of knotted wool and silk. Traditional designs included flowers, leaves, and various geometric shapes. They featured soft colors and elegant patterns.*

△ **The Battle of Lepanto in 1571** *was fought in the Gulf of Corinth between a Turkish fleet of about 273 galleys and a Christian fleet of 200 galleys and heavier galleasses. The Turks were defeated. They lost at least 20,000 men, the Christians about 8,000. This was the last great sea battle between fleets of galleys.*

◁ **The Ottoman sultans lived in the walled Topkapi Palace,** *which was surrounded by beautiful gardens. Begun in 1562, the Palace is now a museum of Ottoman treasures, including a library of 40,000 documents.*

The Mughal Empire

The Mughal dynasty ruled a mighty empire in India for nearly three hundred years. Its founder, Babur, was followed by an even greater ruler, Akbar, under whose reign there was a great flowering of Mughal art and learning.

Babur was a Muslim chieftain from Afghanistan who made his name by capturing Samarkand, once the capital city of his ancestor Tamerlane. But Babur's eyes were on a greater prize. With his army, and the cannon that his gunners used with great skill, he moved into northern India. In 1526 Babur defeated the sultan of Delhi's army at the battle of Panipat, thus founding the Mughal dynasty. Babur was a shrewd and able ruler, but he died four years after his triumph. His son Humayun succeeded him, but he faced dangerous rebellions and, after a reign of ten years, was driven out of India and remained in Persia for fifteen years.

The golden age of Mughal India began in 1556 under the rule of Akbar. Then only 13, he was Babur's grandson and inherited Babur's talents. Akbar defeated several Hindu kingdoms, but did not antagonize them. A great military leader, he widened the empire still further by war and skillful diplomacy and his capture of Bengal, with its riches of rice and silk, was the high point of his career. A conqueror who crushed rebellions, Akbar was also famed as a wise and just ruler. He tolerated all religions, even

△ **The Taj Mahal** *was built between 1631 and 1648 for the favorite wife of India's Mughal emperor, Shah Jahan. 20,000 workers and artists helped create this most beautiful building. It is made of white marble.*

▷ **A Sikh today.**
The Sikh religion was founded in the Punjab region of northern India in the early 1500s by Guru Nanak. The Sikhs fought for freedom from Mughal rule, inspired by their gurus (teachers).

50

permitting Hindus and Portuguese Christians to discuss their faiths at his court. He introduced new styles in art and architecture, making his royal court of Fatehpur Sikri a center of learning for the Mughal empire that he ruled until his death in 1605.

Akbar was succeeded by his son Jahangir, who preferred the company of painters and poets to ruling a large empire. In 1627 his son, Shah Jahan, succeeded him and set about enlarging the empire. He, too, was a great patron of the arts and paid for many splendid buildings, such as the Taj Mahal near Agra. But Shah Jahan had a tragic end, when in 1657 he fell ill and an argument broke out among his sons over who should rule. His third son, Aurangzeb, won the struggle and killed his other brothers, imprisoning his father and seizing the throne. Shah Jahan died in captivity and was buried next to his wife in the Taj Mahal.

Aurangzeb was the last great Mughal ruler, expanding the empire to its greatest extent. Unlike his predecessors, however, Aurangzeb was a strict Muslim and extracted taxes from non-Muslim subjects. He also destroyed many Hindu shrines. After Aurangzeb's death in 1707 the Mughal empire began to break up. He was hailed as the greatest of all the Mughal emperors.

△ **Akbar leads his troops in battle.** *This 1568 painting shows Mughal soldiers, equipped with firearms, storming an enemy fortress. War elephants were used like tanks by armies in India during Akbar's brilliant wars of conquest.*

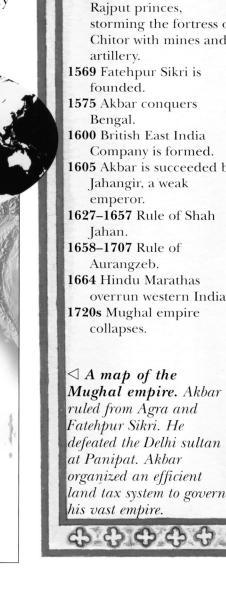

AFGHANISTAN
Kabul
Amritsar
Panipat
Delhi
Indus River
Ganges River
Agra
Calcutta
Diu
Bombay
BAY OF BENGAL
Goa
Madras
INDIAN OCEAN
Pondicherry
Cochin
● European trading posts
■ Extent of Mughal empire in 1700
CEYLON (SRI LANKA)

MUGHAL EMPIRE

1526 Foundation of the Mughal dynasty. Victory at Panipat against the sultan of Delhi, Ibrahim Lodi, gives Babur control of northern India.

1529 Akbar defeats the Afghans.

1530 Humayun becomes emperor.

1540 After Humayun is defeated by Sher Shah, a ruler of eastern India, he is exiled to Persia (until 1555).

1542 Akbar, grandson of Babur, is born.

1556 Start of Akbar's reign; he wins a second battle of Panipat against the Hindus.

1565 Akbar extends his rule to southern India. A great fort is built at Agra.

1567 Akbar subdues the Rajput princes, storming the fortress of Chitor with mines and artillery.

1569 Fatehpur Sikri is founded.

1575 Akbar conquers Bengal.

1600 British East India Company is formed.

1605 Akbar is succeeded by Jahangir, a weak emperor.

1627–1657 Rule of Shah Jahan.

1658–1707 Rule of Aurangzeb.

1664 Hindu Marathas overrun western India.

1720s Mughal empire collapses.

◁ **A map of the Mughal empire.** *Akbar ruled from Agra and Fatehpur Sikri. He defeated the Delhi sultan at Panipat. Akbar organized an efficient land tax system to govern his vast empire.*

Ming China

In the 1300s the Mongol grip on China grew weak. A revolt drove out the last Yüan (Mongol) emperor, and in 1368 a Buddhist monk took his place and called himself Ming Hong Wu founding a new dynasty. The Ming dynasty ruled China for almost 300 years.

Under Hong Wu, Chinese self-confidence and national pride reasserted itself. Initially an able and efficient ruler, though despotic later, the first Ming emperor established good government that ensured a long period of peace and prosperity for China. Hong Wu made Chinese society more equal by abolishing slavery, confiscating large estates and redistributing them among the poor, and demanding higher taxes from the rich. China began to reassert its power over its neighbors and a strong army was maintained to withstand foreign attacks.

Hong Wu was succeeded by emperors who continued the good works he had begun. They sponsored the arts, so making the Ming period one of great creativity, especially in porcelain. In the early 1400s, Chinese ships (then the largest in the world) made voyages as far as Africa and Arabia in fleets under the command of admiral Zheng He. The Ming emperors were also great builders and from 1421, they lived within the walls of the Forbidden City in

△ *Chinese soldiers fight against invading Japanese samurai. In the 1590s the Japanese tried to invade Korea, which the Chinese regarded as their allies.*

▽ **The Forbidden City in Beijing.** *Yung Lo, third Ming emperor, made Beijing his capital in 1421. The emperor lived in seclusion inside the Forbidden City. No foreigner and no Chinese outside the imperial household was allowed to enter the Forbidden City.*

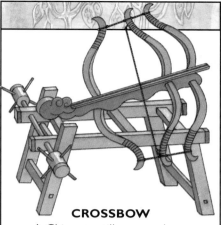

CROSSBOW

A Chinese artillery crossbow. A powerful bow like this could fire an arrow up to 650 feet (200 m), and pierce a wooden shield. The Chinese developed a number of other ingenious weapons, including gunpowder rockets and bombs, which they first used about AD 1000.

Beijing, a huge complex of palaces, temples, and parks into which no foreigner was admitted. Few Chinese ever saw inside the Forbidden City, apart from the emperor's family and the officials and servants of the royal household.

China's first contacts with European traders began in the 1500s, when Portuguese ships arrived. By 1557 the Portuguese had a trading settlement in Macao, and Matteo Ricci, a Jesuit missionary, came to China in 1583. Western traders were eager to buy Chinese porcelain and silk and a new drink, tea, which first reached Europe in 1610.

The Chinese had seldom looked far beyond their borders and after the mid-1500s the government banned voyages overseas. As the most powerful empire in the world, Ming rulers regarded China as the center of the world. They defended their territory and weaker subject-peoples against foreigners such as Hideyoshi of Japan, whose armies tried to invade Korea in the 1590s but later withdrew.

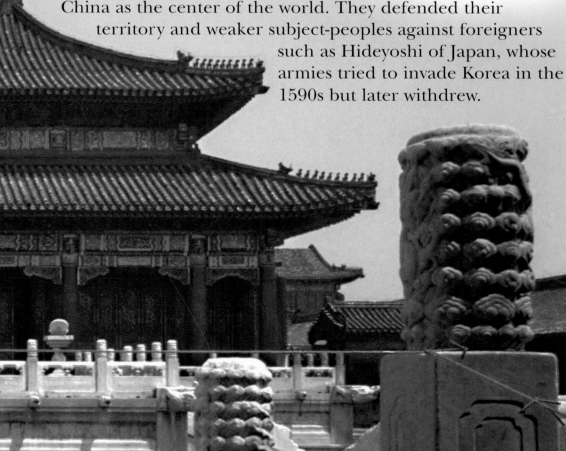

MING CHINA

1368 Foundation of the Ming dynasty in China.

1398 Death of the first Ming emperor, Hong Wu, who has extended his rule to all China and to Mongolia and Manchuria.

1405–1433 Zheng He leads seven voyages westward to explore India and East Africa. The Chinese demand tribute from the countries their ships visit, regarding them as inferior.

1421 The capital is moved from Nanjing to Beijing.

1449 The Ming emperor is captured by the western Mongols, a rare setback for the Ming armies. He resumes the throne in 1457.

1505–1560 A period of poor government by two cruel and pleasure-loving emperors.

1514 Portuguese traders arrive in China, followed by the Dutch in 1522.

1551 Chinese government bans voyages beyond Chinese waters.

1557 The Portuguese set up a trading base at Macao.

1560 Ming forces drive off Mongols and pirate raids, until peace and prosperity are restored. China's population approaches 150 million.

1575 Spanish begin trade with China.

1592–1598 Ming armies help Koreans fight off Japanese invaders.

1644 The last Ming emperor, Ssu Tsung, commits suicide.

△ *Italian missionary Matteo Ricci learned the language and customs of China. He visited Beijing in 1607, presenting two clocks to the emperor.*

Oceania

The people of Oceania—Australia, New Zealand, and the Pacific islands—lived by hunting and food gathering, fishing, and farming. They had come from southern or eastern Asia thousands of years before, traveling between the islands by canoe.

The first aboriginal peoples of Australia probably arrived there from the islands of Southeast Asia about 40,000 years ago. They lived by hunting and gathering and were isolated from the rest of the world. They developed a sophisticated way to exploit the wide variety of environments found in Australia, using boomerangs for hunting and gathering seeds, grubs, roots, tubers, and fruit. They developed a rich cultural life that included the myths of the Dream Time and beautifully ornate rock paintings often on sacred sites.

The Polynesians are the most widely spread people in the world. Their ancestors first lived in eastern Asia and, about 3,500 years ago, set sail in open canoes to find new lands to live in. They set out into the unknown in canoes loaded with the essentials of their life—coconuts, taro, yams, bananas, breadfruit, pigs, and chickens—and used their skills and luck to colonize the vast Pacific Ocean. Their canoes reached as far as Easter Island in the western Pacific and the Hawaiian Islands in the north.

▽ *Flightless birds, called* **moas,** *lived in New Zealand. There were a number of moa species, the tallest being 10 feet (3 m) tall. The last moas died out in the 1700s.*

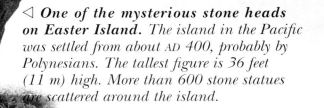

◁ **One of the mysterious stone heads on Easter Island.** *The island in the Pacific was settled from about* AD *400, probably by Polynesians. The tallest figure is 36 feet (11 m) high. More than 600 stone statues are scattered around the island.*

△ **The Maoris of New Zealand** built wooden stockades, called pas. Warriors fought from platforms on the walls, and to capture an enemy's fort was a great triumph. The victors took the food stored inside.

One of the last places they colonized was New Zealand.

Polynesian Maoris first came to New Zealand probably in about AD 750. As their culture developed, there were frequent blood-feuds and wars between Maori groups. The Maoris built hill-forts with stockades and platforms from which warriors hurled weapons (and insults) at their enemies outside. They decorated their faces and bodies with tattoos to show their standing in the community—the more tattoos, the higher the position.

Australia was settled by Aborigines in prehistoric times and later visited by Indonesian traders, but was otherwise isolated. A Portuguese ship may have strayed far enough south for its crew to sight New Zealand or Australia in the 1500s. A mysterious large island is shown on European maps made in the 1540s. The first known landing in Australia by Europeans was made in 1606 and European explorers only reached New Zealand in 1642.

▷ *A tattoed Maori warrior chief, painted in the 19th century. Maori weapons included clubs, stabbing spears, and long staves. Both men and women were tattooed, to show their rank. Fighting was part of Maori culture, and tribal feuds were common.*

▽ *A Maori war canoe sets out on a raid. Like other Pacific islanders, the Maoris built canoes for sea travel. People moved from island to island across the Pacific Ocean in wooden canoes, often twin-hulled like modern catamarans. Some settlements were the result of accidental voyages but others, of planned migrations in fleets of large canoes.*

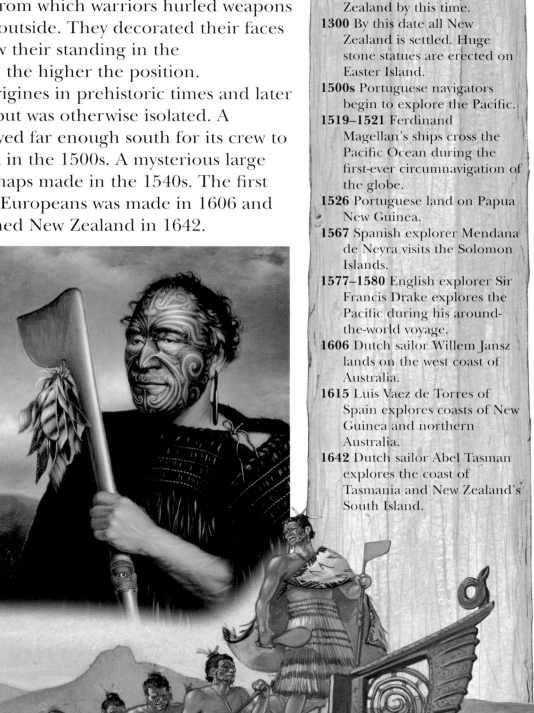

OCEANIA

c. **400** First settlers land on Easter Island.

c. **750** Maoris start to settle New Zealand by this time.

1300 By this date all New Zealand is settled. Huge stone statues are erected on Easter Island.

1500s Portuguese navigators begin to explore the Pacific.

1519–1521 Ferdinand Magellan's ships cross the Pacific Ocean during the first-ever circumnavigation of the globe.

1526 Portuguese land on Papua New Guinea.

1567 Spanish explorer Mendana de Neyra visits the Solomon Islands.

1577–1580 English explorer Sir Francis Drake explores the Pacific during his around-the-world voyage.

1606 Dutch sailor Willem Jansz lands on the west coast of Australia.

1615 Luis Vaez de Torres of Spain explores coasts of New Guinea and northern Australia.

1642 Dutch sailor Abel Tasman explores the coast of Tasmania and New Zealand's South Island.

The Thirty Years War

The religious conflicts that started after the Reformation continued into the 17th century. The most serious was the Thirty Years War. It began in 1618 as a protest by the Protestant noblemen of Bohemia (now part of the Czech Republic) against their Catholic rulers, the Habsburg Holy Roman emperors.

The noblemen chose a Protestant to become King Frederick of Bohemia, but in 1619 Ferdinand II became the new Holy Roman emperor. Rebellion against Ferdinand's rule soon spread to Germany and, determined to turn his whole empire back to Catholicism, Ferdinand sent his army to attack Bohemia.

The Bohemians were hoping for help from other Protestant countries in Europe, but at first this did not arrive. In 1620 Ferdinand's army defeated Frederick's so completely that Frederick and his family were forced to flee to the Netherlands. Soon Catholicism was the only religion allowed in Bohemia. A year later Spain, also ruled by the Habsburgs, joined the war on the side of the Holy Roman empire and sent an army to fight the Protestant Dutch. By 1625 Spain seemed likely to win and so the Dutch asked Denmark and England for help. Many English soldiers, however, died of plague before they could fight and by 1629 Habsburg armies had also defeated the Danes.

▽ **King Gustavus II Adolphus** *of Sweden leading his troops into battle. A brave and inspiring leader, he always fought at the head of his men. He went to war against the Habsburgs because he believed the Protestant religion was in danger of being destroyed. He also thought that the Swedish economy, which depended heavily on trade, was being threatened by a Spanish plan to extend their power to the Baltic Sea, which Sweden itself wanted to control.*

CARDINAL RICHELIEU

The French statesman Richelieu (1585–1642) started his rise to power as adviser to Marie de'Medici, the mother of French king Louis XIII. In 1629 he became Louis's chief minister and began building up the power of the French crown. He ruthlessly suppressed Protestantism in France, but supported the Protestant states in the Thirty Years War in order to defeat Spain and make France the most powerful country in Europe.

△ *In 1618, a group of Bohemian nobles threw two Catholic governors out of a window in Prague Castle. This act, called the Defenestration of Prague, sparked off the Thirty Years War.*

▷ *This map shows how Europe looked after the Treaty of Westphalia was signed in 1648. France was the dominant power, while Switzerland, many states in Germany, and part of the Netherlands became independent.*

THIRTY YEARS WAR

1618 War starts with the Defenestration of Prague.
1619 Ferdinand II is crowned Holy Roman emperor.
1620 Ferdinand's army enters Bohemia and defeats Protestant king Frederick.
1621 Fighting breaks out between Dutch and Spanish in the Rhineland.
1625 Denmark and England join in the war on the side of the Dutch. The Danes do most of the fighting.
1629 Denmark and England withdraw from the war.
1630 King Gustavus II Adolphus of Sweden joins the war on the side of the Protestants.
1631 Swedish victory at the battle of Breitenfeld.
1632 Gustavus is killed after the battle of Lutzen. His chancellor, Oxenstierna, takes command, but is not as successful.
1634 Sweden withdraws following defeat at Nordlingen.
1635 Richelieu takes France into the war against Habsburgs.
1637 French and allies start to defeat Spain.
1643 Following French victory at Rocroi, Olivares (Spain's prime minister) falls from power.
1648 The Treaty of Westphalia brings an end to the Thirty Years War.
1659 Spain and France cease fighting; France becomes the most powerful country in Europe.

Believing the Protestant religion to be in danger, the Swedish king Gustavus II Adolphus led his army to war against Spain and the Holy Roman empire in 1630. He defeated them at Breitenfeld in 1631 and his army was victorious again at Lutzen in 1632. But Gustavus was killed just after the battle of Lutzen, and two years later Sweden also withdrew from the war.

Finally France, although Catholic, entered the war in order to curtail Habsburg power. At first Spain was victorious, but from 1637 the French and their Protestant allies were able to defeat them. The war ended in 1648 with the Treaty of Westphalia, which gave religious freedom and independence to Protestant states. The long war devastated many states in Germany. Some lost over half their population through disease, famine, and fighting.

Tokugawa Japan

The Tokugawa, or Edo, period in Japan marked the end of a series of civil wars and brought a long period of stability and unity. In 1603, Tokugawa Ieyasu became the first of the Tokugawa shoguns (powerful military leaders and effective rulers of Japan). He and his descendants held office until 1867.

Tokugawa Ieyasu was born in 1543, a time when the Japanese warlords were fighting among themselves for control of the country. When Ieyasu was seven, he was sent as a hostage to the Imagawa family at Sumpu. There he learned the skills of fighting and government. When the head of the Imagawa family was killed in battle, Ieyasu returned to his own lands and began a long and well-planned struggle for power. By 1598 he had the biggest army in Japan. He also had the best organized and most productive estates in the country, centered on the fishing village of Edo. In 1603, after defeating his enemies, the emperor appointed Ieyasu to the position of shogun, giving him power to run the country on the emperor's behalf.

△ *Kabuki drama developed as a popular art form in 17th century Japan. Plays were performed to music, and costumes and makeup were very elaborate, especially for the female roles, which were always in fact played by men.*

TOKUGAWA JAPAN

1543 Birth of Tokugawa Ieyasu.

1550 Ieyasu is sent as a hostage to the Imagawa family.

1560 Ieyasu returns to his own lands and allies himself with the warlord, Nobunaga.

1582 Nobunaga commits suicide. He is succeeded by Hideyoshi.

1584 After several small battles, Ieyasu allies himself with Hideyoshi.

1598 Hideyoshi's death starts a new struggle for power among Japan's warlords. Ieyasu is one of the leaders.

1600 Ieyasu defeats his rivals at the battle of Sekigahara.

1603 The emperor appoints Ieyasu shogun and the Tokugawa period begins.

1605 Ieyasu abdicates as shogun but continues to advise his successors on how to run the country.

1613 The population of Edo is estimated to be 150,000, including 80,000 samurai.

1616 Death of Ieyasu.

1635 All the daimyos are forced to have a house in Edo and spend several months of each year there to make sure that they are not secretly plotting against the shogun.

1637 Christianity is banned in Japan and all foreigners, apart from the Dutch, are forced to leave.

1680 The production of silk, cotton, paper, and porcelain flourishes at this time.

1700s Merchants and tradesmen prosper for much of this century, but the daimyos and samurai become less wealthy than they had been.

1830s Peasants and samurai rebel against the Tokugawas.

1867 The last Tokugawa shogun is overthrown.

The emperor lived in Kyoto, but Ieyasu set up his government at Edo. He turned the village into a huge, fortified town, which later became known as Tokyo. He reorganized the country into regions called domains, each of which was led by a daimyo. The daimyo had to control the local groups of warriors, known as samurai, and also promise to support Ieyasu as shogun. This helped to bring peace to Japan. Ieyasu abdicated in 1605, but continued to hold real power until his death in 1616.

At first, Japan was open to foreigners and often visited by Portuguese, English, and Dutch traders. Missionaries converted many Japanese to Christianity. Ieyasu thought the new religion might undermine his rule and from 1612 missionaries were discouraged. In 1637 they were banned altogether and all Japanese Christians had to give up their religion or be put to death. At the same time, the shogun also decided that it would be easier to keep law and order in Japan if there was no foreign influence at all, so he banned all traders, apart from the Dutch who were allowed to send one trading ship each year to the port of Nagasaki.

Despite Japan's isolation from the rest of the world the country flourished. The population and food production increased, but taxes were heavy and many small crimes were punishable by death. Eventually rebellions started and in 1867 the Tokugawa dynasty was overthrown.

△ *Tokugawa Ieyasu (1543–1616) as shogun encouraged agriculture and Confucianism in Japan. He firmly controlled the nobles and their families.*

JAPANESE SOCIETY

Under the Tokugawas society was rigidly controlled—people were expected to commit suicide if they were disgraced in any way. Wealthy women were treated as ornaments. They had to wear very high shoes and long flowing gowns, which made it almost impossible for them to walk, while complicated hairstyles made it difficult for them to move their heads.

◁ *Samurai warriors were trained to fight from childhood. Their main weapons were bows and arrows, single-edged swords and daggers. They fought on foot or on horseback and wore armor and masks to make them look more frightening as well as for protection.*

△ *Himeji castle was built by the warlord Hideyoshi, who ruled Japan as dictator from 1582 until his death in 1598. The castle was his stronghold in the civil wars that tore Japan apart. Under the Tokugawas, the power of the warlords was greatly reduced.*

The Dutch Empire

Until 1581, the Netherlands, or Low Countries, was made up of 17 provinces, which included Belgium, Luxembourg, and the Netherlands. From 1482 they were part of the Holy Roman empire, ruled by Philip of Burgundy. When he died in 1506 they passed to his son, Charles. Charles became king of Spain in 1516, so they became a Spanish possession. The majority of the people in the northern provinces followed the Protestant religion and Charles's son, Philip II, persecuted them for this.

When they refused to give up Protestantism, he used terror tactics to try and persuade them. This led to a series of revolts from 1568 to 1581, led by William of Orange. Then the seven northern provinces declared their independence from Spain, calling themselves the Republic of the United Netherlands.

Seafaring, trade, finance, and fishing were the main ways of making a living in the Netherlands and following the declaration of independence in 1581, these all increased in importance. Amsterdam became the chief city and was home to many wealthy merchants and bankers.

△ **Traders from the Dutch East India Company** buying goods from the locals at the Cape of Good Hope at the tip of southern Africa. They needed these supplies to continue their journey to the East Indies.

DUTCH WEST INDIES

DUTCH GUIANA

DUTCH EAST INDIES

◁ **A flowering in Dutch art** was sparked off by wealth from trade and an end to Spanish rule. This painting is by Jan Vermeer (1635–1675), who lived in the town of Delft. Most of his paintings were of everyday subjects, such as this woman writing a letter, but they show the costumes and furnishings in great detail and rich colors.

△ **This map shows** the Dutch trading empire. The Dutch East Indies (now Indonesia) were rich in spices. Sugar, rice, and slaves were traded in Guiana (now Suriname).

▷ **Coffee, tea, cinnamon, and cloves** were some of the most valuable goods traded by the Dutch East India Company.

THE DUTCH EMPIRE

1568 Dutch led by William of Orange begin revolt against Spanish rule.

1576 Spanish troops destroy Antwerp. Many inhabitants move to Amsterdam.

1577 The Netherlands makes a pact with England to fight against the Spanish.

1579 Seven northern provinces of the Netherlands form the Union of Utrecht.

1581 The Republic of the United Netherlands declares independence. William of Orange is elected ruler.

1599 Dutch take control of the Moluccas from Portugal.

1602 Dutch East India Company is founded.

1621 Dutch West India Company is founded.

1648 Spain recognizes Dutch independence at the end of the Thirty Years War.

1651–1674 Three Anglo-Dutch wars between the Netherlands and England are fought over trade.

1689 William III of Orange and his wife Mary, daughter of James II of England are offered English throne. The Netherlands starts to decline as England becomes more powerful.

△ *William of Orange (1533–1584) led the Dutch in several revolts against Spanish rule. He was elected the first ruler of the Republic of the United Netherlands and was killed by a Spanish agent.*

Although Spain did not yet recognize their independence, the Dutch started to build up a trading empire. In 1599 they began to take control of the Moluccas, or Spice Islands, from the Portuguese and in 1602 the Dutch East India Company was set up to encourage more trade with the islands of the East Indies. In 1619 the Company set up its headquarters in Batavia (now Djakarta) on the island of Java. Then, helped by its own army and ships, the Company drove the Portuguese and English merchants out of the area. The Dutch East India Company went on to take control of Ceylon (now Sri Lanka) and several ports in India. In 1652 it set up a colony at Cape Town on the southernmost tip of Africa to supply its ships sailing between the Netherlands and the East Indies.

Other Dutch merchants sailed westwards and, in 1621, they set up the Dutch West India Company. This took control of several islands in the Caribbean, as well as Guiana on South America's mainland, some islands off the coast of Venezuela and parts of Brazil. The company traded in slaves, tobacco and sugar.

This trading empire helped to make the Dutch very wealthy people. Their trade was jealously guarded, however, and this led to wars with England in the second half of the 17th century.

△ *The cultivation of tulips started in the Netherlands in 1562 when a cargo of bulbs arrived from Turkey. In the 1630s the flowers became so popular people invested large sums to develop new varieties.*

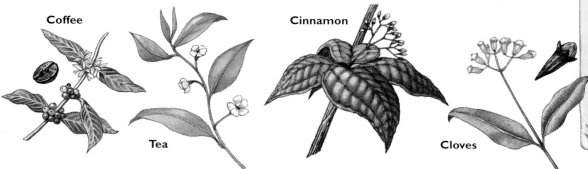

Coffee

Cinnamon

Tea

Cloves

61

Colonizing North America

The Spanish and French were the first Europeans to explore North America. French traders and missonaries explored the north, which they named Canada, while to the south, the Spanish founded what is now New Mexico, exploring California and Texas.

In the late 16th century, small groups of Europeans began to settle in North America. The first serious attempts at colonization were made by Sir Walter Raleigh, an English explorer, in the 1580s in an area he called Virginia. These early colonies all failed, but in 1607 Raleigh set up a more successful colony named Jamestown. Although the colonists had to struggle against hunger, disease, and battles with the Native Americans, whose land they were occupying, the colony managed to survive, encouraging other people to join them.

Probably the most famous early settlers are the Pilgrim Fathers, who left Plymouth in England in 1620. A group of religious dissenters, they were looking for a place to practice their religion in peace. Landing near Cape Cod in Massachusetts, they founded a small settlement and called it Plymouth Plantation.

▷ *Many Native Americans* *helped early settlers to survive. They taught them which crops were best suited to the land and climate and how to raise them. They also traded goods with the settlers.*

◁ *Sir Walter Raleigh (1552–1618), a favorite of Elizabeth I, named Virginia in honor of her. He introduced tobacco and potatoes to Britain. In 1615 he led a failed expedition to South America and was executed by James I on his return.*

△ *The* **Mayflower**, *the ship the Pilgrim Fathers and their families sailed on from England to America in 1620. They planned to land in Virginia, but were blown off course by storms and landed much farther north, near Cape Cod. It was the middle of winter when they landed and only 54 of the original 102 passengers survived until spring.*

Like many of the first settlers, they relied heavily on help from and trade with the Native Americans to survive. Four years later, the Dutch West India Company founded the colony of New Netherlands on the Hudson River and in 1625 they built a trading post on Manhattan Island, calling it New Amsterdam.

Meanwhile the French were starting to colonize Canada. Samuel de Champlain founded Quebec in 1608 and from there he explored beyond the St. Lawrence River as far as Lake Huron, claiming all the land for France. Later, other French explorers in the south traveled along the Mississippi River and claimed the whole river valley for France, calling it Louisiana after the French king Louis XIV.

Many of the colonists earned their living by farming, producing food for themselves and crops for export to Europe, such as tobacco, indigo, and rice. There were also many traders and trappers who either exchanged European goods, such as guns and alcohol, with the Native Americans for animal furs, or hunted and trapped the animals for themselves.

△ *The first settlements were built near a good water supply. The settlers cut down trees to build simple log cabins to live in and barns for their animals. The cleared land was fenced in and used for growing crops such as corn and squash. Turkeys were kept for food and tobacco was grown for export.*

EUROPEANS FIGHT FOR NORTH AMERICA

The English, French and Spanish claimed large areas of North America for themselves, even though there was already a large population of Native Americans there. Some tried to convert the Native Americans to Christianity while others came to trade, especially in furs, or to farm. As colonization increased, bitter battles were fought with the Native Americans and between colonists over who owned the land.

COLONIZING NORTH AMERICA

1513 Juan Ponce de Leon claims Florida for Spain.

1535–1542 Francisco de Coronado claims New Mexico, California, Arizona, and Texas for Spain.

1536 Jacques Cartier explores the St. Lawrence River in Canada, and claims it for France.

1584 Sir Walter Raleigh begins colonization of Virginia.

1608 French explorer Samuel de Champlain founds Quebec.

1609 The Spaniard Juan de Onate establishes Santa Fé as the capital of New Mexico.

1610 Henry Hudson discovers Hudson Bay in Canada.

1612 Settlers in Virginia start to plant tobacco.

1614 John Rolfe, a Virginia colonist, marries Pocohontas, a Native American princess.

1619 The first slaves from Africa arrive in Virginia to work on tobacco plantations.

1621 The Pilgrim Fathers hold the first Thanksgiving Day celebration following their first successful harvest.

1630 By this date there are around 16,000 English settlers in Massachusetts.

1636 Harvard College is founded in Cambridge, Massachusetts.

1641 The French start trading for furs in Michigan.

1664 The English capture New Amsterdam from the Dutch and rename it New York.

1670 The Hudson Bay Company is set up to encourage trade, especially in furs, between Canada and England.

1673 Two Frenchmen, Jacques Marquette and Louis Joliet, explore the Mississippi River from its source to Arkansas.

1679 Fur traders from France become the first Europeans to see the Niagara Falls.

1682 The explorer La Salle claims the whole Mississippi river valley for France.

1683 The first German settlers arrive in Pennsylvania.

1689 The first of three wars breaks out between British and French colonists in North America. It lasts until 1697, with each side wanting to control all the lands occupied by Europeans.

The English Civil War

The English Civil War broke out during the reign of Charles I, who came to the throne in 1625. Charles believed in Divine Right—God had given him the right to rule and so he was not answerable to parliament or to the people. He soon came into conflict with parliament over such issues as raising taxes, religion, and his right to imprison opponents.

Determined to have his own way, Charles dissolved parliament in 1629 and ruled without it for the next 11 years. With the help of three ministers, he found ways of raising money without taxation.

In 1639, however, rebellion broke out in Scotland. Charles did not have enough money to fight a war. He could only raise taxes through parliament, so in April 1640 he recalled its members. But parliament would not give Charles the money he needed unless he let them elect the chief officers of the state. Charles refused and tried to arrest his five leading opponents in the House of Commons.

PURITANS

People of the Puritan faith were Protestants who wanted to purify the Church of England of its pomp and ritual. They dressed in simple, modest clothes without jewelry or makeup and disapproved of entertainment such as dancing and the theater. They spent much of their time at prayer. The Pilgrim Fathers who sailed to America were Puritans and many more followed them to escape religious persecution.

▽ **The execution of Charles I** took place on a scaffold outside the banqueting hall of Whitehall Palace. A large crowd gathered to watch the event on January 31, 1649.

△ **Oliver Cromwell** (1599–1658) was a country gentleman and Member of Parliament before the Civil War. He helped recruit, train, and command the New Model Army. As Lord Protector he tried to impose parliamentary rule in Scotland and Ireland by force.

△ **Royalist soldiers** were also called Cavaliers. They wore their hair long and dressed flamboyantly, wearing wide-brimmed hats with feathers and shirts of fine linen trimmed with lace and bright colored jackets. Most Royalists were Catholics or members of the aristocracy.

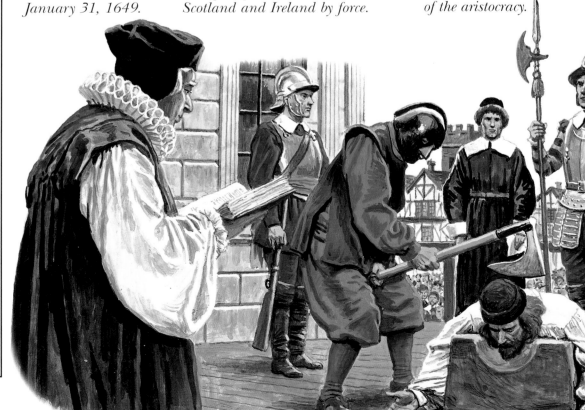

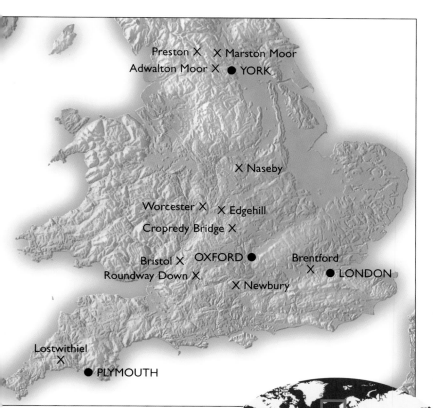

◁ *This map shows the main battles of the war. The pink areas are lands held by the king after the battle of Marston Moor (1644) in which he lost control of the north. Parliament controlled the rest of the country.*

▽ *Parliament's soldiers were known as Roundheads because of their short hair cuts. They wore plain woolen jackets over linen shirts. Iron breastplates and helmets protected them from serious injury.*

This action made civil war unavoidable.

Both sides raised large armies of volunteers and the first major battle took place on August 22, 1642 at Edgehill in the English Midlands. That battle ended with no clear victory for either side and, over the next four years, fighting took place in almost every part of the country. As well as the major battles, there were many skirmishes and sieges in which both civilians and soldiers suffered. Towns and even families were divided in their support, with rich and poor people equally likely to support either side. At first the king's forces, or Royalists, were the more successful. Parliament's supporters, or Roundheads, were led by able generals such as Oliver Cromwell who commanded a professional army, called the New Model Army. The Roundheads eventually defeated Charles's forces in 1645. Charles surrendered to the Scots, who handed him over to parliament, but he managed to escape and plotted with the Scots to start a second civil war, which broke out in 1648. It was quickly crushed and Charles was tried for treason. He was found guilty and executed in January 1649.

England became a commonwealth (republic), which at first was ruled by parliament. But its members quarreled, so from 1653 Oliver Cromwell ruled as Lord Protector. When he died in 1658 he was succeeded by his son Richard, who was weak and soon removed from office. The people wanted a king once more and so in 1660 Charles I's son was invited back from exile to reign as Charles II.

ENGLISH CIVIL WAR

1625 Charles I succeeds James I and marries Henrietta Maria, a Spanish princess.

1629 Parliament tries to curb Charles's power and is dismissed.

1637 Charles forces the English Prayer Book on Scotland.

1639 Rebellion breaks out in Scotland.

1640 Charles calls a new parliament in April, but dismisses it after three weeks. He recalls parliament again in November.

1641 Charles makes peace with the Scots, but rebellion breaks out in Ireland.

1642 In January, Charles tries to arrest five MPs in the House of Commons, sparking off civil war. The first major battle takes place at Edgehill, Warwickshire.

1645 The New Model Army, led by Sir Thomas Fairfax and Oliver Cromwell, decisively defeat Royalists at Naseby, Northamptonshire.

1646 Charles surrenders to the Scots.

1647 Charles is handed over to parliament. He is seized by the army and escapes to the Isle of Wight.

1648 Charles, aided by the Scots, starts a second civil war, but is quickly defeated.

1649 Charles goes on trial for treason on January 20 and is executed on January 31.

1651 Charles's son goes into exile in France.

1653–1658 Oliver Cromwell rules as Lord Protector.

1660 Restoration of the monarchy; Charles II comes to the throne.

The Slave Trade

Africa had a long history of slavery, but until the early 16th century this was only on a relatively small scale. Before this, most people who were enslaved were taken as prisoners of war or as a punishment for crime. Some were sold to Arab traders who sold them on as servants for a profit. The situation began to change when Europeans started to visit the coasts of Africa.

Elsewhere, European explorers were busy colonizing America and the islands of the Caribbean, setting up huge plantations of crops such as sugar cane. In many places, they enslaved the native population to do the work for them. But bad conditions and European diseases began to wipe out the native people, so the colonists started to look for workers to replace them. Some convicts were brought from Europe, but they were few in number and soon fell ill and died. The colonists then looked to Africa for slaves and the slave trade began on a much larger scale.

Soon huge numbers of people were being captured in the interior of Africa. Chained together so they could not escape, they were forced to march to the coast. There they were sold to European slave traders, put on to ships and taken across the Atlantic. Conditions on board ship were terrible with not enough light, air, food or water.

THE SLAVE TRADE

1441 The first Portuguese ship brings gold and slaves back from West Africa to Europe.

1448 Portuguese set up the first trading post in Africa. Slaves are taken there to be sold.

1493 Christopher Columbus introduces sugar cane from Europe to the Caribbean.

1502 Spanish take the first slaves from Africa to America to work on plantations.

1570s The Portuguese take slaves from Africa to Brazil to work on sugar plantations and in processing plants.

△ *Harriet Beecher Stowe (1811–1896) wrote* Uncle Tom's Cabin *in 1852 to raise support against slavery in the southern United States.*

1619 The first African slaves arrive in Virginia to work on tobacco plantations.

c. **1680** The average plantation in Barbados has 60 slaves.

1681 By now there are about 2,000 slaves in Virginia.

1683 Almost all the native peoples of the Caribbean, have been wiped out.

1700s The slave trade is at its peak. Cities such as Bristol, Liverpool, and Nantes grow rich on the profits.

1730 By now, about 90 per cent of Jamaica's population are of African origin.

1780s People start to campaign against slavery.

▽ *On a sugar plantation some slaves worked in the fields and others worked in the processing factories. For all slaves, the work was heavy, conditions were bad, and hours were long. Even those who worked in the plantation owner's house were often badly treated, underfed, and beaten.*

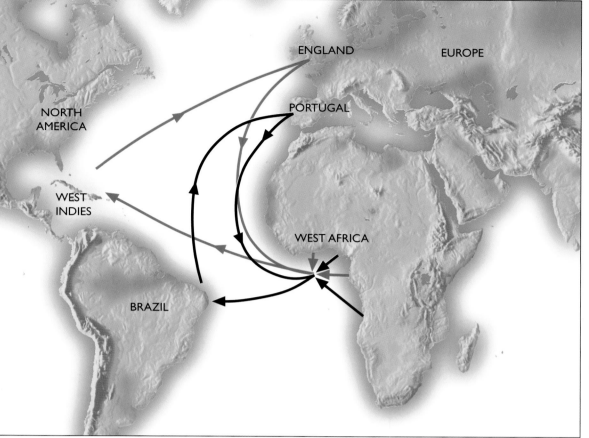

ENGLAND   EUROPE

NORTH AMERICA

PORTUGAL

WEST INDIES

WEST AFRICA

BRAZIL

A SLAVE AUCTION
When African slaves arrived in the Caribbean, South America or the colonies of North America they were sold at auction to the highest bidder. Africans from different cultures, who spoke different languages, were thrust together. Because they could not understand each other, this prevented them making plans to escape.

△ **This map shows** the triangular trade route taken by slave ships. Ships sailed from Europe to Africa with guns and cloth to buy slaves. The slaves were carried on the 'Middle Passage' to the Americas where they were sold. They returned home with sugar, rum and cotton.

◁ **Slave ships** were designed to carry more than 400 people, packed in as tightly as possible, on the two month voyage from West Africa to the Americas.

The slaves were still chained together and packed into so small a space that they could not move about. As many as a third died on each eight-week journey. The ones who did survive were often separated from their families and sold to different slave owners.

Slaves faced a hard life on the plantations where the work was heavy and the hours were long. Their accommodations were poor and they were often badly fed. Many were also whipped or beaten for the smallest mistake and many died soon after arriving on the plantations. Even the strongest rarely survived for more than ten years and very few ever saw their homeland again.

The slave trade reached its peak in the 18th century, when between six and seven million people were shipped from Africa to America. The impact on traditional African societies was devastating, destroying entire kingdoms while others grew rich and rose to power on the trade. From the 1780s onward, however, some Europeans began to realize how cruel slavery was and started to campaign against it.

▽ **Slaves were often brutally ill treated.** This slave is wearing a heavy iron collar to prevent him lying down to make sure that he could not rest while he was working. Many slaves were worked to death.

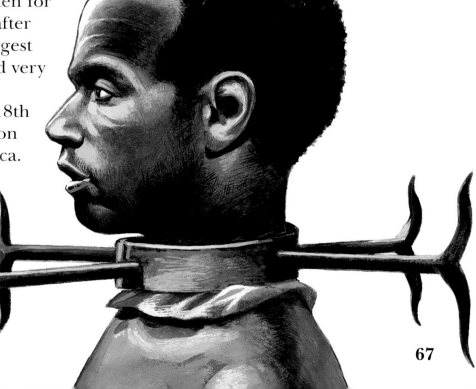

Louis XIV

Louis XIV of France was the most powerful of all European monarchs in the 17th century. An absolute ruler, he made decisions without regard to the common people or even to the nobility.

Louis XIV came to the throne in 1643 when he was just five years old. His mother ruled on his behalf as regent until 1651. During this period, there were constant arguments between her and the council of nobles who wanted a share of the power. There was also a rebellion against the crown in 1648 when the people revolted against the heavy taxes they had to pay. When this revolt spread to the nobles, Louis fled from Paris and did not return until 1653. He was determined that a similar rebellion should never happen again.

In 1661, when he was old enough to rule alone, Louis dismissed the council of nobles and took the government of France into his own hands. He chose his own advisers and met with them each morning to discuss what had to be done. His chief adviser was Jean Colbert, controller-general of finance. France was already the most powerful country in Europe and, by reorganizing taxes and reforming the legal system, Colbert made it the most efficient, too. To increase its wealth, Colbert set up new industries and improved communications with with a network of new roads, bridges, and canals.

▽ *The palace of Versailles, 18km southwest of Paris, was built on the site of a royal hunting lodge between 1662 and 1710. The centre of government, the nobility were encouraged to live there, too, under the king's watchful eye.*

LOUIS XIV

1638 Birth of Louis, son of Louis XIII of France and his wife Anne of Austria.

1643 Louis succeeds to the throne as Louis XIV.

1648 At the end of the Thirty Years War, France is the most powerful nation in Europe.

1653 Prime minister Jules Mazarin finally puts down the five-year uprising known as the Fronde and Louis returns to Paris.

1660 Louis marries Marie-Therese of Austria, daughter of the king of Spain.

1661 Mazarin dies and Louis takes control of France.

1662 Work starts on rebuilding Versailles. In some years Louis spends a quarter of the country's income on the palace.

1667 Start of war with Spain over the Netherlands. Louis gains control of Flanders, but has to retreat in 1668.

1672 Start of six-year Dutch war, which ends in victory for France.

1678 Louis moves his court to Versailles.

1685 Persecution of the Huguenots forces many of them to leave France.

1689–1697 War of the Grand Alliance, led by Britain against France, ends in French defeat.

1701–1713 War of the Spanish Succession in which Louis fights for control of the Spanish empire. Louis ensures the Spanish throne for his grandson, but brings France close to collapse.

1715 Death of Louis XIV at the age of 77.

THE PLAYS OF MOLIERE

Louis XIV was a great patron of the arts and literature. One of his favorite dramatists was Jean Baptiste Molière (1622–1673), often called the father of modern French comedy. From 1659 to 1673 Molière wrote and directed many plays at Versailles. He also acted in his plays and died shortly after collapsing on stage during a performance.

To protect France's position as Europe's dominant power, Colbert increased the size of the navy from 20 to 270 ships. He also enlarged France's merchant fleet to encourage trade.

These policies should have made France very rich, but Louis spent vast sums of money on building a magnificent new palace at Versailles near Paris. He also spent much of the money on wars. Louis wanted to expand French territory to reach the Alps, the Pyrenees, and the Rhine River, which he thought of as France's natural frontiers. To help him do this he greatly expanded the army and engaged in three major wars between 1667 and 1697.

The peasants and workers were heavily taxed to pay for Louis's extravagance, while the nobles and clergy paid nothing. Two bad harvests in a row left thousands starving, but any protests were quickly and severely crushed. After years of religious tolerance, the Huguenots, or French Protestants, were again persecuted by their Catholic rulers and from 1685 they were threatened with imprisonment or death if they did not give up their faith. As a result, around 300,000 fled abroad. As many of them were skilled craft workers, the French economy suffered from their loss.

When Louis died in 1715, his five-year-old great-grandson succeeded him. The boundaries of France were firmly established, but the country was financially weak after all the years of warfare.

△ **The Hall of Mirrors**, the most magnificent room at Versailles. The palace's ornate gilded statues, glass, tapestries, and paintings all stressed the king's magnificence and its style was copied throughout Europe.

▷ **Louis XIV (1638–1715)** was glorified by artists and writers as the Sun King. He was jealous of his personal reputation, or glory, which he considered to be inseparable from that of France, the country he ruled for 72 years.

69

Revolution & Industry

The world in turmoil 1700–1900

The two centuries between 1700 and 1900 were a time of conflict, revolution and change in many parts of the world. Some changes were political, while others were economic or social. Empires were won and lost, kings and governments toppled, and agriculture, industry, and transportation developed rapidly.

The countries of northwest Europe grew more powerful, while Spain and Portugal declined. The 13 American colonies declared their independence from Britain in 1776 to become the United States of America. They were helped by the French, who in 1789 had their own revolution, overthrowing their king and becoming first a republic and then an empire. By 1793 this action had led to wars between France and several other European countries, including Austria, Britain, the Netherlands, Portugal, Prussia, Russia, and Spain. The wars lasted until 1815 when the French emperor Napoleon was finally defeated. The Spanish and Portuguese colonies in South America took advantage of the wars in Europe to gain their independence, and by 1830 they were all free of foreign rule. Later conflicts in Europe united the separate states of Germany and of Italy into two countries, while conflict over slavery in the United States of America led to a four-year civil war.

Revolutions in agriculture, industry, and transportation affected the lives of even more people, especially in Europe and America. Canals and railways made travel overland easier, while steam-powered ships were

faster and more reliable than sailing ships had been. New methods of farming made it possible to feed more people, and large numbers left the countryside to make a living in the rapidly expanding towns. Factories in towns used machines to produce vast quantities of goods once made by hand. To provide raw materials and a ready market for these factory goods, many European countries began to build up new empires overseas. Britain tightened its control on India throughout this period and laid claim to Australia and New Zealand and many islands in the Pacific. In the Scramble for Africa, between 1880 and 1900, the European powers divided up the whole continent of Africa among themselves. China, Japan and Russia stayed largely isolated from the rest of the world and gradually stagnated. Millions of Europeans settled in the United States of America and forced the Native Americans to leave the lands they had lived in for thousands of years.

REVOLUTION & INDUSTRY

1644 Manchus overthrow the Ming dynasty of China.

1682–1725 Peter the Great rules Russia.

1730 Four-crop rotation begins in England.

1740 Frederick the Great becomes king of Prussia, which then dominates Europe.

1756–1763 Seven Years War: France, Austria, and Russia clash with Britain and Prussia.

1768 James Cooke sets out on the first of three voyages to the Pacific.

1776 On July 4, the Continental Congress in America adopts the Declaration of Independence.

1789 On July 14, a mob seizes the Bastille in Paris and the French Revolution starts.

1791 Thomas Paine's *The Rights of Man* published.

1804 Napoleon declares himself emperor of France.

1808 Independence struggles begin in South America.

1821 Napoleon dies in exile.

1837–1901 Queen Victoria's reign, during which the British empire includes a quarter of the world's people.

1848 Year of Revolutions affects most of Europe.

1856 Indian Mutiny.

1869 Union Pacific Railroad links east and west coasts of America.

1861 The American Civil War begins.

The Russian Empire

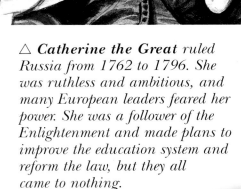

Peter the Great transformed Russia from an isolated, backward nation into a major European power. Nearly 40 years after his death, another great ruler, Catherine the Great, carried on his ambition.

Peter the Great, or Peter I, became czar of Russia in 1682 when he was just ten years old. At first he ruled with his half-brother Ivan V. When Ivan died in 1696, Peter ruled on his own until 1725. Russia had been expanding rapidly since 1639, but it was still a very backward country compared with the rest of Europe. Peter was determined to change this and for 18 months he toured western Europe, studying what was happening there. He met kings, scientists, and craft workers, as well as people who knew about industry, farming, and shipbuilding. In the Netherlands he even disguised himself as an ordinary workman and took employment in a shipyard for a while.

When Peter returned to Russia, he put the knowledge he had gained to use. He built up the Russian navy and established a modern iron industry. He encouraged other industries and farming, improved and expanded the army and built new roads and canals to help trade.

Peter also realized Russia needed a seaport that was not ice-bound in winter, but this meant it had to be on either the Baltic or Black seas, neither of which was in Russian territory. In 1721 Peter won a war against Sweden and gained Estonia and Livonia, both of which were on the Baltic. To reflect Russia's growing wealth and his own power, Peter also moved the capital north from Moscow to St. Petersburg.

△ *Catherine the Great ruled Russia from 1762 to 1796. She was ruthless and ambitious, and many European leaders feared her power. She was a follower of the Enlightenment and made plans to improve the education system and reform the law, but they all came to nothing.*

◁ *Peter the Great ruled Russia from 1682 to 1725. An immensely tall (nearly 7 feet) and strong man, his physical presence matched his character. Energetic and strong-willed he could be brutal, even imprisoning and torturing his own son.*

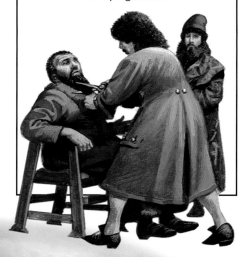

In the countryside, however, the serfs (peasants) were worse off as Peter increased the amount of tax they had to pay. In spite of this, Russia was more secure and advanced at Peter's death in 1725 than it had been when he came to power.

In 1762, another powerful ruler came to the throne. Catherine II (the Great) was Prussian by birth, but married the heir to the Russian throne in 1745. He was murdered six months after becoming czar and Catherine declared herself empress, even though the crown should have gone to her son. Like Peter I, she encouraged western ideas and used warfare to gain territory for Russia, fighting the Ottoman empire in 1774 and 1792, and Sweden in 1790. She also claimed much of Poland when it was partitioned (divided up). Conditions did not improve for the serfs, however. They were still heavily taxed and often faced starvation in order to pay the government. Those who complained were severely punished. A revolt in 1773 was harshly put down to discourage rebellions.

▽ **Russian peasant houses** *made of wood gave little protection from the worst of the weather. Life was a constant struggle for the serfs. They paid heavy taxes and, if the harvest was bad, they often went hungry.*

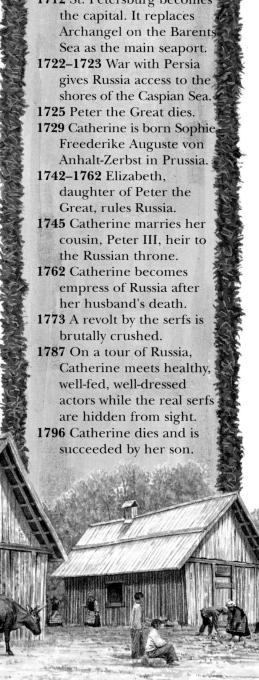

RUSSIAN EMPIRE

1638 Peter the Great is born.

1696 Peter becomes sole ruler of Russia.

1700–1721 Great Northern War against Sweden.

1703 St. Petersburg is founded. Peter calls it his "window on Europe."

1712 St. Petersburg becomes the capital. It replaces Archangel on the Barents Sea as the main seaport.

1722–1723 War with Persia gives Russia access to the shores of the Caspian Sea.

1725 Peter the Great dies.

1729 Catherine is born Sophie Freederike Auguste von Anhalt-Zerbst in Prussia.

1742–1762 Elizabeth, daughter of Peter the Great, rules Russia.

1745 Catherine marries her cousin, Peter III, heir to the Russian throne.

1762 Catherine becomes empress of Russia after her husband's death.

1773 A revolt by the serfs is brutally crushed.

1787 On a tour of Russia, Catherine meets healthy, well-fed, well-dressed actors while the real serfs are hidden from sight.

1796 Catherine dies and is succeeded by her son.

△ **St. Petersburg** *was designed and built by European architects. It had many palaces, churches, and government buildings. Its broad, tree-lined main streets were crossed by waterways and bridges.*

◁ **A carriage with runners**, *like a sleigh, gliding through the snow. Russian winters were so cold and snowy that carriage wheels had to be removed and replaced by runners.*

Manchu China

The Ming dynasty had ruled China since 1368, but in the early 17th century, rebellions against high taxes and an unpopular government began. At the same time, tribes in Manchuria, northeast of China, were uniting.

By 1618 the Manchu were strong enough to take control of and hold on to the Ming province of Liaotung. When a rebellion in China led to the capture of Beijing, the capital, in 1644, Ming officials asked the Manchus to help them defeat the rebels. Instead, the Manchus seized power and set up a new dynasty, known as the Qing, which ruled China for more than 250 years.

The Manchus considered themselves superior to the Chinese and lived apart from them. They made Chinese men wear their hair in pigtails and marriages between the Chinese and the Manchus were forbidden. From the start, however, they adopted the Chinese way of government and employed former Ming officials. Gradually they also

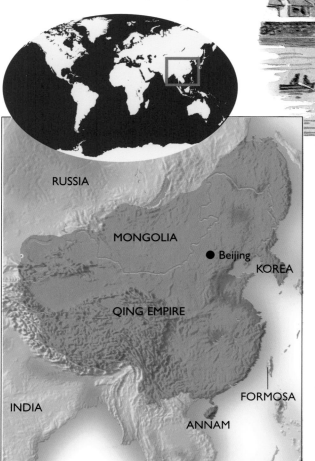

RUSSIA

MONGOLIA

● Beijing

KOREA

QING EMPIRE

INDIA

FORMOSA

ANNAM

△ *The only port Westerners were permitted to use* in the early 19th century was Canton. The Chinese, however, imposed many controls. For example, traders were only allowed to live and store their goods in a very small area around the port.

◁ *This map shows* the extent of the Qing dynasty's empire in orange It is much larger than China today whose boundary is shown in blue.

adopted the Chinese way of life, which made their rule more acceptable to the Chinese people.

Under the Qing dynasty, China flourished once more. Its empire grew to three times the size it had been under the Ming, and the population tripled from 150 million to 450 million people. Production of silk, porcelain, lacquerware, and cotton expanded, and trade, especially with Europe, increased greatly. The Chinese still considered their products to be better than anything else in the world and accepted only gold and silver in exchange for them. China's wealth came from farming, as it could produce almost all the food its people needed, and it grew tea for export. It could also provide all the tools and other equipment the farmers used to grow their crops.

During the 18th century, however, it became increasingly difficult for China to ignore European imports. Europeans, and especially the British, urgently wanted to find markets for their new products. Although the emperor Qianlong tried to restrict Europeans traders to just one port, they wanted to sell their goods to all parts of China. In 1792, Britain sent its first ambassador to the Chinese court with a request to be allowed to trade more widely. But the emperor would not give his permission, as he wanted China to remain isolated from the influence of other countries. This policy gradually changed China from a rich and successful country into a poor and backward one.

▷ **Beautifully shaped vases** *made from fine porcelain and decorated with patterns of leaves, flowers, and animals were exported to the West. Porcelain, lacquerware and silk were in great demand in Europe and America during the Qing dynasty.*

▽ **Only the emperor** *was allowed to wear a silk gown embroidered with a five-clawed dragon. On taking control of China the Manchu made the Chinese adopt their tradition of wearing their hair in a pigtail as a sign of loyalty. The Manchu wore superior clothes to the Chinese.*

◁ **Beijing** *expanded greatly under the Ming who added many palaces and temples, building a new wall and moat around the city. The Qing left the inner city unaltered, but new palaces and temples were added outside the city wall, to the west of the capital.*

75

The Enlightenment

The Enlightenment was a period from the late 17th century into the 18th century, when new ideas about government, personal freedom and religious beliefs began to develop in Europe.

The Enlightenment was influenced by the growth in scientific knowledge that began in the mid-17th century. People looked for reasons why things happened as they did. Modern chemistry and biology grew out of this questioning and our knowledge of physics and astronomy increased greatly. Medicine also improved as people began to study the human body and how it worked.

During the 18th century people began to look at the whole world and the role of people within it. The French philosopher and writer François Marie Voltaire

THE ENLIGHTENMENT

1632–1704 Life of English philosopher John Locke. He believed that all men were equal and free and that the authority of government comes only from the consent of the governed.

1687 Sir Isaac Newton publishes his *Philosophiae Naturalis Principia Mathematica* in which he sets out his theories about light and the visible spectrum, the three laws of motion, and the existence of gravity.

1724–1804 Life of German philosopher Immanuel Kant. He spends his life trying to discover the laws which govern the way people live.

1743 Benjamin Franklin sets up the American Philosophical Society in Philadelphia. Its members are interested in science as well as philosophy.

1743–1794 Life of French chemist Antoine Lavoisier, the first to establish that combustion (burning) is a form of chemical action.

1751 The first volume of the *Encyclopédie* is published.

1751 Carl Linnaeus publishes his *Philosophia Botanica*.

1755 Samuel Johnson's *Complete Dictionary of the English Language* is published. It contains over 43,000 words.

1768 The *Encyclopaedia Britannica* is first published.

1788 *The Times* newspaper is first published in London.

1791 Thomas Paine's *The Rights of Man* is published. This work greatly influences America in its fight for independence from Britain.

1792 Mary Wollstonecraft's *A Vindication of the Rights of Women* is published. It argues for equal opportunities in education for everyone.

▷ *A botanical drawing of sunflowers from* Philosophia Botanica *by Carl Linnaeus, published in 1751. Linnaeus was a Swedish botanist who was the first to classify the plant and animal kingdoms, defining and grouping living things into species. Linnaeus wrote many books on the subject.*

▽ *The* Encyclopédie, *compiled by French writer and critic Denis Diderot, was written by experts in many different subjects and aimed to further all branches of knowledge. The first volume was published in 1751. The work was completed in 1772 and comprised 17 volumes of text and 11 volumes of pictures.*

△ *A reconstruction of* **Endeavour**, *the ship that British captain James Cook set out in to explore the South Pacific in 1768. Scientists and skilled artists on board recorded the plants, animals, and people they met on the voyage.*

The scene below shows a lecture being given in the salon, or drawing room, of Madame Geoffrin in Paris, in 1725. Noblewomen such as Madame Geoffrin were great patrons of learning and the arts. By persuading well-known scholars, writers, and philosophers to give private lectures to them and their friends in their homes, they encouraged the discussion of new ideas. Women such as Marie Anne Lavoisier also helped advance science. She assisted her husband, Antoine Lavoisier, in his experiments on gas and later edited his work.

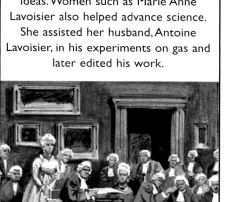

attacked the Church and governments of the day. Another Frenchman, Jean-Jacques Rousseau, criticized civilization itself, saying people should not try to obtain more possessions or power than they needed. Both challenged the idea of absolute monarchy and the tradition that the nobility and clergy were entitled to special privileges. Other great thinkers of the Enlightenment included the economist Adam Smith, the historian David Hume, the philosopher Immanuel Kant, and the writers Mary Wollstonecraft and Samuel Johnson.

These new ideas, together with those of other scholars and philosophers of the time, spread rapidly. Many had their thoughts published in books or pamphlets. Others wrote letters to the newspapers or gave lectures. The wealthy and well educated in France often met in the drawing-rooms of noblewomen to discuss the latest books, plays, and issues of the day.

People began to question the way they were governed. A belief that everyone had the right to knowledge, freedom, and happiness inspired the American War of Independence and the French Revolution and eventually led to an end to slavery and the breakup of Spain's empire in South America.

▽ *François Marie Voltaire (1694–1778), novelist, playwright, scientist, and philosopher. He famously said, "I may disagree with what you say, but I will defend to the death your right to say it."*

▷ *Ballet in the 18th century was performed in public for the first time. Ballerinas began to wear clothes that were less constricting and easier to dance in.*

The Agricultural Revolution

Until the end of the 17th century, farming methods in Europe remained unchanged from the Middle Ages. Most people still lived in the country and were able to grow just enough food to feed themselves with a little spare to sell at the local market.

The land people farmed was in small strips, scattered over three or four large open fields that surrounded each village. To keep the land fertile, one field had to remain unplanted, or fallow, each year and so produced nothing. This system worked quite well while the population was small in number and most people could grow at least some of their own food. As the population began to increase, however, more people moved to live in the newly expanding towns where there was no land on which to grow crops. This meant that, if everyone was going to be fed, better ways of growing crops and organizing farms had to be found.

Some of the earliest experiments in agriculture were carried out in the Netherlands, in order to create more land that was suitable for farming. The Dutch drained water from

▽ *Miles of stone walls* were built across many parts of Britain as more fields were enclosed. Some stone was dug out of the fields, but the rest had to be cut from quarries. Elsewhere, hedges and brick walls were erected.

▽ *New, larger breeds* of farm animals were bred during the 18th century. Artists often painted portraits of the best of them, together with their proud owners, as in this picture called Mr. Healey's Sheep.

CROP ROTATION

Crop rotation increased the fertility of the soil without having to leave any fields lying fallow with grass for a year. Using four fields, a farmer planted wheat in the first, turnips in the second, barley in the third, and clover in the fourth. Each year the crops were rotated, so in the following year wheat was grown in the second field, turnips in the third, barley in the fourth and clover in the first. The clover put goodness back into the soil, while the turnips broke it up at a deeper level, so improving it for wheat and barley.

▷ *A seed drill* made a series of even holes into which seeds fell. A worker then raked over the holes. Before this, seeds were scattered on the ground by hand. They fell unevenly and often failed to germinate, or were eaten by hungry birds.

THE AGRICULTURAL REVOLUTION

1701 British inventor Jethro Tull invents the seed drill.

1715 By this date the Dutch have reclaimed over 400,000 acres of land.

1730 Introduction in England of four-crop rotation to make better use of land.

1759–1801 Enclosure Acts passed by British parliament enclose nearly 7,500,000 acres of common land.

1790 A professorship of agriculture and rural economy is set up at Edinburgh University.

1796 A school for farmers is set up at Keszthely in Hungary. There students learn from the experiences of others.

1800 By this date the weight of the average cow in Britain has more than doubled from 100 years earlier as a result of careful breeding.

1840 German farmer Justus von Liebig publishes the first book on using chemicals in farming.

lakes and reclaimed land from the sea, using pumps powered by windmills to keep the water out. This cost a great deal of money, so Dutch farmers could not afford to leave any of their fields unplanted. Instead, they experimented with crop rotation, in which four different crops were planted in the same field over a four-year period. This idea was copied in Belgium and Britain who also reclaimed large amounts of low-lying land near the sea. Other experiments involved farm machinery. The plow was improved and the horse-drawn seed drill and hoe were invented. These allowed several rows of seeds to be sown and later weeded all at the same time.

In many areas, the land itself was reorganized. The large, open fields were divided up into smaller ones, separated by fences, hedges, or walls. Laws were passed in Britain giving landowners the right to enclose common land, which had previously been used for grazing by everyone in the village. Sometimes whole villages were demolished and the people forced to move away to make more space for the new system of enclosed fields.

Farmers also began to experiment with breeding bigger and more profitable cattle, sheep and pigs. They grew crops such as turnips which would feed the animals over the winter when the grass stopped growing. This made sure that there would be plenty of animals to breed from again in the following spring.

The population of Europe continued to rise and more people left the countryside to live in towns and cities. By the end of the 18th century, however, the revolution in agriculture made sure that there was enough food to feed them all.

△ *The fantail windmill* was invented in 1745. Before this, a windmill's main sails needed moving whenever the wind changed so that they faced into the wind and worked efficiently. The fantail was attached to the main sails and moved them when the wind shifted.

79

Austria and Prussia

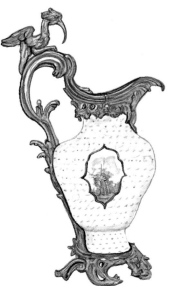

Europe in the 18th century was dominated by absolute monarchs. Rulers of all they surveyed, they built lavish palaces and attracted artists and intellectuals to their "enlightened" courts. Two of the richest and most powerful European states at that time were Austria and Prussia.

Austria was ruled by the Habsburgs, a family that had dominated Europe since the 13th century. Through a series of wars, inheritances, and marriages, the Habsburgs came to rule a vast area of land that by the 16th century had become too large for one person to rule alone. The Habsburg emperor, Charles V (and I of Spain) divided his lands so that one half was governed from Madrid in Spain while the other was governed from Vienna in Austria. In 1700 the Spanish Habsburgs died out, but the Austrian Habsburgs continued to assert their power.

In 1740 Maria Theresa came to the Austrian throne. She pulled Austria back from virtual bankruptcy, restoring its power and under her rule Austria became the artistic center of Europe. Artists from all over Europe came to work on its grand building projects.

△ *Maria Theresa (1717–1780) inherited the throne of Austria in 1740. Three other rulers claimed the throne and war broke out among her rivals. Her position was secured in 1748 when the war was ended.*

▽ *Wolfgang Amadeus Mozart (1756–1791) playing at the court of Maria Theresa. Mozart first played at court when he was only six years old. Born in Salzburg, he later settled in Vienna where he became a friend of the composer Franz Joseph Haydn (1732–1809).*

△ *The Schonbrunn Palace in Vienna was built between 1696 and 1711. Then on the edge of the city, it was the Habsburgs's summer palace. Originally planned to rival Versailles, it had 1,440 rooms and was set in formal gardens, surrounded by a park.*

Maria Theresa was succeeded in 1780 by her son Joseph II, who was a follower of the Enlightenment. He was concerned with the living conditions of his poorer subjects and began reforms such as freeing the serfs and abolishing privileges.

Frederick II (the Great) became king of Prussia in 1740. He inherited a well-organized state with an efficient and powerful army, which he used to increase Prussia's power. Frederick was an outstanding general, his greatest victory being at Rossbach (1757) when he routed a combined French and Austrian army twice the size of his own. Under his leadership, Prussia emerged from struggles to dominate Europe as a major power. He introduced economic reforms, religious freedom, and abolished torture in the belief that only a ruler with absolute power could improve society.

Holy Roman Empire

◁ *The Seven Years War (1756–1763) was a clash of interests between European powers. France, Austria, and Russia opposed Prussia and Britain. At the end of the war Prussia gained Silesia seized from Austria and Britain took control of France's colonies in India and America.*

▽ *Frederick the Great (1712–1786) of Prussia was a cultured man, but also a stern administrator and very ambitious. He encouraged the study of science and agriculture and also improved education for middle class boys.*

AUSTRIA AND PRUSSIA

1700 By this date Austria has reconquered Hungary from the Ottomans. The last Spanish Habsburg monarch dies and Spain is ruled by the Bourbons of France.

1701 Frederick III Elector of Brandenburg is crowned Frederick I, King of Prussia.

1711 Charles VI, Archduke of Austria, becomes Holy Roman emperor.

1713 Frederick William succeeds as king of Prussia. He centralizes government and creates a powerful regular army.

1740 Charles VI dies and his daughter Maria Theresa inherits the Austrian throne. War breaks out as rivals challenge her right to rule. Frederick II (the Great) becomes king of Prussia and seizes Silesia from Austria.

1756–1763 Seven Years War. France, Austria, and Russia clash with Britain and Prussia.

1757 Battle of Rossbach. Prussia defeats a much larger Austrian and French army.

1758 Frederick defeats Russians at Zorndorf.

1765 Maria Theresa rules Holy Roman empire with her son Joseph.

1772 First partition of Poland by Austria, Prussia, and Russia.

1780 Maria Theresa is succeeded by Joseph.

1781 Joseph introduces major reforms and frees the serfs.

1786 Frederick the Great dies.

1795 Final partition of Poland between Austria, Prussia, and Russia. Poland ceases to exist until 1919.

81

Birth of the USA

BIRTH OF THE USA

763 End of the Seven Years War between France and Britain. Britain gains control of France's territory in Canada and India.

1765 Protests start against British taxes in the American colonies.

1770 At the Boston Massacre, British troops fire on a crowd of colonists and kill five of them.

1773 At the Boston Tea Party, colonists board three ships in Boston harbor and throw their cargoes overboard as a protest against the tax on tea.

1775 The American War of Independence starts.

1776 On July 4 the Continental Congress adopts the Declaration of Independence. British forces capture and burn New York.

1777 British army is defeated at Saratoga, New York. France joins war on America's side.

△ *Thomas Jefferson (1743–1826) was a lawyer and politician who helped to draft the Declaration of Independence. In the war he was an ambassador in Europe. From 1801 to 1809 he was president of the United States.*

1777 British capture Philadelphia, Pennsylvania.

1778 The British capture Savannah, Georgia.

1779 Spain joins the war on America's side.

1780 The Dutch join war on America's side. British victory at Charleston, South Carolina.

1781 After a siege at Yorktown, Virginia, the British army surrenders.

Before 1750, fighting frequently broke out between British and French colonists in North America over trade and wars in Europe. This fighting was brought to an end when British control of all Canada was agreed by the signing of the Treaty of Paris at the end of the Seven Years War (1756–1763).

With the threat from the French removed, British colonists in America no longer relied on Britain for defense. But Britain needed American taxes to pay for governing their new French territories. By this time there were about two million people living in Britain's 13 colonies in America. They produced most of the food and goods they needed, but taxes were imposed on imported goods, such as tea, and legal documents.

By 1770 the colonists were becoming increasingly unhappy with the British government. Even though they had to pay British taxes they had no say in how government was run. The colonists declared that "taxation without representation is tyranny." Britain reacted by sending more soldiers and, in April 1775, an armed confrontation between colonists and British troops took place at Lexington in Massachusetts.

▽ *George Washington became commander of the American forces in 1775. On Christmas night 1776, he led his troops across the ice-strewn Delaware River and went on to defeat the British at the battle of Trenton, one of the first major American victories in the War of Independence. In 1789, he was elected the first president of the United States, serving two terms.*

PAUL REVERE

Paul Revere is one of the heroes of the War of Independence. He is shown here on his brave ride from Boston to Lexington to warn of the approach of British soldiers. Although he was captured, his mission was successful. He has been famously immortalized by American poet Longfellow who wrote: "Listen my children and you shall hear Of the midnight ride of Paul Revere."

The colonists formed an army of their own, commanded by George Washington and on June 17 the two armies clashed at Bunker Hill, near Boston. The British were successful, but the War of Independence had begun.

Fighting continued and on July 4, 1776 the colonial leaders passed the Declaration of Independence from Britain. The British government refused to accept this. Under Washington's continuing command, the colonists' army increased in size, becoming better equipped and better trained, and began defeating the British. France, Spain, and the Netherlands all joined in on the colonists' side, making it difficult for Britain to keep its army supplied. The six-year war ended in 1781 when the British surrendered at Yorktown. Two years later, Britain recognized an independent United States of America.

△ *British troops,* trained for fighting in European wars, found fighting in America very different. Standing in close-packed ranks, firing volleys of shot, they presented good targets for the American sharpshooters. The British won the battle of Bunker Hill (1775), but at a terrible cost of 1,000 casualties against 400 American casualties. British infantrymen (left) wore red long-tailed coats and so were known as "redcoats."

▽ *The Declaration of Independence* was signed on July 4, 1776, by delegates from the 13 colonies. It separated them from Great Britain and created the United States. It is recognized as one of the great documents of history.

The French Revolution

△ *Maximilien Robespierre (1758–1794) was a lawyer who was elected to the Estates General in 1789. In 1793, he started the Reign of Terror and during the following nine months thousands of opponents of the Revolution were put to death, until he himself was denounced and guillotined.*

In the 18th century, society in France was divided into three classes, known as estates. The first estate was the nobility, the second was the clergy, and the third was everyone else. Only people in the third estate paid taxes, however, and discontent grew as taxes kept increasing.

In 1788, a bad harvest made food scarce and pushed up prices leaving many poorer people facing starvation. The government was also short of money, as a result of extravagant kings and costly wars. Many well-educated members of the third estate knew about the ideas of the Enlightenment and some had helped America in its war of independence from Britain. This made them realize how unfair the system was in France. When the French king, Louis XVI, called a meeting of the Estates General (the nearest France had to a parliament) in 1789 to try and raise more money, the third estate started to rebel. They said that if they had to pay taxes, they should have a say in the way the country was run. Louis XVI refused this request and locked them out of the room at Versailles in which the Estates General was meeting.

The third estate decided to hold its own meeting on a tennis court at Versailles. Calling themselves the National Assembly, its members refused to move until the king listened to their demands. Unrest was growing elsewhere—in Paris a mob attacked the Bastille, a royal prison, and soon riots broke out all over France.

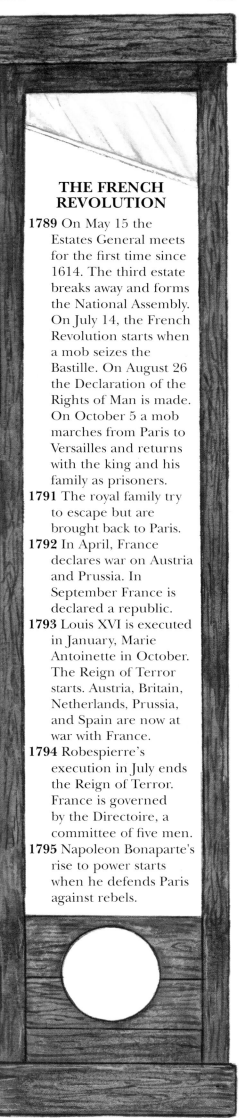

▷ *The Place de la Concorde today is an important site in the heart of Paris, but in 1793 it was where the guillotine stood. Another important revoutionary site, the Bastille, was demolished soon after its capture on July 14, 1789.*

The National Assembly then made its Declaration of the Rights of Man. These included liberty, equality and the right to resist oppression. Louis XVI refused to agree to this and so he and his family were arrested and brought back to Paris, where they were held in the Tuileries until 1793. Finally, as the king still refused to give more power to the people, he was put on trial and executed.

This was the start of the Reign of Terror, led by Maximilien Robespierre, which lasted until 1794. During that time thousands of people were arrested and put to death. Austria, Britain, the Netherlands, Prussia, and Spain all declared war on France. Frightened by this turn of events, Robespierre's colleagues ordered his execution. A new government, the Directoire, was set up. The threat of civil war in 1795 lead to the rise to power of an ambitious French general—Napoleon Bonaparte.

THE FRENCH REVOLUTION

1789 On May 15 the Estates General meets for the first time since 1614. The third estate breaks away and forms the National Assembly. On July 14, the French Revolution starts when a mob seizes the Bastille. On August 26 the Declaration of the Rights of Man is made. On October 5 a mob marches from Paris to Versailles and returns with the king and his family as prisoners.

1791 The royal family try to escape but are brought back to Paris.

1792 In April, France declares war on Austria and Prussia. In September France is declared a republic.

1793 Louis XVI is executed in January, Marie Antoinette in October. The Reign of Terror starts. Austria, Britain, Netherlands, Prussia, and Spain are now at war with France.

1794 Robespierre's execution in July ends the Reign of Terror. France is governed by the Directoire, a committee of five men.

1795 Napoleon Bonaparte's rise to power starts when he defends Paris against rebels.

MARIE ANTOINETTE
Marie Antoinette (1755–1793) was the daughter of Marie Theresa of Austria and married Louis XVI in 1770 when he was heir to the French throne. Young and pretty, she was popular at the start of Louis's reign in 1774. But Marie was extravagant and soon the people turned against her. On hearing that Parisians were rioting over bread shortages, she is quoted as callously saying "let them eat cake."

◁ *During the Reign of Terror around 500,000 people were arrested and 17,000 of them were put to death by public execution on the guillotine. Many of the victims were aristocrats, whose deaths attracted large crowds. Their bodies were buried in unmarked graves.*

Oceania

OCEANIA

1605 The Dutch explorer Willem Janzoon lands briefly on the northeast coast of Australia but does not venture inland.

1642 Anthony van Diemen, the Dutch governor-general of Batavia, sends Abel Tasman to explore the South Pacific. Tasman sees Tasmania, which he names Van Diemen's Land.

1644 Tasman's second journey, during which he sails along the north coast of Australia.

1686 The English explorer William Dampier reaches Australia.

1699 The British Admiralty sends Dampier on a second voyage to Australia; he returns in 1701.

1768 Captain James Cook's first voyage to the South Pacific; it lasts until 1771.

1772 Captain Cook's second voyage to the South Pacific. This voyage also lasts for three years.

1776 Captain Cook's third and last voyage to the South Pacific. It ends in tragedy in 1779 when he is killed in a quarrel with the Hawaiians.

1788 The first penal colony is set up in Australia and convicts are transported there from Britain.

1793 The first free settlers from Britain arrive in Australia. They settle in the area of Botany Bay.

1803 Settlers from Britain start going to Tasmania for the first time.

1813 By this date merino sheep have been introduced into Australia and the settlers have spread farther north and west, beyond the Blue Mountains.

1840 Maori leaders sign the Treaty of Waitangi with the British. It offers them land rights and full British citizenship. The treaty is not honored and war breaks out (1843–1848).

1851 The discovery of gold in Victoria results in the Gold Rush and brings many more settlers to Australia.

The first European to see the continent of Australia was the Dutch explorer Willem Janzoon, who landed on its northeast tip in about 1605. Over the next 20 years, other Dutch explorers also landed briefly on the north and west coasts of Australia, but, like Janzoon, none of them ventured inland.

Another Dutchman, Abel Tasman, was sent from Batavia (Indonesia) in 1642 to find out more about the extent of the great southern continent. On this voyage, Tasman sailed to Tasmania, New Zealand, Tonga, and Fiji. Two years later he sailed south again, traveling along the north coast of Australia. But he thought the land looked too poor and did not think that any Europeans would want to live there.

In the 18th century, the British navigator, James Cook, made three famous voyages to the Pacific. His first voyage left in 1768 and with him went scientists and skilled artists to record the plants, animals, and people they met. It took him around New Zealand, then to the eastern and northern coasts of Australia. Cook landed at Botany Bay on the southeast coast and claimed the territory for Britain, even though it was already inhabited by Aboriginal Australians. On his second journey he explored many of the Pacific Islands and in 1776, on his third voyage, he went to New Zealand once more, then explored the Pacific coast of South America before going to Hawaii.

In 1788 the British government started transporting convicts to the penal colony of Port Jackson, which had been set up in Australia. Some convicts stayed on when their

▽ *Captain James Cook* and the crew of the Endeavour *meeting Maoris in New Zealand for first time. Between 1769 and 1770, Cook spent six months charting the coast of New Zealand, also attempting to establish good relations with the people he visited.*

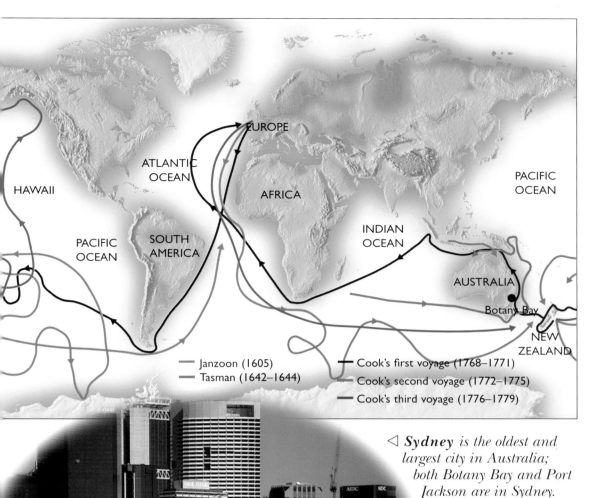

◁ **This map shows** the routes followed by Willem Janzoon and Abel Tasman, as well as the three voyages made by James Cook. These three men did more than any other Europeans to map the coasts of the Pacific Ocean.

Janzoon (1605)
Tasman (1642–1644)
Cook's first voyage (1768–1771)
Cook's second voyage (1772–1775)
Cook's third voyage (1776–1779)

THE MAORIS

When James Cook arrived in New Zealand, there were around 100,000 Maoris living there. They were skilled sailors and woodworkers who had migrated to New Zealand from the Pacific Islands of Polynesia about 800 years earlier. At first they lived by hunting, but by the 18th century most were self-sufficient farmers, living in villages and growing sweet potatoes and other crops. They used stone and wood for their tools and weapons, and this put them at a disadvantage when European settlers started to arrive. In 1840 the first British colonists founded Wellington on land bought from the Maoris. Britain claimed New Zealand and sent a governor to sign an agreement with the Maoris, called the Treaty of Waitangi, granting them land rights and offering British citizenship. Their rights were not protected, however, and war broke out. It ended in defeat for the Maoris in 1848.

◁ **Sydney** is the oldest and largest city in Australia; both Botany Bay and Port Jackson are in Sydney. With its fine natural harbor, it developed from a penal colony into a thriving town, which by 1850 had a population of 60,000. Schools, hospitals, churches, and court houses were built and several parks laid out.

sentences were completed and from 1793 they were joined by free settlers in ever increasing numbers. These settlers had little respect for the Aboriginal Australians whose homelands they were stealing. They did not understand Aboriginal beliefs that the people belonged to the land and not the other way around and they had no respect for Aboriginal sacred places. Instead, missionaries were sent to try and convert the Aboriginals to Christianity. Settlers in New Zealand treated the Maori population in the same way and soon the native peoples began to die in large numbers. Many were shot by the settlers or killed by the diseases they brought. Others simply lost the will to live as they lost a way of life they had followed for thousands of years.

▷ **Aboriginal paintings** on rocks and tree bark often depicted animals and people, in highly stylized forms. They were painted in pigments made from colored earths and were drawn in order to keep the spirits of the creator ancestors alive.

87

Napoleon

The empire
Dependent states
X   Battles

Borodino X
X Friedland
Smolensk
X Leipzig
Waterloo   X Lutzen
X Jena
Hohenlinden X   X Wagram
Austerlitz X
Vittoria
Marengo X
X Torres Vedras
X Trafalgar

△ *This map shows the French empire under Napoleon I and the dependent states that were virtually part of it. The main battles of the Napoleonic Wars are also shown.*

▷ *Josephine de Beauharnais (1763–1814) married Napoleon in 1796. The widow of a French general executed in 1794, she had important political connections. Their marriage was annulled in 1809, because she failed to produce a son.*

Napoleon Bonaparte was born on the island of Corsica in 1769. The son of an Italian nobleman, he made his name in the French army, rising to become the emperor of France. The start of the 19th century was dominated by war as he set out to achieve his aim of ruling Europe.

At the age of 15 Napoleon went to military school in Paris, becoming an officer in 1785. A supporter of the French Revolution, he gained his first victory in 1793 when he siezed the port of Toulon from French rebels being aided by British and Spanish troops. Following this, Napoleon fell from favor with the French leadership until 1795, when he was recalled to Paris to defend the city against rebels who threatened to cause a civil war. In 1796 he was given command of the army in Italy and by 1797 he had conquered Milan and Mantua.

NAPOLEON'S ACHIEVEMENTS

Apart from the Code Napoleon (which forms the basis of many countries' legal systems today) Napoleon also changed how wars were fought with new tactics and formations. Much of his success was based on his popularity and in 1802 he introduced the Legion of Honor to reward outstanding service to the state.

1825   1850   1875   1900

Other Italian states, including Sardinia and Naples, surrendered and Napoleon was put in command of the invasion of Egypt.

The French hoped that invading Egypt would disrupt the British trade route to India and so cause massive unemployment and unrest in Britain. In 1798 the French army defeated the Egyptians at the battle of the Pyramids and the Ottomans at the battle of Aboukir Bay, before the British navy under Nelson defeated the French navy at the battle of the Nile.

Napoleon returned to France, determined to overthrow the Directoire, or committee, that ruled the country. France needed a strong leadership after the instability following the Revolution and many welcomed his return. In November 1799, the Directoire was overthrown and in 1802 Napoleon became First Consul. Two years later, he proclaimed himself Emperor of France. He was determined to reorganize France, and in 1804 he introduced the Code Napoleon, which enshrined in law some of the principles of the French Revolution. The code protected property rights, established the equality of all people before the law, and allowed people to practice their religion freely.

△ *At the Battle of Austerlitz* in December *1805, a French army of 73,000, under the command of Napoleon and his generals Soult and Bernadotte, defeated an army of 87,000 Austrians and Russians. The enemy was lured into a valley where many were killed.*

NAPOLEON

1769 Birth of Napoleon at Ajaccio, Corsica.

1785 Napoleon becomes an officer in the French army.

1795 Napoleon defends Paris against rebels and prevents civil war breaking out.

1797 A French army led by Napoleon drives Austrians from much of north Italy and negotiates a peace.

1798 Nelson defeats the French fleet at the battle of the Nile, in Egypt.

1799 Napoleon returns to France and seizes power. Austria, Britain, Russia, and Turkey join forces to fight the French.

1801 By this date, only Britain is still at war with France.

1802 Napoleon plans to invade Britain, even though the two countries have signed a peace agreement this year.

1803 Britain declares war on France once more.

1804 Napoleon declares himself emperor of France.

1805 Nelson defeats French fleet at battle of Trafalgar. Napoleon's army defeats the Austrians and Russians at the battle of Austerlitz.

1806 Napoleon's army defeats the Prussians at Jena.

1807 Napoleon's army defeats the Russians at Friedland. France controls Portugal.

1808 The Peninsular War starts when Napoleon places his brother Joseph on the throne of Spain. British forces arrive in Portugal.

1809 Napoleon wins a decisive victory over the Austrians at Wagram. Napoleon marries the Austrian emperor's daughter, Marie Louise.

1811 Birth of Napoleon's son, Napoleon II, in March.

1812 Napoleon's army invades Russia but is defeated by the harsh climate. In Spain the French army is defeated at Salamanca.

Napoleonic Wars

As well as ruling France, Napoleon continued leading its army. He was a brilliant general and had thousands of conscripted men at his command.

Between 1803 and 1805 France was at war with Britain. Napoleon knew that the only way to win was to land his army in Britain and to do so he needed control of the seas. He persuaded the Spanish to help, but in October 1805 the combined fleet of France and Spain was defeated at Trafalgar by the British fleet, under the command of Lord Nelson. Napoleon then decided to blockade the transport of British goods across Europe. When Portugal refused to agree to this, Napoleon marched his army through Spain to invade Portugal in 1807. The following year he removed the king of Spain from the throne and gave it to his brother, Joseph Bonaparte.

Britain sent troops to Portugal under the command of Arthur Wellesley (later Lord Wellington). At first Napoleon seemed undefeatable and by 1812 he had control of a vast area of Europe. In the same year, however, he attempted a disastrous invasion of

△ *A cartoon of the Duke of Wellington who was given a dukedom in 1814 after defeating Napoleon's armies in Spain. In 1815, Wellington defeated Napoleon again, at Waterloo.*

South American Independence

By 1800 Spain and Portugal still ruled vast colonies in North and South America. Most colonists hated being ruled by foreigners and paying taxes to distant governments. Some colonies had tried to break free, but none had succeeded. As the Napoleonic Wars in Europe brought chaos to Spain and Portugal, the colonies decided to try again to fight for independence.

The main fight against Spanish rule was led by Simón Bolívar from Venezuela and José de San Martin from Argentina. San Martin gained freedom for his country in 1816, but Simón Bolívar's fight was longer and more difficult. He had joined a rebel army that captured Caracas, capital of Venezuela, in 1810, but was then defeated by the Spanish. Bolívar became the army's leader in 1811 and spent three years fighting the Spanish. When he was defeated a second time, he went into exile in Jamaica. There he realized he could not defeat the Spanish

△ *At the battle of Ayachucho in 1824, Simón Bolívar's army defeated the Spanish, finally securing independence for Peru.*

▷ *José de San Martin freed Argentina from Spanish rule, then led his army over the Andes mountains to help the people of Chile gain their independence, too.*

Russia and his army in Spain and Portugal suffered its first setbacks. By 1813 Napoleon's empire was collapsing and in 1814 he was forced to abdicate. He managed to escape from his exile on the island of Elba, landing back in France in 1815. Given a hero's welcome, he raised a new army and marched into Belgium to defeat the Prussians at the battle of Ligny. But he was then defeated at the battle of Waterloo and exiled to St. Helena.

△ **Napoleon**, *as well as being commander of the French army, was also admiral of the French navy, in whose uniform he is shown here. In 1806, he tried to disrupt British trade by using his ships to blockade all ports under French control, but this was not successful.*

army in an open battle, so, in 1819, he led his army over the Andes from Venezuela to Colombia where he defeated the Spanish in a surprise attack at the battle of Boyoca. Two years later, he freed Venezuela and in 1822 he freed Ecuador and Panama from Spanish rule. He then made them all part of a new state, called the Republic of Gran Colombia, with himself as president. Finally Peru was liberated and part of it was renamed Bolivia after Bolívar.

NAPOLEONIC WARS

1813 Napoleon's army is forced out of Spain after its defeat at Vitoria in June. In October his forces are heavily defeated at the battle of Leipzig.

1814 In April Napoleon is forced to abdicate and is exiled to the island of Elba, off the coast of Italy.

1815 In March Napoleon escapes from Elba and returns to France to raise a new army. He is defeated at the battle of Waterloo on June 18th.

1821 Death of Napoleon in exile on the island of St. Helena in the South Atlantic.

◁ **Napoleon's tomb** *in the Hotel des Invalides, Paris. When Napoleon died, he was buried in a simple grave on St. Helena, but in 1840, his remains were dug up and reburied in the chapel of St. Louis, in the Invalides. Inside the red stone sarcophagus, lie six coffins, one inside the other.*

SOUTH AMERICAN INDEPENDENCE

1808 Independence struggles begin in South America.

1816 José de San Martin leads Argentina to independence from Spain.

1817 At the battle of Chacabuco in Chile, San Martin and Bernado O'Higgins are victorious over the Spanish.

1818 Chile becomes independent from Spain.

1819 Colombia wins independence from Spain.

1821 Simón Bolívar's victory over the Spanish at Carabobo ensures independence for Venezuela.

1822 Brazil wins independence from Portugal.

1824 Bolívar wins independence for Peru.

1825 New republic of Bolivia is named after Bolívar.

1828 Uruguay wins independence from Spain.

◁ **Bolivians today** *wear dress that combines ancient patterns with Spanish influences. After independence, conditions for most people changed very little.*

The Industrial Revolution

SPINNING JENNY

James Hargreaves, inventor of the spinning jenny, was a poor spinner and weaver. He named his new machine after his daughter, Jenny. Other hand-spinners feared the machine would put them out of work, and so they broke into Hargreaves' house and destroyed the machines he had there, forcing him to move to another town.

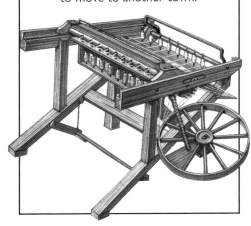

▽ *A pithead at Liverpool in England, painted in 1792. In the center is a steam pump used to drain water from the mine. Steam engines were used to power all kinds of machinery in factories and mines.*

The Industrial Revolution began in Britain in the mid-18th century, transforming society as people moved from the countryside to the town in order to work in factories.

Two events in the early 18th century helped make the Industrial Revolution possible. The first was Abraham Darby's discovery that coke instead of charcoal was a better fuel for smelting iron. The second was Thomas Newcomen's improved steam engine, used to pump water out of coal mines. These two inventions meant that more coal and better quality iron could be produced for industry.

Until the 1760s most goods were hand-made by people working at home or in small workshops. Many were spinners and weavers, producing woolen or linen cloth. Others made small metal items, such as nails, pins and knives. From the start of the century, however, there had been a rising demand for cotton cloth for clothes that were more comfortable to wear and easier to wash than either wool or linen. At first cotton was imported from India as rolls of ready-made cloth, but then raw cotton was imported and British spinners and weavers started manufacturing the cloth themselves.

In 1733 the invention of a flying shuttle speeded up the weaving process so much that ordinary spinning wheels could not produce

enough yarn to keep the weavers supplied. Then, in 1764, James Hargreaves invented the spinning jenny, which allowed one person to spin eight threads at once. Five years later, Richard Arkwright invented the spinning frame. This could spin more threads but needed water power to run it as it was too heavy to turn by hand. Factories were built near fast-flowing streams to house these new machines and soon the cotton industry began to develop on a very large scale. By 1790, James Watt's improvements to the steam engine meant that steam power could be used to drive machinery. This also increased the demand for coal to heat the water to make steam and for iron to make the engines and other machinery. Coal mines became bigger and deeper and iron works and foundries expanded, while canals (and later railroads) were built to bring raw materials to the factories and take the finished goods away.

Towns boomed as people moved in to be near their place of work. Both housing and working conditions were often poor and many people, including children, suffered from malnutrition, disease, or accidents at work.

▽ *The first public railroad*, *from Stockton to Darlington in England, opened in 1825. From 1830, steam locomotives were used to draw covered passenger carriages.*

△ *Children worked in coal mines from the age of five. Older children pulled heavy loads from the coal face to the bottom of the shaft, while younger children sat all day in total darkness, opening and closing doors to let the air circulate.*

INDUSTRIAL REVOLUTION

1698 Thomas Savery develops a steam engine to pump water out of mines.

1709 Abraham Darby discovers smelting iron with coke.

1712 Thomas Newcomen improves Savery's engine.

1733 John Kay invents the flying shuttle, greatly speeding up weaving.

1742 First cotton factories set up in Birmingham and Northampton.

1759 Bridgewater Canal built to take coal from the mines right to the center of Manchester is begun.

1764 James Hargreaves invents the spinning jenny.

1769 James Watt designs more efficient condensing steam engine. Richard Arkwright invents spinning frame powered by water. Josiah Wedgwood builds a pottery in Staffordshire.

1779 Samuel Crompton invents the spinning mule, a cross between the spinning jenny and the spinning frame. First iron bridge is built.

1799 Steam engines are now being used to drive machinery in paper, flour, and textile mills.

1808 Richard Trevithick demonstrates his steam locomotive in London.

1811 Start of "Luddite" protests against new machinery.

1815 Humphrey Davy invents the safety lamp—it warns miners of explosive gas.

1825 The first passenger railway from Stockton to Darlington opens.

1842 Act bans all women and children under the age of ten working underground in coal mines.

Europe in Turmoil

At the end of the Napoleonic Wars, many parts of Europe were in a state of chaos. Many people were living in poverty, partly as a result of the wars, but mostly because the population of Europe had almost doubled in number in just a century.

There was not enough land for everyone to make a living in the countryside, while in the towns there were more people than there were jobs. Even those who did have work were often badly paid, poorly housed and inadequately fed, while the people they worked for were wealthy and lived in luxury.

Although the French Revolution was long since over, many people remembered its promises of liberty and equality. Very few poor people had the right to vote and so the only way they could bring about change in their countries was by revolution. Revolt broke out in France in 1830 and quickly spread to other countries as a growing number of people were able to read about events in newspapers. These revolts were soon crushed, but the desire for change did not go away. Ordinary people still wanted a say in government and a share in the wealth enjoyed by the rich.

In 1848 so many revolutions and protests broke out again throughout Europe that it was known as the Year of Revolutions. But this time they were not all for the same reasons. In Britain the Chartists demonstrated for political reforms and votes for all men.

EUROPE IN TURMOIL

1830 Riots break out as ordinary people demand a say in government.

1831 Belgium declares independence from the Netherlands.

1832 Greece becomes independent from the Ottoman empire.

1838 In Britain, the People's Charter is published to demand political reforms. Its supporters become known as Chartists.

1844 Friedrich Engels makes a study of the lives of workers in Manchester, England.

1848 The Year of Revolutions affects most of Europe.

1852 In France, the Second Republic is replaced by the Second Empire.

▽ *Riots broke out in Berlin in 1848. Women and children were brutally attacked by Prussian soldiers as demands for reform and a united Germany were crushed.*

◁ *The revolutions of 1848* *were sparked off by a small, local revolt in Palermo on the island of Sicily on January 20. This inspired a revolt in France on February 24. Soon the spirit of protest had spread across Europe. Only Spain, Russia, and Scandinavia remained calm.*

▽ *This map shows* *the main centers of unrest during 1848, "the Year of Revolutions". By the end of 1849 all the revolts had been quashed but governments had been forced to listen to their people's complaints and realize the importance of nationalism.*

In Ireland some people agitated for their country to become an independent republic, free from Britain. In France some rioters in Paris, who were demanding votes for all men and a new republic, were shot and killed by soldiers, but in Belgium, Denmark, and the Netherlands reforms were made peacefully.

The revolutions in Germany and Italy had a different cause, however, as both nations were made up of a number of separate states, each with its own government. Many German people wanted all the German states to be united into one country, while many Italians wanted their country to be united, too. In contrast, there were many other groups of people in the vast Austrian empire who were not Austrian. They had their own languages and their own ways of life and they wanted the empire to be broken up into a number of separate and independent states to reflect this.

Despite the numbers of people and countries involved, all the revolutions in 1848 were squashed by the end of the following year. Only the French achieved one of their aims—their king, Louis Philippe, abdicated and the monarchy was briefly replaced by the Second Republic. The ideas that drove these revolutions and unrest did not go away, however. Many governments realized that they would have to make some reforms, while scholars, philosophers and economists began to look for different ways of governing countries and distributing wealth more fairly. The most famous political thinkers of this time were the German socialists Karl Marx and Friedrich Engels who, in 1848, published their ideas as *The Communist Manifesto*.

FEARGUS O'CONNOR

Feargus O'Connor (1794–1855) was elected to the British parliament in 1832 as member for County Cork in Ireland. When he lost his seat in 1835, he began agitating for votes for all men. He led the Chartists from 1841 until 1848 and was renowned for his brilliant speeches.

Exploring Africa

Although Europeans had been trading with Africa since the 16th century, they knew very little about the interior of the continent. They hardly ever ventured beyond the trading posts on the coast, partly because traveling was difficult in many places and partly because they were afraid of catching deadly diseases or being attacked by wild animals.

As the views of the Enlightenment became better known, the situation began to change. In Britain especially, people became more curious about the interior of Africa and in 1788 an association was formed in London to encourage exploration and trade in Africa. At the same time, many Europeans started to campaign for slavery to be abolished. They also thought that Africans should become Christians and so, from around 1800, increasing numbers of missionaries were sent out. Many went to Cape Colony (now part of South Africa), which the British took from the Dutch in 1806. This was the largest European settlement in Africa with a population of around 21,000 people.

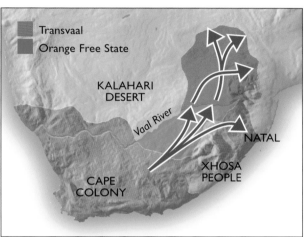

Transvaal
Orange Free State

KALAHARI DESERT

Vaal River

NATAL

CAPE COLONY

XHOSA PEOPLE

△ **Henry Stanley found David Livingstone** encamped at Ujiji on the shores of Lake Tanganyika in 1871. They spent several months exploring together, before Stanley returned to England.

◁ **This map shows** the route of the Great Trek, when the Boers went in search of new lands north of the Vaal River (Transvaal). Some Boers tried to settle the Zulu lands of Natal, but were defeated. Later, the British took over Natal.

△ **The Victoria Falls,** also called Mosi-oa-tunya (the Smoke that Thunders), on the Zambezi River. The first European to the see the falls was David Livingstone in 1855, who named them after the British queen Victoria.

◁ **Zulu warriors** attacking British soldiers. Warfare was an important part of Zulu life and from the 1820s they were the most powerful state in southern Africa. Armed with spears and round-headed clubs called knobkerries, their fighting tactics enabled them to kill many Boers and British soldiers, before eventually being defeated themselves in 1879.

Most of the colonists were Dutch farmers, known as Boers. By 1835 many of them were unhappy with living under British rule and decided to set off on the Great Trek into the interior. After much hardship the trekkers formed two new republics, the Transvaal and the Orange Free State. But the trekkers came into conflict with the Zulus, whose homelands they had moved into. The Zulus attacked the Boers and the Boers retaliated. Eventually the Zulus were defeated by the British in 1879.

Many British expeditions explored Africa's interior along its great rivers between 1768 and 1875. From 1768 to 1773, James Bruce explored Ethiopia, and in two expeditions from 1795 to 1806 Mungo Park explored the Niger River. From 1852 to 1856 David Livingstone crossed the continent following the Zambezi River, and Richard Burton, John Speke, and James Grant set out to look for the source of the Nile. Livingstone also set out to look for the source of the Nile in 1866, but lost contact with Britain for almost three years. Another expedition, sent out to look for him and led by journalist Henry Stanley, found him on the shores of Lake Tanganyika. After Livingstone's death, Stanley decided to continue exploring. His expedition of 1879 along the Congo River was paid for by the king of Belgium, who wanted to establish an overseas empire for himself. This was the start of the Scramble for Africa, in which Europe took control of almost the entire continent.

European Colonization of Asia

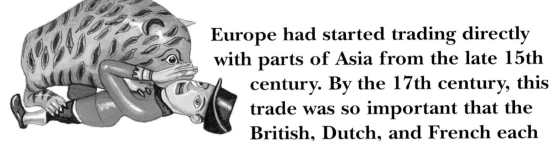

Europe had started trading directly with parts of Asia from the late 15th century. By the 17th century, this trade was so important that the British, Dutch, and French each set up East India Companies to control and protect it.

The Dutch concentrated on the islands of Indonesia, while the British and the French fought over India until 1763, when the British East India Company took control.

In the 1830s, however, the Dutch decided they wanted to control more than just trade with Indonesia, and so they started to oversee agriculture on the islands. Where the local people had grown the crops they needed to feed their families, with a little spare to sell at market, the Dutch set up plantations on which crops were grown for cash. These crops included coffee and indigo (a plant from which a blue dye is made). By doing this, enormous profits were made by Indonesian princes and Dutch colonists. For the

HONG KONG

For nearly 70 years, China had restricted trade with the rest of the world. To force the country to open up its ports, Britain went to war against China from 1839 to 1842. Britain won and five ports were opened and Hong Kong Island became a British colony. Kowloon was added to the colony in 1860 and, in 1898, China gave the New Territories to Britain on a 99-year lease. With its fine harbor, Hong Kong became a center of finance and trade, exporting textiles and clothing.

▷ *This map shows British control of India, which began in 1757. The dependent states were ruled by Indian princes under British protection. Until 1947, India also included the countries of Pakistan and Bangladesh.*

▽ *Officials of the East India Company were usually very wealthy and enjoyed a luxurious lifestyle. They had many servants to help them at work and in their homes, and were often carried from place to place in enclosed litters, called palanquins, like royalty.*

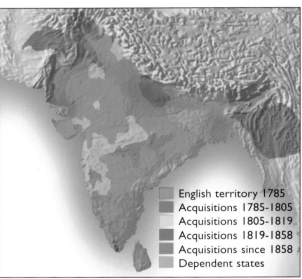

English territory 1785
Acquisitions 1785-1805
Acquisitions 1805-1819
Acquisitions 1819-1858
Acquisitions since 1858
Dependent states

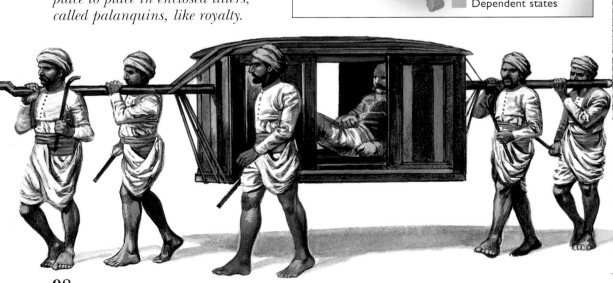

△ *Many Europeans, when they went to India, tried to live exactly as they would have done at home. Here Lady Impey, wife of the British Chief Justice of Bengal, is shown supervizing Indian tailors in 1782. Although in India, the decor and furnishings are typically British.*

ordinary people, however, there was hardship as they no longer had the time or the land to grow the crops they needed.

As well as controlling India (which then included Pakistan and Bangladesh) through the East India Company, Britain also began to build up colonies in Southeast Asia during the 18th and 19th centuries. One of the earliest was Singapore on the tip of the Malay peninsula, which came under British control in 1819. By 1867 Malacca and Penang had also become British colonies and in 1896 the remaining Malay states formed a federation under British advisors. Ruling through the local sultans, the British were able to control Malaya with few problems. Like the Dutch, however, they exploited the country's natural resources by setting up rubber plantations and mining the vast deposits of tin found in Malaya. Between 1824 and 1885 Britain also tried to take control of Burma (Myanmar) in order to protect India, part of which had been invaded by the Burmese in 1824. The Burmese resisted British colonization in a series of three wars, but they were finally defeated in 1885 and Britain took control of much of their country.

France, too, became involved in Asia again in the late 1850s when it began to take control of Indochina (now Cambodia and Vietnam). Many local people tried to resist French rule and colonization, but by 1888 they had all been defeated.

COLONIES IN ASIA

1786 The British take control of Penang in Malaysia.

1789 The French East India Company ceases to exist.

1819 Foundation of the British colony of Singapore.

1824 Start of the Anglo-Burmese wars.

1841 Sultan of Brunei gives Sarawak to James Brooke.

1842 China cedes Hong Kong to Britain at the end of the First Opium War.

△ *Chintz was made in India for export to Europe. The beautifully printed cotton was made into dresses and furnishing.*

1856 Indian Mutiny leads to British government taking control of India from the East India Company.

1884 French victory at the battle of Bac-Ninh in Indochina.

1885 Burma becomes part of India at end of the third Anglo-Burmese War.

1887 French form Indochina, from Cambodia and Cochinchina, Tonkin, and Annam (Vietnam).

1893 Laos is added to Indochina.

▷ **Britain invaded Burma** *not only to protect India, but also to gain access to Burma's valuable natural resources of teak, oil, and rubies. In spite of having a larger and better-equipped army, however, the British had to fight three wars before they finally took control.*

The British Empire

Queen Victoria succeeded to the British throne in 1837 and reigned for almost 64 years. At the time of her accession, trade and industry had already helped to make Britain one of the richest and most powerful countries in the world.

Britain was also a land of great contrasts, with landowners and industrialists living in luxury, while the poor led very hard lives both in the towns and in the countryside.

Much of Britain's wealth came from her colonies, which were eventually known as the British empire. The earliest colonies had been established in the 17th and 18th centuries in places as far apart as Canada, India, Australia, and the Caribbean. More were added by the Treaty of Vienna at the end of the Napoleonic Wars. During Victoria's reign, still more colonies were added, including New Zealand, many islands in the Pacific and Atlantic oceans, parts of the Far East and large areas of Africa, until, at its greatest extent, the empire contained a quarter of the world's land and a quarter of its people.

The colonies mainly provided raw materials for British factories and a ready market for their goods. At first, colonies were often run by trading companies, such as the East India Company in India and the Hudson's Bay Company in Canada, but gradually they all came under direct rule from Britain. India was the most prized and Britain went to great lengths to protect its trade routes with India.

△ *Queen Victoria (1819–1901) was just 18 years old when she inherited the British throne from her uncle, William IV. After her husband's death in 1861 she went into deep mourning and was not seen in public for many years.*

▽ *Victoria's family tree. Queen Victoria married Prince Albert in 1840. Several of their nine children made dynastic marriages with the royal families of Europe.*

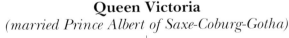

Queen Victoria
(married Prince Albert of Saxe-Coburg-Gotha)

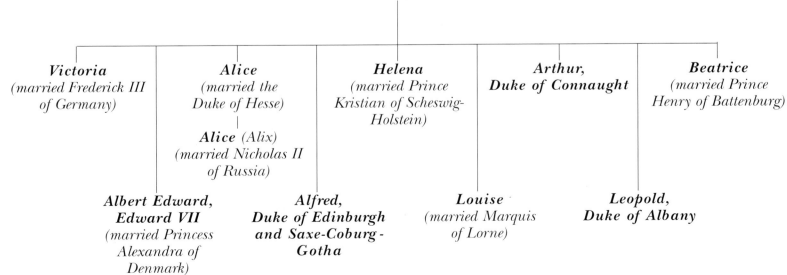

Victoria
(married Frederick III of Germany)

Alice
(married the Duke of Hesse)

Alice *(Alix)*
(married Nicholas II of Russia)

Helena
(married Prince Kristian of Scheswig-Holstein)

**Arthur,
Duke of Connaught**

Beatrice
(married Prince Henry of Battenburg)

**Albert Edward,
Edward VII**
(married Princess Alexandra of Denmark)

**Alfred,
Duke of Edinburgh and Saxe-Coburg-Gotha**

Louise
(married Marquis of Lorne)

**Leopold,
Duke of Albany**

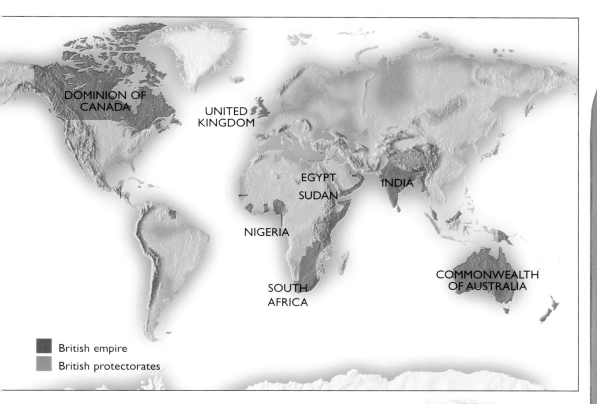

THE BRITISH EMPIRE

1763 Britain takes control of Canada

1788 First British settlement established in Australia.

1808 Sierra Leone becomes a British colony.

1815 Treaty of Vienna gives Cape Colony (South Africa), Ceylon (Sri Lanka), Mauritius, Malta, and French islands in the Caribbean to Britain.

1829 Britain claims the whole of Australia.

1830 Britain starts to control the Gold Coast (Ghana).

1839–1842 Britain fights Opium Wars to open China to trade.

1840 By the Treaty of Waitangi Britain takes New Zealand.

1843 In West Africa, the Gambia becomes a British colony.

1845 English landowners do little to help their Irish tenant farmers as the Great Potato Famine strikes Ireland.

1851 The Great Exhibition is held in London. Exhibits from all parts of the empire are intended to show off Britain's success as an industrial and trading nation.

1853–1856 The Crimean War.

1857–1858 The Indian Mutiny leads to India being ruled directly from Britain.

1860 Lagos (Nigeria) is added to the empire.

1867 Canada becomes a British Dominion.

1875 Britain buys shares in the Suez Canal Company to control trade route to India.

1876 Victoria is crowned Empress of India.

1878 Britain takes Cyprus.

1882 Britain controls Egypt.

1886 Britain takes Burma.

1899 Britain controls Sudan.

1901 Death of Queen Victoria.

△ **This map shows** the British empire in 1821. It was called "the empire on which the Sun never sets," because it was the largest empire the world had ever seen and spread right across the globe.

▷ **The potato famine** of 1845 to 1846 was caused by blight ruining the Irish potato crop. About one million died of hunger and many more lost their homes and emigrated to the United States.

THE CRIMEAN WAR

The Crimean War (1853–1856) was fought between Russia on one side and Turkey, France, and Britain on the other to limit Russia's domination of the Black Sea. Bad administration led to hundreds of thousands of lives being wasted. More men died in hospital than in battle until Florence Nightingale and 30 volunteers arrived to work in the military hospitals. On her return to England, she set up the first training school for nurses.

This was especially true after the opening of the Suez Canal in 1869, which cut 4,000 miles (6,400 km) off the journey from Britain to India. As British rule became established, the economies of many of the colonies were also changed as plantations were set up to produce tea, sugar, coffee, and spices for the British market. Other plantations produced rubber or cotton. Many people also migrated from Britain to Canada, Australia, and New Zealand, where they set up farms producing wheat, cattle and sheep to export to Britain.

Toward the end of Victoria's reign, however, Britain began to lose its place as the world's leading industrial nation. Colonies, such as Canada and Australia became self-governing, but remained part of the empire until 1947 when it ended.

The American West

Since the United States had declared its independence from Britain in 1776, many settlers had arrived from Europe. At first most made their homes in the eastern states, but a few traveled farther west toward what are now Ohio, Michigan, Indiana, and Illinois.

Many more people moved into the area around the Great Lakes after 1825 when the opening of the Erie Canal made the transport of people, farm products, and manufactured goods much easier. Until 1803, however, the area to the west of the Mississippi River, known as Louisiana, was controlled by the French, who sold it to the US in that year. Soon explorers and traders began to venture farther west, setting up routes, or trails, which would later be followed by settlers.

In 1848, at the end of the Mexican-American War, people started traveling to the newly acquired land in the west.

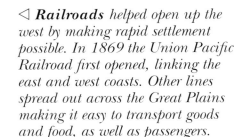

◁ **Railroads** *helped open up the west by making rapid settlement possible. In 1869 the Union Pacific Railroad first opened, linking the east and west coasts. Other lines spread out across the Great Plains making it easy to transport goods and food, as well as passengers.*

GOLD RUSH

Gold was discovered in California in 1848, when it was still a province of Mexico. As the news spread, thousands of would-be miners rushed to the site in 1849. They used large pans to wash the river gravel, hoping to find gold among the pebbles. Some made fortunes, but many did not. With the influx of people from all over the world, cities such as San Francisco rapidly expanded, taking on a cosmopolitan air.

Known as pioneers, they made the journey in long trains of covered wagons. They took with them food and clothing, tools and furniture, not just for the journey but also to help them set up their new homes. When they reached their destination, each family chose a place to settle and started clearing the land ready for farming. The trees they chopped down were cut into timber and used to build homes. Tree stumps were pulled up and the land plowed and seeds were sown. If the crops did not grow, then the family would have to go hungry or gather food from the wild as there were no towns or shops where they could buy supplies.

In spite of these hardships, the number of people heading west increased. The discovery of gold in California in 1848, and in Nevada and Colorado in 1859, brought thousands of prospectors from all around the world. Then, in 1862, the government passed the Homestead Act. In exchange for a small fee, this act gave 160 acres (65 ha) of land to each family who would settle and farm for at least five years. Many thousands took up the offer, especially just after the Civil War. Soon towns and cities sprang up all over the Great Plains and west. But the land the government sold so cheaply was taken from the Native Americans who had lived there for thousands of years.

◁ **Bison** (also called buffalo) lived on the Great Plains and were hunted by Native Americans who depended on them for food, shelter and clothing. The white settlers killed them in vast numbers.

THE AMERICAN WEST

1803 The Louisiana Purchase. US buys the vast area west of the Mississippi from France.

1821 Opening of the Santa Fe Trail from Missouri to New Mexico.

1825 Opening of the Erie Canal.

1835 Texas claims independence from Mexico.

1836 Mexicans defeat the Texans at the Alamo, then are defeated themselves by Texan forces at San Jacinto.

1842 Border dispute between Canada and the US is settled.

1845 Texas becomes the 28th state of the US.

1845 Many Europeans emigrate to the US, especially from Ireland and Germany.

1846 War breaks out between the US and Mexico over land boundaries.

1848 Signing of the Guadalupe-Hidalgo Treaty ends the Mexican-American War. US, gains California, Nevada, Utah, and Arizona, plus parts of New Mexico and Texas.

1849 Height of the Gold Rush.

1858 John Butterfield opens a stage route to the west.

1859 Many new mines open up in Nevada and Colorado.

1862 The Homestead Act encourages farmers to move to the Great Plains.

1867 US buys Alaska from Russia.

1869 The Union Pacific Railroad is completed.

1882 Huge copper deposits are discovered at Butte, Montana.

1893 The Great Northern Railroad reaches Seattle.

◁ **Long trains of covered wagons** took pioneers westward. Made of wood, they had massive wheels and strong axles and were pulled by teams of oxen or mules. Inside was food, clothing, tools, and furniture. Water was stored in a barrel slung on the side. Wagons were always in danger of attack by Native Americans whose land was being taken.

The American Civil War

★ ★ ★ ★ ★

GENERAL ROBERT E. LEE

Robert Edward Lee (1807–1870) was born in Virginia. The most talented military strategist of his day, towards the end of the Civil War he became commander in chief of the southern Confederate forces. Before the war, Lincoln offered him command of the Union army of the North, but he turned it down when Virginia withdrew from the Union. Although his side lost, he was an outstanding leader and probably the most able general of the war.

In the United States, by the early 19th century, the northern and southern states had slowly drifted apart for economic and social reasons. In the North, industry and trade had developed and towns and cities had increased. In the South, however, there was little industry and vast plantations relied on slave labor to grow cotton for export.

In the North, slavery had been banned since 1820, but the plantations of the South needed a huge labor force and relied on slaves who were still being brought from Africa. When Abraham Lincoln was elected president in 1861, his party was opposed to slavery and wanted it banned. Many people in the South saw this as a threat to their way of life and, in 1861, 11 southern states announced that they were breaking away from the Union to form their own Confederacy. When the United States government told them they had no right to do this, civil war broke out.

The other 23 states remained in the Union, so the North had more soldiers and more money, as well as the industry to provide the weapons and supplies they needed for war.

▽ *At the battle of Bull Run, Virginia, 1861, Confederate forces (right) under generals "Stonewall" Jackson and Beauregard defeated the Union army (left). It was the first major battle of the Civil War.*

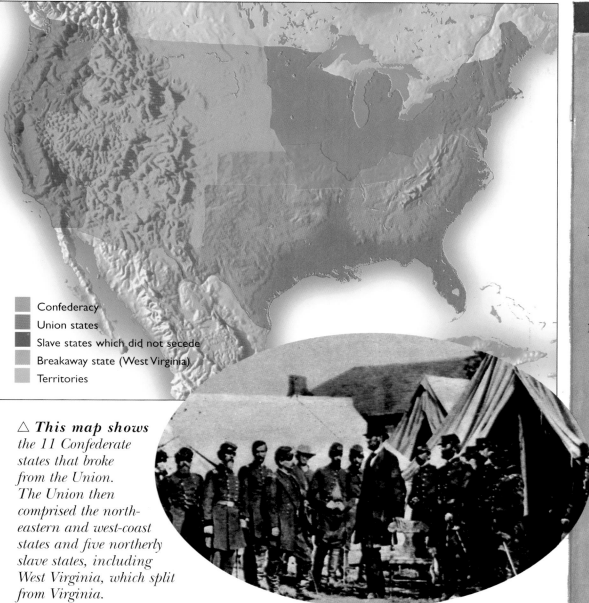

■ Confederacy
■ Union states
■ Slave states which did not secede
■ Breakaway state (West Virginia)
■ Territories

△ **This map shows** the 11 Confederate states that broke from the Union. The Union then comprised the north-eastern and west-coast states and five northerly slave states, including West Virginia, which split from Virginia.

△ **Abraham Lincoln** (1809–1865) visiting the cemetery after the battle of Gettysburg, where he gave his famous Gettysburg Address in November 1863. Born in Kentucky, he is remembered as one of the great US presidents.

The North also controlled the navy and so was able to blockade southern ports and prevent the South getting help or supplies from abroad. It also prevented the South from exporting cotton, so cutting off its wealth.

In spite of this, the early battles of the war were won by the South, which had brilliant generals and great enthusiasm for the fight. In July 1863, however, the war turned in favor of the North when Unionist troops defeated Confederate forces at the battle of Gettysburg, Pennsylvania, and another Unionist army captured the Confederate town of Vicksburg, Mississippi. In this same year Lincoln announced the abolition of slavery throughout the United States, which was later approved by Congress in 1865.

The war continued until April 1865 when the Confederate general Robert E. Lee surrendered at Appomattox, Virginia. By this time, much of the South was in ruins. On both sides thousands of people had died, many in battle, but many more from disease and hunger. Five days after the surrender, Lincoln was shot by an assassin. Though the war was over, much bitterness remained in the South. Many southerners moved west and, even though the slaves were set free, with few resources their conditions hardly improved.

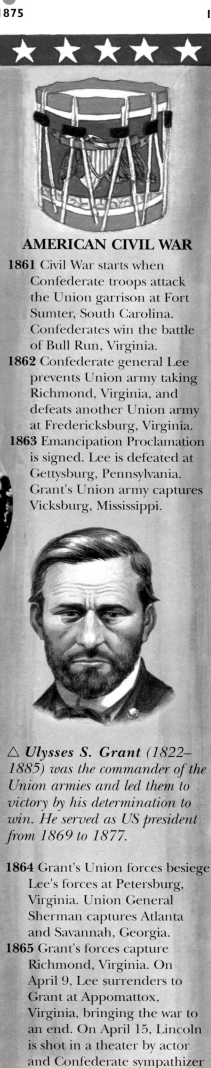

AMERICAN CIVIL WAR

1861 Civil War starts when Confederate troops attack the Union garrison at Fort Sumter, South Carolina. Confederates win the battle of Bull Run, Virginia.

1862 Confederate general Lee prevents Union army taking Richmond, Virginia, and defeats another Union army at Fredericksburg, Virginia.

1863 Emancipation Proclamation is signed. Lee is defeated at Gettysburg, Pennsylvania. Grant's Union army captures Vicksburg, Mississippi.

△ **Ulysses S. Grant** (1822–1885) was the commander of the Union armies and led them to victory by his determination to win. He served as US president from 1869 to 1877.

1864 Grant's Union forces besiege Lee's forces at Petersburg, Virginia. Union General Sherman captures Atlanta and Savannah, Georgia.

1865 Grant's forces capture Richmond, Virginia. On April 9, Lee surrenders to Grant at Appomattox, Virginia, bringing the war to an end. On April 15, Lincoln is shot in a theater by actor and Confederate sympathizer John Wilkes Booth.

Native Americans

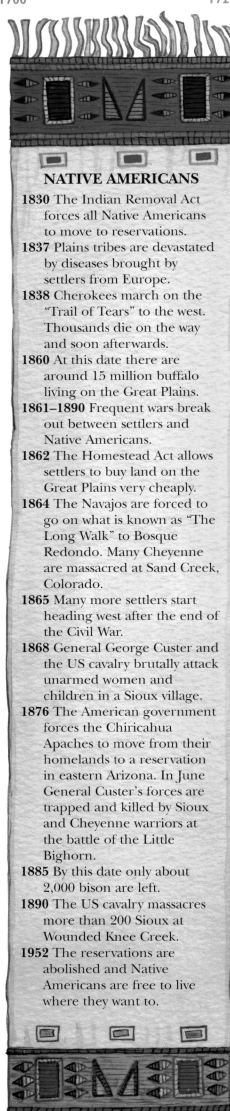

NATIVE AMERICANS

1830 The Indian Removal Act forces all Native Americans to move to reservations.

1837 Plains tribes are devastated by diseases brought by settlers from Europe.

1838 Cherokees march on the "Trail of Tears" to the west. Thousands die on the way and soon afterwards.

1860 At this date there are around 15 million buffalo living on the Great Plains.

1861–1890 Frequent wars break out between settlers and Native Americans.

1862 The Homestead Act allows settlers to buy land on the Great Plains very cheaply.

1864 The Navajos are forced to go on what is known as "The Long Walk" to Bosque Redondo. Many Cheyenne are massacred at Sand Creek, Colorado.

1865 Many more settlers start heading west after the end of the Civil War.

1868 General George Custer and the US cavalry brutally attack unarmed women and children in a Sioux village.

1876 The American government forces the Chiricahua Apaches to move from their homelands to a reservation in eastern Arizona. In June General Custer's forces are trapped and killed by Sioux and Cheyenne warriors at the battle of the Little Bighorn.

1885 By this date only about 2,000 bison are left.

1890 The US cavalry massacres more than 200 Sioux at Wounded Knee Creek.

1952 The reservations are abolished and Native Americans are free to live where they want to.

When the Europeans first reached North America in the 16th century, they found the land inhabited by many different tribes of Native Americans. Each had its own language and way of life, but they all lived in harmony with their environment, never taking more from it than they needed to survive.

They did not have horses or wheeled vehicles and, although they had some knowledge of using metal, most of their tools and weapons were made from wood or stone. On the west coast, where trees and fish were plentiful, Native Americans built wooden canoes and went fishing for their main food supply, while on the east coast they grew corn and tobacco in small plots around their villages and trapped animals in the surrounding woods. On the Great Plains they hunted buffalo (bison), while in the deserts of the southwest they built small dams to irrigate the land for growing corn, beans, and squash.

The arrival of the Europeans soon had a disastrous effect on Native Americans. They had no resistance to diseases, such as measles and smallpox, that Europeans brought with them. Many were also killed in disputes over land. But the worst problems started in the 19th century when a huge influx of Europeans began to arrive in the United States.

In 1830 the American government passed the Indian Removal Act. This forced all Native Americans in the eastern states to leave their homelands to go and live on reservations far from the land that they knew, while their lands were taken over by European settlers. One of the first to suffer were the Cherokees, many of whom died on what became known as the Trail of Tears.

▷ **The Sioux** were the largest nation of the Great Plains. They lived in tepees made of wooden poles covered in buffalo hide. Tepees could be quickly put up or taken down and were easy to transport, making them ideal for hunters following the herds of buffalo across the plains.

GERONIMO

Apache chief Geronimo's (1829–1909) first name was Goyanthlay, which means "One Who Yawns." When Mexican troops killed his family, he became a fierce warrior, feared by both Mexican and American soldiers. He eventually surrendered and in 1905 took part in President Roosevelt's victory parade.

△ *Native Americans fought a series of wars from 1861 to keep their land and stave off starvation. Experts in mounted marksmanship since the Spanish introduced guns and horses in the 17th century, their battle tactics often struck terror into the hearts of their enemies.*

▽ *Native Americans today are proud of their heritage and try to keep their rituals, customs, and languages alive. They have also staged protests to regain lost land.*

The situation grew worse throughout the century as more European settlers arrived and began to claim still more land to the west. On the Great Plains they did not share the Native Americans' respect for their environment. Instead settlers hunted buffalo for sport and between 1860 and 1885 they hunted the animals almost to extinction. Native American resistance was put down harshly by the US Army, although the Sioux managed to defeat 250 cavalrymen at the battle of the Little Bighorn in 1876. The final defeat of the Native Americans came in 1890 when more than 200 unarmed Sioux men, women, and children were killed at Wounded Knee Creek.

Unification of Italy

▽ *Garibaldi handing the Kingdom of the Two Sicilies to Victor Emmanuel in 1860. Victor Emmanuel was proclaimed the first king of a united Italy in 1861.*

GIUSEPPE GARIBALDI

Giuseppe Garibaldi (1807–1882) took part in a revolt in Italy in 1834 and had to spend the next ten years in exile in South America. He returned to Italy in time for the revolutions of 1848, but went back into exile when they did not succeed. On his return, Garibaldi gave his support to Victor Emmanuel and in 1860 he set out from Genoa with 1,000 volunteers to free Sicily and Naples

At the start of the 19th century, Italy was united under the control of Napoleon. After his defeat in 1815, its separate states were given back to their former rulers with only Piedmont–Sardinia remaining independent.

The states were ruled by foreigners, with Austria having the most power. During the 1820s and 30s opposition to foreign rule grew and the Risorgimento movement encouraged people to campaign for an independent and united Italy. Revolutions broke out in many states in 1848, but they were soon crushed. In 1858, Piedmont–Sardinia allied itself with France and defeated Austria. This was followed in 1860 by a successful revolt led by Guiseppe Garibaldi and his army of Redshirts.

Unification of Germany

Like Italy, Germany was also made up of many different states in the early 19th century. Following Napoleon's defeat in 1815, however, they joined together to form the German Confederation. This was made up of 38 states, of which Austria and Prussia were the most powerful.

From the start, Austria and Prussia competed against each other for leadership of the Confederation and in 1866 Prussia declared war on Austria. Their two armies met at Sadowa on the Elbe River on July 3 and the Prussians were victorious. The war ended on July 26 and the German Confederation was divided when Otto von Bismarck, the chief Prussian minister, set up a separate North German Confederation dominated by Prussia.

The French felt threatened by the growing power of Prussia, and on July 19, 1870 their emperor, Napoleon III, declared war on Prussia. On September 1 Napoleon III's army of 100,000 men was heavily defeated at the battle of Sedan on the French border and Napoleon III was taken prisoner. Three days later the people of Paris rose up against him and the French Second Empire was overthrown. The Prussian army then besieged Paris.

OTTO VON BISMARCK

Bismarck (1815–1898) started his rise to power in Prussia after the collapse of the Revolution of 1848. Becoming Prussian foreign minister in 1862, he determined to unite the north German states and make Prussia the ruler of a united Germany. To achieve this, he went to war with Austria and France. Germany was finally united in 1871 and Bismarck became its first chancellor.

▷ *The unification of Italy* took only ten years. The last region to join was that around Rome, known as the Patrimony.

Piedmont–Sardinia
Area added 1860
Area added 1866
Area added 1870

He conquered the island of Sicily first and then went on to conquer Naples. Meanwhile, the northern states had joined up with Piedmont–Sardinia and accepted Victor Emmanuel II as their king. Garibaldi handed Naples and Sicily to him in November 1860 and in 1861 Italy was declared a kingdom. Only Venice and Rome remained under foreign control and they became part of Italy in 1866 and 1871 respectively.

UNIFICATION OF ITALY

1815 After being briefly united under the control of Napoleon I, the Italian states are divided once more and given back to their former rulers.

From 1820s In the Risorgimento, secret societies are formed to oppose foreign rule.

1848 Unsuccessful revolutions break out in many states to try and bring about unification.

1849 Victor Emmanuel II becomes king of Piedmont–Sardinia.

1852 In Piedmont–Sardinia, Count Camillo Cavour forms his first government under Victor Emmanuel II. It is his hard work that unifies northern Italy.

1860 Garibaldi and his Redshirts set out to conquer the Kingdom of the Two Sicilies.

1861 Victor Emmanuel II becomes king of a unified Italy.

1866 Venice becomes part of Italy.

1871 Rome becomes part of Italy.

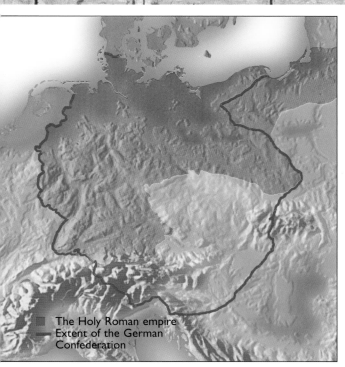

The Holy Roman empire
Extent of the German Confederation

◁ *This map shows* the mass of independent German states before unification. For many centuries, these states had formed the core of the Holy Roman empire, which was conquered by Napoleon I in 1806.

▽ *Napoleon III* (1808–1873) was the nephew of Napoleon I (Bonaparte) and came to power in France in 1848. In 1851 he declared himself emperor and set about transforming Paris and encouraging industry. After the Franco-Prussian War, his empire collapsed and he went into exile.

UNIFICATION OF GERMANY

1815 Thirty-eight German states form the German Confederation.

1848 Unsuccessful revolutions break out in many states to bring about unification.

1862 Bismarck becomes Prussia's foreign minister and determines to make Prussia the most powerful state in the German Confederation.

1864 Austria and Prussia declare war on Denmark over control of Schleswig-Holstein. The Danes are defeated and Schleswig-Holstein becomes part of the German Confederation.

1866 Prussia wins the Seven Weeks War against Austria. The North German Confederation is set up. Venice is taken from Austria and given to Italy.

1870–1871 Franco-Prussian War is won by Prussia.

1871 Creation of the German Second Empire, ruled by William II, the former king of Prussia.

When the Franco-Prussian War finally ended on May 10, 1871, Germany had taken control of Alsace and Lorraine from the French and the German Second Empire had been declared, with William II, King of Prussia, as its emperor and Otto von Bismarck as its chancellor.

Scramble for Africa

SCRAMBLE FOR AFRICA

1880 Leopold II, King of Belgium, claims the Congo as his own personal territory.

1882 Britain takes control of Egypt to secure access to the Suez Canal.

1884 The Conference of Berlin divides Africa up among seven European countries.

1889 The British conquer the Matabele and take their land, calling it Rhodesia.

1890 The Italians take control of Eritrea from where they try, but fail, to conquer Abyssinia (now Ethiopia).

1891 Tanganyika (now Tanzania) becomes a German protectorate. The French make northern Algeria part of France.

1893 The French take control of Mali.

1894 Uganda becomes a British protectorate.

1895 Kenya comes under British control and is known as the East African Protectorate.

1899 Start of the Boer Wars between Britain and the Boer people for control of southern Africa.

1910 The Union of South Africa is formed.

1911 The British colony of Rhodesia is divided into Northern Rhodesia (now Zambia) and Southern Rhodesia (now Zimbabwe).

1912 Morocco is divided into Spanish and French protectorates.

Most European nations had been content to have trading colonies around the coast of Africa. Only the British and the Boers in South Africa had moved inland and set up new settlements. In 1880 less than 5 percent of the continent was ruled by European powers. But within 20 years the situation had changed completely in what is known as the Scramble for Africa.

Seven European nations took control of the whole of Africa, apart from Liberia and Ethiopia. They were helped to do this by the opening of the Suez Canal, which linked the Mediterranean to the Red Sea and cut many miles off the journey to the east coast of Africa and India. They were also helped by improvements in transportation (steamships were more reliable than the old sailing ships) and medicine that made it possible for Europeans to survive some of the diseases they met in Africa.

By 1884 Belgium, Britain, France, Portugal, and Spain had already started to claim new colonies in Africa or expand their old ones. The newly unified countries of Germany and Italy also wanted their share of the continent. To try and prevent any serious conflict, the European powers attended an international conference on Africa held in Berlin that same year.

▽ **At Isandhlwana**, *southern Africa, the Zulus resisted the British, wiping out 1,700 British soldiers at the start of the Zulu War in 1879. Later they were themselves defeated at the battle of Rorke's Drift.*

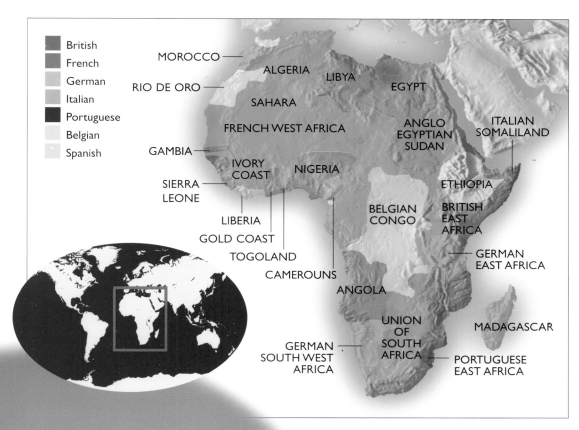

British
French
German
Italian
Portuguese
Belgian
Spanish

MOROCCO
ALGERIA
LIBYA
EGYPT
RIO DE ORO
SAHARA
FRENCH WEST AFRICA
ANGLO EGYPTIAN SUDAN
ITALIAN SOMALILAND
GAMBIA
IVORY COAST
NIGERIA
SIERRA LEONE
ETHIOPIA
LIBERIA
BELGIAN CONGO
BRITISH EAST AFRICA
GOLD COAST
TOGOLAND
CAMEROUNS
GERMAN EAST AFRICA
ANGOLA
UNION OF SOUTH AFRICA
MADAGASCAR
GERMAN SOUTH WEST AFRICA
PORTUGUESE EAST AFRICA

◁ **This map shows** *Africa in 1914, when the European powers had finished establishing colonies there. Only two countries on the continent remained independent: Ethiopia and Liberia.*

CECIL RHODES

Cecil Rhodes (1853–1902) was born in Britain and went to Natal in southern Africa when he was 17. He became a member of the Cape Colony parliament in 1881, becoming prime minister in 1890. He owned a large diamond mining company and helped to bring more territory under British control, but he failed in his ambition to give Britain an empire in Africa that stretched from the Cape to Egypt.

◁ **The Suez Canal** *was opened in 1869. This, together with the later construction of railways, made it much easier to travel to the east coast and the interior of Africa.*

The conference allowed the European powers to divide Africa among themselves, with no regard for the African peoples, their cultures or any natural boundaries. Any resistance to this by the Africans was crushed by large and well-equipped armies that were sent out from Europe and many thousands died in the fighting. Others suffered hardship and hunger as their traditional ways of life were destroyed and they were forced to work as cheap labor in mines and on plantations, growing crops such as cotton, tea, coffee, and cocoa for export to Europe. Large areas of rain forest were cut down for their timber and many species of wild animals were hunted almost to extinction by white settlers who hunted for sport to pass the time.

In the British and German colonies, schools and medical centers were set up for the local people. Some were run by the government, others were run by missionaries who then expected the Africans to become Christians. In other colonies, however, the Africans were treated little better than slaves and nowhere did they have the right to vote or say how their country should be run.

◁ **Patriotic posters** *encouraging men to join the army appeared in Britain during the Boer Wars (1899–1902). A bitterly fought battle, around 20,000 Boer women and children died in British concentration camps in South Africa.*

▷ **On the Great Trek** *during the 1830s many Boers left Cape Colony and headed north in search of new farmland away from British rule. The African peoples, caught in the struggle between these two groups of warring whites, suffered greatly.*

The Modern World

Towards the Millennium 1900–1990s

At the start of the 20th century, large areas of the world were controlled by European powers. Britain, France, Belgium, the Netherlands, Portugal, and Spain had built up great empires, while newly-united Germany wanted to expand the territory it controlled and this caused the outbreak of World War I in 1914.

Poor social and economic conditions led to rebellion in Ireland in 1916 and revolution in Russia in 1917. World War I ended in 1918 with defeat for Germany and its allies, but the peace that followed was an uneasy one. Growing unemployment in the 1920s was made worse by the Wall Street Crash in 1929 and the Great Depression that followed. A civil war in Spain from 1936 to 1939 brought the Fascists to power there, while in Germany and Italy Fascist parties were elected to government by promising people full-time employment, an escape from poverty and a renewed sense of national pride.

In 1939 World War II broke out, initially between Britain and France on one side and Germany on the other. Soon most of the countries in Europe, the British Commonwealth, the Soviet Union, the United States, and Japan were also involved. The conflict lasted until 1945 and the peace that followed saw great changes in the world and the way it was ruled. The US and the Soviet Union emerged as superpowers, while Europe was divided between the capitalist West, supported

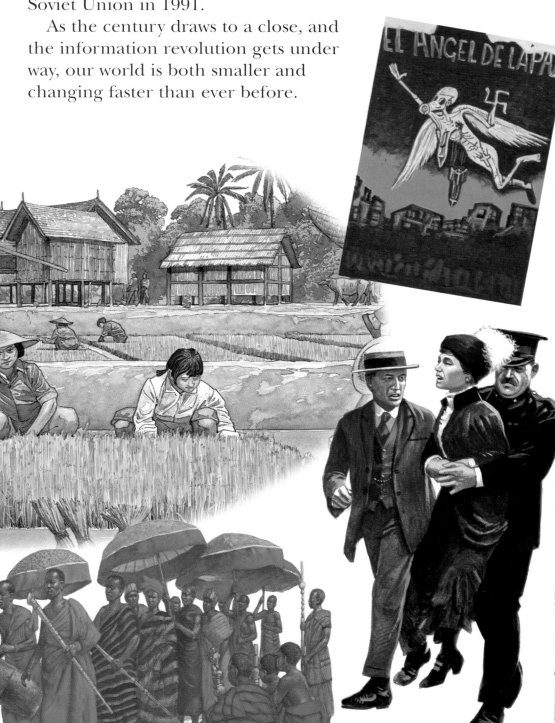

by the US, and the communist East, supported by the Soviets. Communists also came to power in China, and the European empires broke up as their colonies were granted independence. What became known as the Cold War broke out between the two superpowers and, although neither fought the other directly, both were involved in an arms race and a space race. They both also tried to expand their spheres of influence to Asia, Africa and South America, before the Cold War abruptly ended with the fall of communism and the collapse of the Soviet Union in 1991.

As the century draws to a close, and the information revolution gets under way, our world is both smaller and changing faster than ever before.

THE MODERN WORLD

1914 Austria declares war on Serbia and Germany on Russia and World War I begins.

1917 The Russian Revolution starts when the Bolsheviks led by Lenin seize power. They gain control of all of Russia only in 1921, after a bloody civil war.

1918 World War I ends with the loss of more than 8.5 million soldiers.

1921 Anglo-Irish Treaty gives Ireland independence, leaving Northern Ireland under British rule.

1929 Wall Street Crash sparks the Great Depression.

1933 Nazis led by Adolf Hitler come to power in Germany.

1936–1939 Spanish Civil War ends with victory for the Nationalists under Francisco Franco.

1939 Germany overruns Czechoslovakia, and then Poland, and World War II begins.

1941 The US enters the war following the Japanese attack on their naval base at Pearl Harbor.

1945 Germany surrenders. Japan surrenders after atomic bombs are dropped on Hiroshima and Nagasaki. United Nations formed. Europe is divided and the Cold War begins.

1947 Pakistan and India gain independence from Britain.

1948 The state of Israel is founded and the Arab League declares war.

1949 Communists led by Mao Zedong gain control of China.

1960s Most countries in Africa gain independence.

1965–1973 The Vietnam War.

1969 US astronaut Neil Armstrong is first to land on the moon.

1990 Germany is reunited.

1991 Soviet Union collapses and Cold War ends.

1994 Free elections in South Africa.

Votes for Women

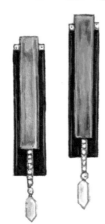

Women's right to vote was first suggested by British author Mary Wollstonecraft in her book _A Vindication of the Rights of Women_, published in 1792. At that time, most people had no say in the way they were governed. Groups, such as the Chartists in Britain, began campaigning for political reform in the 1830s, but they were only concerned with obtaining the vote for all men. Women were not included.

In the middle of the 19th century, however, a movement began in the United States with the aim of winning voting rights for women across the world. Its first meeting was held at Seneca Falls in New York state in 1848, when a convention on women's rights was led by Lucretia Mott and Elizabeth Cady Stanton. Many other public meetings followed, even though they were often fiercely opposed by those who did not want women to have the right to vote. The speakers included women such as Sojourner Truth and Harriet Tubman, both of whom had been born slaves.

The movement gained in strength throughout the rest of the 19th century and in 1890 Wyoming became the first state to allow women to vote in local elections. Three years later New Zealand became the first country in the world to allow women to vote in national elections. (The electoral bill was passed by only two votes.) In Britain, this triumph encouraged various women's suffrage (right to vote) societies to unite in 1897.

△ **Suffragettes campaigning** in the British general election of 1910. Not all those who supported women's right to vote were women, a few were men, including some politicians. Suffragettes campaigned on behalf of the politicians they knew would support their cause.

▽ **Many women campaigned peacefully** for the right to vote. Known as suffragists (to distinguish them from the more militant and derogatory term suffragettes), they marched through the streets, holding rallies to gain support for their cause.

At first their campaigns were peaceful, but in 1903 one of their members, Emmeline Pankhurst, set up a new society called the Women's Social and Political Union (WSPU). It believed in actions rather than words and the WSPU held public demonstrations and attacked property in protest against women's lack of rights. Many of its members were arrested and sent to prison, where they often went on hunger strike to bring attention to their cause. In 1913 one member of the WSPU, Emily Davison, was killed when she threw herself under the King's horse at the Derby horse race.

With the outbreak of World War I in 1914, the WSPU gave up its active protests and its members involved themselves in the war effort. Many women took on jobs traditionally done by men, proving that they were just as capable. In 1918 the vote was given to all British women over the age of 30, even though the age for men was only 21. Women in the US were given the right to vote in 1920 and in 1928 the voting age for British women was lowered to 21.

△ **Emmeline Pankhurst**, founder of the WSPU, was arrested and imprisoned several times for destroying property. Other tactics included nonpayment of taxes, disrupting political meetings, and public demonstrations.

▷ **Suffragettes in prison** who went on hunger strike were forcibly fed by doctors and prison officers. Those who became too ill to endure prison life any longer were released, but they were rearrested as soon as their health improved.

VOTES FOR WOMEN

1848 First women's rights convention held at Seneca Falls, New York.

1890 Wyoming allows women to vote in local elections.

1893 New Zealand gives women the vote in national elections.

1897 The National Union of Women's Suffrage Societies is formed in Britain.

1902 Australia gives women the right to vote.

1903 Emmeline Pankhurst forms the Women's Social and Political Union.

1905 The first two suffragettes are sent to prison in Britain.

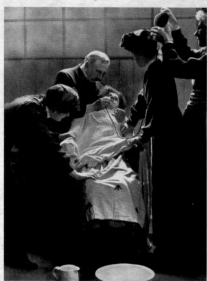

1906 Finland gives women the vote. In 1907, the first women representatives are elected to the Finnish parliament.

1913 Suffragette Emily Davison is killed when she throws herself under the King's horse at the Derby. Norway gives women the vote.

1917 Russia gives women the right to vote.

1918 British women over the age of 30 are given the vote. Canadian women are given equal voting rights with men.

1919 Germany, Austria, Poland, and Czechoslovakia all give women the right to vote.

1920 Women in the US are given the vote.

1944 France gives women the right to vote.

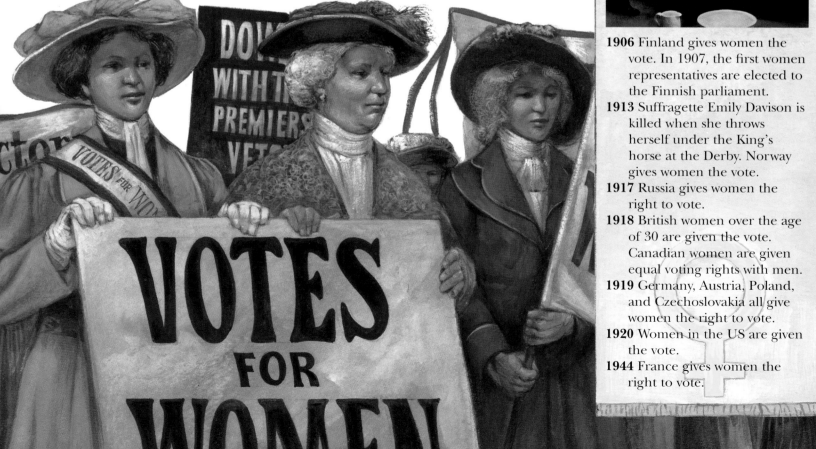

World War I

Toward the end of the 19th century, there was growing rivalry among the nations of Europe. Germany was quickly becoming a major industrial and military power and many countries, especially France and Britain, felt threatened by this.

At the same time, Turkey's Ottoman empire was breaking up. Newly independent Serbia was gaining power and land and the empire of Austria-Hungary saw this as a threat. As a result, Germany formed the Triple Alliance with Austria-Hungary and Italy and pledged to defend each other in case of attack, while Britain, France, and Russia formed the Triple Entente for the same purpose.

In the early 1900s both Britain and Germany added bigger and better battleships to their navies and all of Europe gradually expanded their armies. By 1914 it only needed one incident to spark off a war. This came when Archduke Franz Ferdinand was assassinated in Sarajevo, Bosnia. Franz Ferdinand was heir to the

WORLD WAR I

1878 Serbia gains independence from the Ottoman empire.

1882 Germany, Austria-Hungary, and Italy form the Triple Alliance to defend each other in the event of war.

1891 France and Russia agree that, if either one is attacked, the other will give it full military support.

1904 Britain forms the Entente Cordiale with France.

1907 Russia joins with Britain and France to form the Triple Entente.

1908 Austria-Hungary occupies Bosnia-Hercegovina to stop Serbia taking control.

1912–1913 Balkan Wars between the Balkan League (Serbia, Bulgaria, Greece, and Montenegro) and the Ottoman empire. Serbia's side is victorious.

1914 June 28 Gavrilo Princip assassinates Archduke Franz Ferdinand in Sarajevo.

July 28 Austria declares war on Serbia. Russia prepares to defend Serbia from Austria.

August 1 Germany declares war on Russia to defend Austria.

August 3 Germany declares war on France, Russia's ally.

August 4 German armies march through Belgium to France. Britain declares war on Germany. World War I begins.

August 26 Germany defeats Russian forces at the battle of Tannenberg.

September At the battle of the Marne the Allies halt German advance on Paris. German victory at the Masurian Lakes leads Russia to retreat from East Prussia.

November At the end of the battle of Ypres German forces are prevented from reaching the English Channel.

YOU ARE THE MAN I WANT'

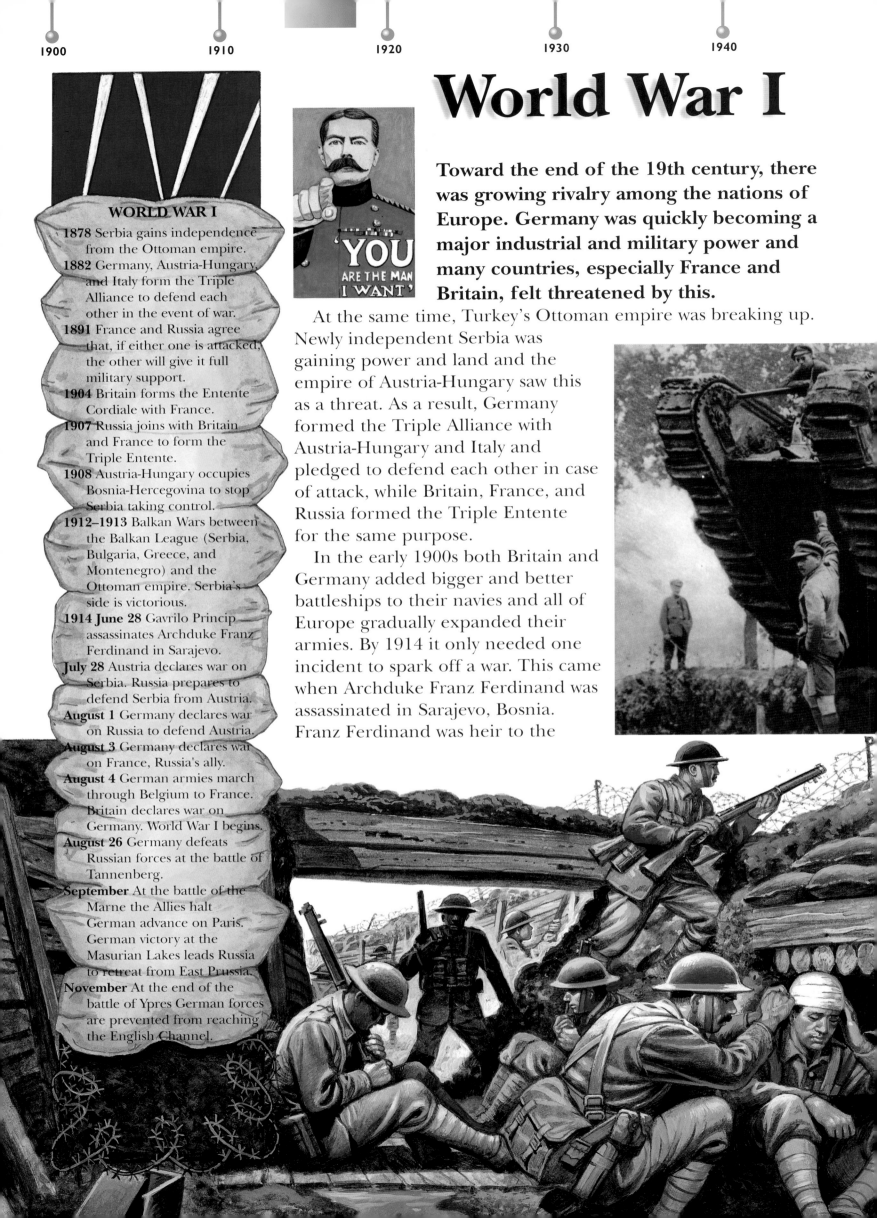

▷ **This map shows** the major battlefronts of World War I. There were dozens of bloody battles on the Western Front, where opposing armies dug in with defensive trenches. There were over a million casualties at the Somme in 1916.

▽ **Tanks** were a British invention that made their first appearance in battle at the Somme in 1916. Their tracks allowed them to travel over barbed wire and across rough ground. From 1917, they helped to break the stalemate of trench warfare.

Allies
Central powers
Neutrals
Battlefronts

Petrograd (St Petersburg)
Moscow
RUSSIA
BELGIUM
GREAT BRITAIN
London
Berlin
GERMANY
Paris
Vienna
FRANCE
AUSTRIA-HUNGARY
Romania
SPAIN
ITALY
IRAN
ALGERIA (FR)
Serbia and Balkan Campaign
Constantinople (Istanbul)
OTTOMAN EMPIRE
TUNISIA (FR)
Dardanelles Campaign
Jerusalem
Palestinian Campaign
Mesopotamian Campaign
LIBYA (IT)
EGYPT (GB)
ARABIA

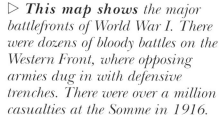

◁ **Archduke Franz Ferdinand** on June 28, 1914, was paying an official visit to Sarajevo as inspector general of the imperial army, when a bomb was thrown at his car. It bounced off and exploded under the next car. As Franz Ferdinand and his wife were leaving to visit the wounded in hospital, they were shot dead by Gavrilo Princip.

◁ **In the trenches** soldiers on both sides were comparatively safe. There they ate and slept, while waiting for orders to go into battle. Dugouts, or underground shelters, offered some protection from enemy shells and the worst of the rain, but the trenches were usually cold, muddy and wet.

throne of Austria-Hungary and the man who shot him was a Serbian protesting Austro-Hungarian rule in Bosnia. Austria-Hungary declared war on Serbia, prompting Russia to mobilize its army to defend Serbia. Germany declared war on Russia and on France, Russia's ally. The following day the German army marched through Belgium to attack France. This drew Britain into the war, since, in 1830, it had made an agreement to defend Belgium if ever it was attacked.

Sopwith Camel

WORLD WAR I PLANES
World War I (1914–1918) was the first war in which airplanes were widely used. Flimsy and unreliable, they were first used to spy on enemy trenches and troop movements. Later, they were used in aerial combat and in bombing raids. Two of the most famous airplanes to be used were the British Sopwith Camel, which was a biplane (which means it had two pairs of wings), and the German Fokker E1, which was a monoplane (single pair of wings). Fokker was a Dutch engineer, but he had built his factory in Germany in 1912 and so supplied planes to the Germans.

People who lived through the war that followed called it the Great War, but it later became known as World War I (1914–1918) as it eventually involved many of the countries of the world. They were divided into two groups, known as the Allies and the Central Powers. The Central Powers were made up of Germany, Austria-Hungary, and Turkey, while the Allies included France, Britain and its empire, Russia, Italy, Japan, and, from 1917, the United States. The war was fought along two main lines, or fronts. These were the Western Front, which ran from Belgium, through France to Switzerland, and the Eastern Front which ran from the Baltic to the Black Sea. There was also fighting in the Middle East and along the border between Italy and Austria.

German Fokker E1 monoplane

Trench Warfare

What made World War I so different from any other war in the past was the fact that most of it was fought from two parallel lines of trenches separated by only a short stretch of ground known as "no-man's land."

Trench warfare was necessary because the power, speed, and accuracy of the weapons used on both sides would have made it impossible to have fought a battle in the open. When soldiers did leave the trenches to launch an attack, often only a few yards of ground were gained and the cost in casualties was enormous. This led to a stalemate situation that lasted from the end of 1914 until the summer of 1918. Even the use of new weapons such as airplanes, tanks, and poison gas did little to change the situation.

At the end of 1917, Russia started peace talks with Germany and German soldiers who had been fighting on the Eastern Front could join those fighting in the west. For a while they outnumbered the Allied forces, but by September 1918 more than 1,200,000 well-trained and well-equipped soldiers from the United States joined the Allied forces in France. This made it possible for the Allies to start defeating the Central Powers. By the end of October, almost all German-occupied France and part of Belgium had been reclaimed, and Turkey and Austria had been defeated. In Germany people were running short of food and fuel. The navy mutinied and there was widespread unrest. On November 9 the German ruler, Kaiser William II, abdicated and on November 11 an armistice was signed between Germany and the Allies, bringing the fighting in World War I to an end.

△ **War leaders** *US president Woodrow Wilson (left), French president Georges Clemenceau (center), and British prime minister David Lloyd-George (right) lead their countries to victory.*

▽ **On the Western Front** *most of the fighting took place in northern France and Belgium. Mules were used to bring supplies to the front and heavy guns were horse-drawn. Dead horses and troops could not be moved quickly and the stench of their rotting flesh hung over the trenches.*

◁ **T. E. Lawrence** *(1888–1935), known as Lawrence of Arabia, worked for British army intelligence in North Africa at the start of the war. In 1916, he joined the Arab revolt against the Ottoman Turks, leading them to conquer Aqaba in 1917 and Damascus in 1918. With only a few thousand Arabs he took on the Turkish army.*

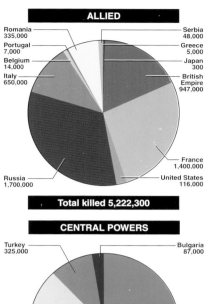

ALLIED

Romania 335,000
Portugal 7,000
Belgium 14,000
Italy 650,000
Russia 1,700,000

Serbia 48,000
Greece 5,000
Japan 300
British Empire 947,000
France 1,400,000
United States 116,000

Total killed 5,222,300

CENTRAL POWERS

Turkey 325,000
Austria Hungary 1,200,000

Bulgaria 87,000
Germany 1,800,000

Total killed 3,412,000

◁ *These charts show* the numbers of Central and Allied soldiers killed during World War I for each of the countries that took part in the war. Germany sustained the greatest losses, followed by Russia, and then France. The number of civilian deaths was comparatively light.

▽ *Going over the top* of the trench was the most dangerous time for soldiers. First, they had to get through their own barbed wire before running through no-man's land to reach the enemy.

In January 1919, the Allies met at the Paris Peace Conference, which formally ended the war. It drew up the Treaty of Versailles, which said that Germany was guilty of starting the war and that it had to pay vast sums of money in compensation to its former enemies. It also had to return Alsace-Lorraine to France and give up its overseas colonies. The same treaty established the League of Nations, which struggled to keep peace in the world throughout the 1920s and 1930s.

WORLD WAR I

1915 British naval blockade of Germany leads to a German submarine blockade of Britain.

April–May Germany uses poison gas for the first time at the second battle of Ypres.

May 22 Italy joins the Allies.

September British and French campaign at Loos fails.

1916 February Start of battle for Verdun, France, lasting for five months.

March Failure of the Gallipoli campaign by Australian, New Zealand, and British forces to capture the Dardanelles and Constantinople.

May Only major sea battle at Jutland in the North Sea ends with both sides claiming victory.

June Russian offensive led by general Brusilov fails to defeat the Germans.

July 1 Start of the battle of the Somme (ends November).

1917 On April 6 the United States joins the war.

July Third battle of Ypres (Passchendaele), Allied offensive gains little.

October Italians are defeated at the battle of Caporetto.

1918 On March 3, Armistice signed between Russia and Germany.

July Germans launch offensive on the Western Front.

August Allies break through German defenses and force them to retreat.

October After Italian victory at Vittorio Veneto, Austria-Hungary surrenders.

November Revolution in Germany. Armistice is signed on November 11 at 11 o'clock. World War I ends.

1919 Treaty of Versailles is signed.

The Russian Revolution

Following defeat in the Crimean War, Czar Alexander II realized Russia was very backward compared with the rest of Europe. To modernize his country he freed the serfs (who were treated little better than slaves), improved government, education, and the army and encouraged the development of industry and the railroads. Many people, however, thought his reforms did not go far enough and in 1881 he was assassinated.

Alexander III succeeded him as czar and promptly undid most of his father's reforms. Unrest began to grow and people such as Vladimir Lenin looked to the writings of Karl Marx, the founder of communism, for ways of changing Russian life. The first serious rebellion broke out in 1905 after troops fired on striking workers in the capital, St. Petersburg. It was soon crushed and the leaders, including Lenin, went into exile. The new czar, Nicholas II, promised more civil rights to his people, but this promise was soon broken.

When World War I started, life for most people in Russia went from bad to worse. The railroads, which had been used to bring food, fuel, and supplies for industry to the cities, were now used to take troops and weapons to the front. The economy almost collapsed and people started to go hungry. The government did nothing to improve the situation and in March 1917 riots broke out again. This time the troops joined the rioters. Nicholas abdicated and his advisers resigned.

A temporary government was set up, with Prince George Lvov as its chief minister. He was succeeded by Alexander Kerensky, but unrest continued. The Bolsheviks,

VLADIMIR ILYICH LENIN

Lenin (1870–1924) was a lawyer who was also involved in political activities. In 1897 he was exiled to Siberia for his political views and in 1898 he became leader of the Bolsheviks who wanted major reforms in the way Russia was governed. He was exiled again from January 1905 to March 1917, but on his return to Russia his strong personality and powerful speeches persuaded thousands of ordinary people to join the revolution.

▷ *Leon Trotsky (1879–1940) was a leader of the Bolshevik revolution and the most powerful man in Russia after Lenin. When Stalin came to power in 1924, Trotsky was dismissed from office, exiled and eventually murdered.*

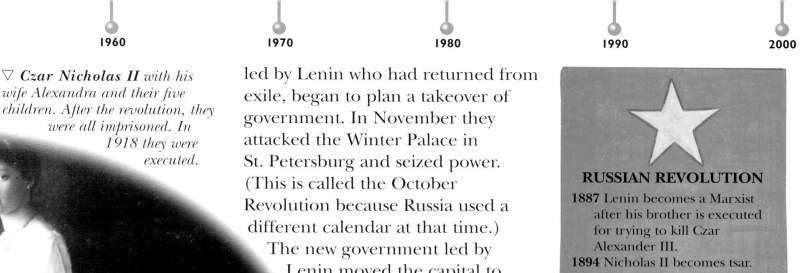

▽ *Czar Nicholas II with his wife Alexandra and their five children. After the revolution, they were all imprisoned. In 1918 they were executed.*

led by Lenin who had returned from exile, began to plan a takeover of government. In November they attacked the Winter Palace in St. Petersburg and seized power. (This is called the October Revolution because Russia used a different calendar at that time.)

The new government led by Lenin moved the capital to Moscow and made peace with Germany. It broke up the landowner's large estates and gave the land to the peasants who worked on it. The workers took control of the factories and the state took control of the banks. Not everyone agreed with this, however, and in 1918 civil war broke out between the Bolshevik Red Army and the anticommunist White Russians. This ended in victory for the Bolsheviks in 1921. The following year, the Union of Soviet Socialist Republics was formed. After Lenin's death in 1924, he was succeeded by Joseph Stalin. Stalin's rule was oppressive and many of his opponents were killed.

▽ *Armed workers led by the Bolsheviks stormed St. Petersburg's Winter Palace in 1917, starting the revolution. They were joined by Russian soldiers, tired of fighting the Germans in World War I.*

RUSSIAN REVOLUTION

1887 Lenin becomes a Marxist after his brother is executed for trying to kill Czar Alexander III.

1894 Nicholas II becomes tsar.

1898 Russian Social Democratic Workers' party is founded.

1904–1905 Russo-Japanese War over Russian expansion into Manchuria, a province of China under Japanese control. The Russians are driven out.

1905 Around 200,000 people march on the Winter Palace in St. Petersburg. The rebellion is put down and Lenin goes into exile.

△ *Rasputin (1869–1916) was a priest who had great influence over the imperial family. He told the czarina he could cure her sick son and persuaded the tsar to ignore the people's complaints.*

1917 Lenin returns from exile and goes to St. Petersburg. Nicholas II abdicates and a republican government is formed. Revolutionaries attack the Winter Palace and the government falls.

1918 Russia withdraws from World War I after signing the Treaty of Brest-Litovsk. The imperial family is executed. Civil war between the Red Army (communists) and White Russians (anti-communists) lasts until 1920.

1922 The Russian empire is renamed the Union of Soviet Socialist Republics.

IRISH HOME RULE

1886–1893 Attempts to give Ireland its own parliament are defeated in London.

1896 James Connolly founds the Irish Socialist and Republican party.

1905 Sinn Fein, the Irish nationalist party, is founded.

1912 The third Irish Home Rule bill is introduced in the British parliament, but World War I starts in 1914 before it can be enacted.

1916 On Easter Monday in Dublin, Irish republicans rise in armed revolt against British rule. Although they are defeated, their cause gains much support when 15 of the rebels are executed.

1918 Newly elected Sinn Fein MPs set up their own parliament in Dublin, rather than going to Westminster in London.

1919 Outbreak of bitter fighting between Irish republicans and British troops.

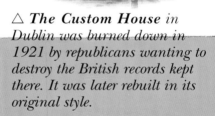

△ *The Custom House in Dublin was burned down in 1921 by republicans wanting to destroy the British records kept there. It was later rebuilt in its original style.*

1921 Anglo-Irish Treaty between the British government and the Irish Republican party separates Ulster from the rest of Ireland.

1922 Outbreak of civil war between supporters of the Anglo-Irish Treaty and those who oppose it. Michael Collins is assassinated.

1937 The Irish Free State becomes Eire.

1949 Eire withdraws from the British Commonwealth and becomes the republic of Ireland.

Irish Home Rule

At the end of World War I, the question of Irish independence from Britain became critical. Many Irish wanted self-government and were increasingly frustrated as two home rule bills put before the British parliament were defeated. Then, in 1912, a third home rule bill was approved, but it was prevented from coming into force by the outbreak of World War I.

Not all the Irish wanted home rule. Most people in the six counties of the north, known as Ulster, wanted to remain part of Britain and be governed from London, while in the south most wanted Ireland to become a completely independent republic. This division between north and south dated back to the 16th century, when a succession of English monarchs had used the planting of Protestant English and Scottish people on lands seized from Irish Catholics as a way of increasing loyalty to the British crown. Conflict between the two sides pushed Ireland to the brink of a civil war, also only prevented by the outbreak of World War I.

During the war, people who wanted Ireland to become a republic continued their campaign. They belonged to various organizations, including the political party Sinn Fein, the Irish Republican Brotherhood, the Irish Volunteers, and the Irish Citizen Army. Led by Padraig Pearse and James Connolly, around 1,600 protesters rose up in armed rebellion on Easter Monday, 1916. They took control of several public buildings in Dublin and declared Ireland a republic. The fighting lasted for four days before they were forced to surrender.

In the British general election of December 1918, Sinn Fein candidates were elected to every Irish constituency outside Ulster. Instead of going to Houses of Parliament in London, however, they set up their

▷ *The Easter rising of 1916 saw fighting erupt on to the streets of Dublin. Barricades were set up with British soldiers on one side and Irish Republicans on the other. Both sides suffered casualties, with 100 British soldiers and 450 Irish Republicans and civilians being killed. Many public buildings in Dublin were destroyed or badly damaged in the conflict.*

own parliament, called the Dail Eireann, in Dublin. It had its own courts, tax system, and postal service, and in 1919 it declared Ireland a republic. This led to three years of war between the military wing of Sinn Fein (later called the Irish Republican Army) led by Michael Collins, and the Royal Irish Constabulary, helped by British soldiers known as the Black and Tans. In July 1921 Michael Collins decided to negotiate with the British government, rather than continue fighting. In December he signed the Anglo-Irish Treaty, which made most of Ireland independent, but left Northern Ireland under British rule. This led to another outbreak of civil war, this time between the Free-Staters, who supported the Anglo-Irish Treaty, and the Republicans who wanted independence for a united Ireland.

The civil war lasted until 1923, when the Republicans decided to accept the division of Ireland for the time being. Their leader, American-born Eamon de Valera, founded a new political party, called Fianna Fail, in 1926, won the Irish general election in 1932, and served as head of government for many years.

△ **This map shows** Ireland after the settlement of 1923. Three of the nine counties of Ulster became part of the Irish Free State; the other six, stayed part of the United Kingdom.

◁ **Black and Tan** was the name given to British soldiers because of the color of their uniforms. Specially recruited by the British government between 1920 and 1921, they were hated by the Irish.

EAMON DE VALERA

Eamon de Valera (1882–1975) was born in the USA, but came to Ireland when he was just two years old. As a teacher he supported a campaign to revive the Irish language. He took part in the Easter rising but escaped execution because of his American birth. He was elected president of Sinn Fein and opposed the partition of Ireland in 1922. In 1926 he formed a new political party, Fianna Fail, and in 1932 he became prime minister of Ireland, becoming its president in 1959.

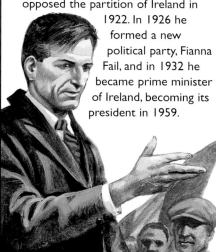

The Great Depression

%

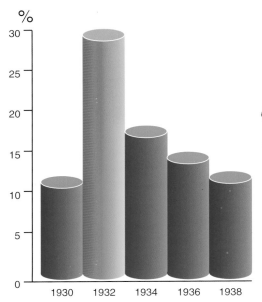

30

25

20

15

10

5

0

1930 1932 1934 1936 1938

△ **Unemployment figures** rose throughout the world during the Great Depression. The worst hit countries were the USA, Britain and Germany, whose economies were heavily based on industry.

▽ **Soup kitchens** serving free food were set up in many cities to feed the hungry. The Depression meant misery for millions who lost their jobs. More than a quarter of the US's population had no income other than what they could get from begging, charity handouts, and limited public welfare.

After World War I, the economies of many European countries were in chaos. Germany had to pay reparations (large sums of money) to Britain and France for starting the war. This led its economy to collapse in the 1920s. Other nations also suffered as they tried to pay back money borrowed to finance their war effort.

Most of the money borrowed to finance the war came from the United States. There, many people were starting to invest in stocks and shares, pushing up the price of shares beyond their real value. Share prices reached a peak in August 1929, then started to dip. When they were still falling in October, investors began to panic and sold their shares for whatever they could get. Reckless selling made prices fall still further and thousands of investors lost all their money. This is called the Wall Street Crash and started an economic crisis as banks and businesses closed down, throwing people out of work.

▽ **Panic in the streets of New York**, October 1929. As the value of shares dropped lower and lower, many investors rushed to the Wall Street Stock Exchange only to discover that they had lost all their money.

124

THE NEW DEAL

Part of the New Deal introduced by President Roosevelt in 1933 included a program to create more jobs. Young people were found work in the national forests, while a series of dams were built on the Tennessee River to provide electricity and prevent soil erosion. There were also welfare (social security) and labor laws to improve working conditions.

The situation was made worse as a severe drought hit the agricultural states of the Midwest. The Dust Bowl was a vast area where the rich topsoil, worn away by droughts and overfarming, turned to dust and blew away in the wind. Nothing would grow, and many farms were abandoned as farmers and their families took what they could and went to start a new life in California.

The US economic crisis soon affected the whole world. The system of international loans depended on the US and collapsed as money loaned overseas was called back home. This brought economic problems to Europe, especially Britain and Germany, both of which had high unemployment. Many countries attempted to protect their own industries by passing laws placing import duties on foreign goods. At the height of the Depression in 1932, world exports of raw materials had fallen by over 70 per cent, ruining the economies of many colonies who depended on the export of food and raw materials for their income.

The US was particularly badly hit. Mass unemployment led to many being made homeless, reduced to living in shanty towns of tin and cardboard, called Hoovervilles after President Herbert Hoover. In 1933, however, a new government led by Franklin D. Roosevelt introduced the New Deal. It included financial support for farmers and a construction program to create more jobs. Banks were more closely regulated and savings better protected. Even so, unemployment remained high throughout the 1930s.

△ *On the Jarrow Crusade* *200 men set out in October 1935 from Jarrow in northern England to London to draw attention to unemployment in their home town. Helped by sympathizers, they marched all the way there on foot.*

GREAT DEPRESSION

1929 In October the New York stock exchange on Wall Street crashes as people panic and sell their shares.

1932 At the height of the Depression there are 12,000,000 unemployed people in the US. Roosevelt is elected president.

1933 Roosevelt introduces the New Deal to protect people's savings and create jobs. In Germany there are 6,000,000 unemployed.

1935 In Britain 200 men march from Jarrow to London with a petition drawing attention to unemployment.

1936 The Depression ends in Germany as public works and munitions production bring full employment.

1939 Around 15 percent of the US's work force is still unemployed.

1941 Full employment returns to the US as it enters World War II.

The Rise of Fascism

Fascism is the name of a political movement that grew up between the wars. Fascist leaders promised strong leadership and were opposed to socialism. They gained massive support by promising to restore national pride and create jobs in countries humiliated by defeat in World War I and the misery of high unemployment.

Italy was the first country to have a Fascist government when Benito Mussolini marched his followers into Rome in October 1922 and threatened to overthrow the government by force if he was not made prime minister. The king agreed to his demand and asked Mussolini to form a new government. Gangs of armed Fascists then terrorized and killed members of other political groups who did not agree with them and by January 1923 Italy had become a one-party state. Two years later, Mussolini started ruling as dictator and became known as "Il Duce."

At that time, Spain was also ruled by a dictator by the name of Miguel Primo de Rivera. He tried to unite the people around the motto of "Country, Religion, Monarchy," but he did not succeed. He fell from power in 1930 and Spain became a republic the following year. But in 1933 Primo de Rivera's son founded the Falangist party, made up of Spanish Fascists.

△ **Benito Mussolini (1883–1945)** *impressed many Italians with his policies at first. After Italy's disastrous efforts in World War II, he was shot while trying to escape.*

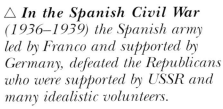

△ **In the Spanish Civil War** *(1936–1939) the Spanish army led by Franco and supported by Germany, defeated the Republicans who were supported by USSR and many idealistic volunteers.*

▷ **Hitler addressing a rally at Nuremburg, 1938.** *Adolf Hitler (1889–1945) was a powerful speaker who knew exactly how to win the support of his audience. He turned Germany into a police state, persecuting his political opponents, trade unionists and Jews, whom he blamed for all Germany's problems.*

126

In 1936, under the leadership of General Francisco Franco, the Falangist party overthrew the elected government in Spain. A terrible civil war broke out in which Franco, supported by Italy and Germany, eventually defeated the Republicans supported by Russia. In 1939 Franco became dictator of Spain.

In Germany, the Nazi party and its leader Adolf Hitler rose to power in 1933. The Nazis won support by promising to build Germany into a great state again. Hitler started a program of public works to create jobs and built up munitions and the armed forces. He imposed total control on the people, banning other political parties, introducing a secret police, and persecuting minorities, especially the Jews. Hitler also wanted to take back lands Germany lost after World War I. These included the Saar area, which he reoccupied in 1935, and the Rhineland, reoccupied in 1936. In 1938, Hitler sent tanks into Vienna to persuade the Austrians to agree to a union with Germany and also threatened to take over the Sudetenland in Czechoslovakia. To try to keep the peace, the Munich Agreement of September 1938 gave the Sudetenland to Germany. The following March, however, Hitler's troops took over the whole of Czechoslovakia and began to threaten Poland.

△ **Neville Chamberlain**, *prime minister of Britain, waiving the Munich agreement in 1938. It was signed in an attempt to keep peace in Europe by recognizing Germany's claim to the Sudetenland.*

RISE OF FASCISM

1922 Fascists led by Mussolini as prime minister come to power in Italy.

1923–1930 Primo de Rivera rules Spain as dictator.

1925 From this date Mussolini rules Italy as dictator.

1929 Mussolini wins the support of the Roman Catholic church by making Vatican City an independent state.

△ **Francisco Franco** (*1892–1975*) *became chief of staff of the Spanish army in 1935. He sympathized with Hitler, but kept Spain neutral in World War II. He was a ruthless dictator and tolerated no opposition to his rule, which lasted until his death.*

1931 Spanish monarchy overthrown as Republican party wins the election.

1932 Sir Oswald Mosley forms the British Union of Fascists.

1933 Nazis led by Adolf Hitler come to power in Germany. In Spain, Primo de Rivera's son creates the Falangist (Fascist) party.

1934 Hitler gains total power as his rivals are assassinated on the Night of the Long Knives.

1935 Italy invades Abyssinia (Ethiopia).

1936–1939 Spanish Civil War between Republicans and Nationalists (Falangists). Nationalists win and Franco becomes dictator of Spain.

1937 German aircraft bomb the Spanish town of Guernica in support of the Nationalists.

1938 On March 13 the Anschluss unites Germany and Austria.

Revolution in China

By 1900, China's crumbling Manchu dynasty was losing control of government and large parts of the country were dominated by foreign powers. The Chinese Nationalist party, the Kuomintang, was founded by Sun Yat-sen to try and unify the country under a democratic government. In 1911, the Manchu dynasty was overthrown. China became a republic with Sun Yat-sen as provisional president.

Sun died in 1925 and Chiang Kai-shek then became president of China and leader of the Kuomintang. By that time the Chinese Communist party had been founded. Its first meeting was held in Shanghai in 1921. Mao Zedong was an early member of the party.

Throughout the 1920s, warlords in the north of China tried to gain control of the country. In order fight them, the Kuomintang and Communists united in 1926 and defeated the warlords. But the following year, in 1927, civil war broke out between the Kuomintang and Communists as Chiang Kai-shek carried out a lightning coup and executed hundreds of Communists. The Communists were forced out of Shanghai and took refuge farther south in the province of Jiangxi.

The Kuomintang then claimed to have united the whole of China under their government in Nanjing. But, in 1931, the Communists, led by Mao, set up a rival government in Jiangxi. In October 1933 Chiang Kai-shek sent his army to Jiangxi with the

△ **The last emperor** of China was Pu Yi, who came to the throne in 1908 at the age of two. His father acted as regent and refused to allow any reforms in the country. Four years later, Pu Yi abdicated and China became a republic.

▽ **The Long March** from Jiangxi in the south to Shaanxi in the north claimed many lives. It took 568 days and, of the 100,000 who set out, about 80,000 died on the journey. The marchers were pursued by the Kuomintang.

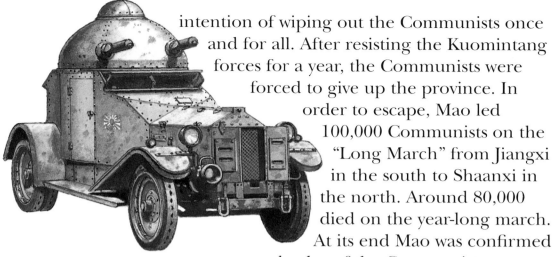

intention of wiping out the Communists once and for all. After resisting the Kuomintang forces for a year, the Communists were forced to give up the province. In order to escape, Mao led 100,000 Communists on the "Long March" from Jiangxi in the south to Shaanxi in the north. Around 80,000 died on the year-long march. At its end Mao was confirmed as leader of the Communists.

During World War II, Japan invaded China and the two sides united to defeat them. When Japan surrendered in 1945, civil war broke out again. This time the Communists waged a successful guerrilla war against the Kuomintang, helped by peasant uprisings throughout China. By January 1949 the Communists had taken control of Tianjin and Beijing from the Kuomintang. They continued moving south, forcing the Kuomintang off the mainland and on to the island of Taiwan. On October 1, 1949 mainland China became the People's Republic of China with Mao as its first president.

△ *A Japanese armored car* *used in the war against China in* *1937. The Japanese were much* *better equipped than the Chinese.*

▽ *Mao Zedong (1893–1976)* *was born into a peasant family in* *Hunan province. While fighting* *in the revolutionary army of 1911* *he became interested in politics* *and in 1923 he became a member* *of the Chinese Communist party.*

▽ *This map shows* the route taken on the Long March from 1934 to 1935. It covered 6,000 miles (9,700 km) and passed through 11 provinces. At the end of the march, with so many dead, Mao Zedong said "It proclaims to the world that the Red Army is an army of heroes."

REVOLUTION IN CHINA

1905 Sun Yat-sen founds the Kuomintang (Chinese Nationalist party).

1911 Collapse of the Manchu empire. Sun Yat-sen becomes president.

1921 Foundation of the Chinese Communist party. Mao Zedong is one of its first members.

1925 Death of Sun Yat-sen. Chiang Kai-shek succeeds him as leader of China.

1926 With Communist help, Chiang Kai-shek defeats the northern warlords.

1927 Start of civil war between the Communists and the Kuomintang. Communists are forced out of Shanghai and into the Jiangxi hills.

△ *Empress Dowager Cixi* *was mother to one emperor and* *aunt to another and ruled as* *regent for both of them. She* *encouraged reactionary policies,* *however, and helped to bring* *about the downfall of the* *Manchu dynasty's empire.*

1931 Communists set up a rival government in the south.

1933 Chiang Kai-shek attacks the Communists in Jiangxi.

1934 Mao leads Communists on the "Long March".

1935 Mao becomes leader of the Communist party.

1937–1945 The Kuomintang and Communists unite to fight against Japan.

1938 Japanese controls most of the east. Mao's Communists control the northwest.

1939 The Soviet army stops the Japanese from advancing farther west in China.

1946 Civil war breaks out again.

1949 The People's Republic of China is proclaimed. Chiang and supporters escape to Taiwan.

129

World War II

World War II started on September 3, 1939, two days after Adolf Hitler had sent troops to invade Poland. Both Britain and France protested and when Hitler refused to withdraw, the two declared war on Germany. The war was fought between the Axis powers (Germany, Italy, and Japan) and the Allies (Britain and the countries of the Commonwealth, France, the United States, and the Soviet Union).

Initially, Hitler had signed a nonaggression pact with the Soviet Union and on September 17, Soviet troops invaded Poland from the east. By the end of 1939, the Soviet Union had also invaded Estonia, Latvia, Lithuania, and Finland, while in the following spring German troops invaded Denmark, Norway, Belgium, the Netherlands, and France. The tactics the Germans used became known as the Blitzkrieg, which means "lightning war," because they overcame any opposition so quickly. Using vast numbers of tanks, they made surprise attacks. Then, as the tanks moved ahead, bomber planes moved in behind to eliminate any remaining defenses. The planes were then followed by infantry to complete the takeover. By June 1940, most of Europe had fallen and Britain stood alone.

WORLD WAR II

1939 Germany annexes Czechoslovakia. Italy annexes Albania. Italy and Germany agree an alliance.

August 23 Germany and USSR sign nonaggression pact.

August 25 Britain, France, and Poland agree an alliance.

September 1 Germany invades Poland.

September 3 Britain and France declare war on Germany.

△ *Many children were evacuated from British cities and sent to live with families in the countryside away from the danger of bombs.*

September 17 USSR invades Poland.

December Battle of the River Plate, South America, is first real battle of the war.

1940 March USSR takes Finland. Germany submarines attack British merchant ships.

April–May Germany occupies Norway, Denmark, Belgium, and the Netherlands.

June Germany occupies France. Allies evacuate from Dunkirk.

August–October Battle of Britain.

November Italy tries to invade Greece. Hungary, Romania, and Slovakia join Axis powers.

▽ *The battle of Britain was fought in the skies above southeast England from August to October 1940. Although Britain had far fewer planes than the Germans it still managed to win. Over 2,600 planes were shot down in the battle.*

When Italy joined the war on Germany's side in June 1940, Hitler planned to invade Britain. In August and September his air force, the Luftwaffe, attacked southeast England and London in daylight raids, trying to crush morale and destroy the British air force. Despite having far fewer planes, however, the British air force managed to defeat the Germans and so prevent the invasion. Even so, many British towns and cities were still bombed in the months that followed.

A new battle front opened in September 1940 when Italian troops moved into Egypt. Britain already had part of its army stationed there to defend the Suez Canal. By February 1941 the Italians had been defeated, but German troops, commanded by Field-Marshall Rommel, then arrived and forced the British troops back to the Egyptian border.

Buoyed up by his successes, Hitler launched an attack on his former ally the Soviet Union in June 1941, invading the country with the help of Finland, Hungary, and Romania. By the end of 1941, however, Allied fortunes were about to change as the United States joined the war, following the unprovoked attack on its navy at Pearl Harbor in Hawaii, by the Japanese air force.

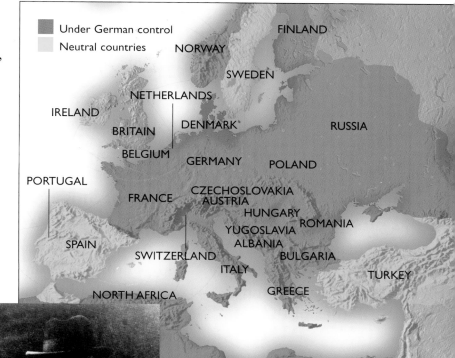

△ *Europe by the end of 1941* *was almost completely under German control. On the continent, only neutral countries managed to remain free. Axis troops had also expanded into North Africa.*

◁ *Winston Churchill (1874–1965) was prime minister of Britain from 1940 to 1945. His strong leadership and rousing speeches encouraged people through the worst days of the war. Here he is shown making a "V" for victory.*

World at War

The attack on Pearl Harbor marked the start of the war in the Pacific and by May 1942 Japan had taken control of all of Southeast Asia including Burma, Singapore, the Philippines, and New Guinea, from where they threatened the north coast of Australia.

The Japanese also took control of many islands in the Pacific, but by August 1942 the USA had defeated their navy at the battles of the Coral Sea, Midway Island, and Guadalcanal and stopped them invading any more territory. More victories for the United States followed, allowing them to take many Pacific islands out of Japanese control. This gave them bases from which they could now bomb Japan.

Meanwhile, British troops led by Field-Marshall Montgomery won a decisive battle at El Alamein, Egypt, in October and November 1942. Montgomery quickly advanced across Libya to meet Allied forces in Algeria and Morocco. The Axis armies, trapped between the Allies, were forced to surrender in May 1943.

German troops in the Soviet Union were also facing great difficulties. Although they had been within sight of Moscow by November 1941, the Russians had started to fight back and in 1943 they defeated the Germans at the battle of Stalingrad (now called Volgograd), but with the loss of many lives on both sides.

◁ *Charles de Gaulle (1890–1970) was a French general who escaped to Britain in 1940 when the Germans invaded his country. In London he quickly became leader of the free French who were determined to continue the fight against Germany. As the resistance movement grew in France, de Gaulle was recognized as its leader, too. After the liberation of France in 1944, he returned to Paris from Algeria and was elected president of France for only a few months. He was again president of France from 1959 to 1968.*

THE SIEGE OF LENINGRAD

German and Finnish forces besieged the Russian city of Leningrad (now St. Petersburg) from September 8, 1941 to January 17, 1944. In that time the people of the city suffered terribly and around one million died of cold, hunger, disease, and injury. They were determined not to let the Germans take control of their city and many of the children, sick, and elderly were evacuated. The remaining population, together with 200,000 Soviet troops, fought back as best they could, until the siege was ended by a successful Soviet attack from outside the city.

◁ *The US naval base at Pearl Harbor in Hawaii was attacked without warning by the Japanese air force on December 7, 1941. Four battleships were destroyed, many more damaged and 3,300 people killed. This attack brought the USA into the war on the side of the Allies.*

It took until August 1944 to expel the last German troops from Soviet soil, by which time they were needed in the west to defend Germany itself from an Allied invasion.

The Allied invasion of Europe started on June 6, 1944 and by July 2 one million troops had landed in Normandy, France and started to advance toward Germany, via Belgium and the Netherlands. Reinforced by the troops returning from the Soviet Union, Germany was able to launch a counterattack in December, but by January 1945 this had been defeated. In March 1945 Allied troops crossed the river Rhine and in the following month they reached the Ruhr, the heartland of German manufacturing and arms production. At the same time, Soviet troops were heading toward Berlin, where opposition to Hitler was growing rapidly. Realizing he was facing defeat, Hitler committed suicide on April 30. Soviet troops captured Berlin two days later and on May 7 the Germans signed a general surrender at Reims in France. This became official on May 9 when it was signed in Berlin.

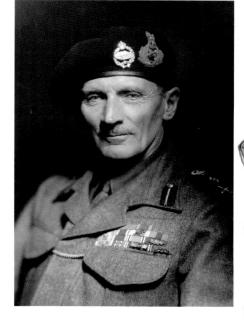

△ *Field-Marshall Montgomery* (1887–1976) was the commander of the 8th Army, which defeated Rommel's forces at El Alamein in Egypt, 1942. He also played an important role in the invasion of Italy and Normandy, accepting Germany's surrender in 1945.

▽ **The bombing of towns** and cities killed and injured many thousands of civilians on both sides. An Allied raid on Dresden in 1945 killed around 80,000 civilians in one night. Even those that escaped injury had their lives severely disrupted as fire destroyed their houses, factories, stores, offices and roads.

WORLD WAR II

1941 February Allies capture 113,000 Italian soldiers in North Africa. German forces arrive to replace them.

April Yugoslavia and Greece fall to Germany.

May German invasion of USSR begins.

December 7 Japan attacks Pearl Harbor. The US declares war on Japan. Italy and Germany declare war on the US.

△ *Heinrich Himmler* was the head of the SS, a military body created to defend Hitler. This also gave him control of the Gestapo (secret police service) and concentration camp guards.

December Japan invades Malaya and Hong Kong.

1942 February Singapore falls to the Japanese; 90,000 British and Commonwealth troops are taken prisoner.

March Dutch East Indies (now Indonesia) fall to the Japanese.

May The Philippines and Burma fall to the Japanese.

August US victory at the battle of Guadalcanal finally ends Japanese expansion. In the Soviet Union the battle of Stalingrad begins.

October In North Africa, Allies defeat Axis forces at the battle of El Alamein, Egypt.

The War Ends

Although the war in Europe was at an end, fighting continued in Asia. In September 1944, US troops began to recapture the Philippines from the Japanese, while a campaign led by the British started to reconquer Burma. An Allied invasion of Japan was planned for late 1945, but before it could be put into operation, an atomic bomb was dropped on Hiroshima in Japan.

The bomb was dropped by the USA on August 6, 1945 and three days later a second atomic bomb was dropped on Nagasaki. Thousands of people died in the two explosions and many thousands more died later from radiation sickness, burns, and other injuries. Five days later, the Japanese government under Emperor Hirohito surrendered and on August 14 World War II ended.

Almost six years of fighting had had a devastating effect on the world. There had been battles at sea, as well as on land and in the air, and the loss of life had been enormous.

▷ **Roosevelt and Churchill** at the Casablanca Conference in 1943. The US president and British prime minister met to discuss the progress of the war and their plans for the invasion of Sicily and the defeat of Japan.

WORLD WAR II

1943 February The battle of Stalingrad ends in defeat for the Germans.
May Axis troops in North Africa surrender.
July Allied troops invade Sicily. Mussolini's government is overthrown and Italy declares war on Germany.
1944 June Allied forces land in Normandy, France, to start invasion of Europe.
July An unsuccessful attempt to kill Hitler is made.

△ **Hirohito (1901–1989)** was emperor of Japan, coming to the throne in 1926. After his country's defeat in World War II the US pressured Japan to have a constitution and the power of the emperor was diminished.

October Allies invade Philippines.
December Start of battle of the Bulge, last German offensive.
1945 February At the Yalta Conference, Allies agree to divide Germany into four zones after the war.
March US captures Iwo Jima.
April Adolf Hitler takes his life.
May Soviet troops enter Berlin. Germany surrenders.
June US forces capture Okinawa.
July Division of Germany agreed at Potsdam Conference.
August Atomic bombs dropped on Hiroshima and Nagasaki. Japan surrenders.
October United Nations formed.

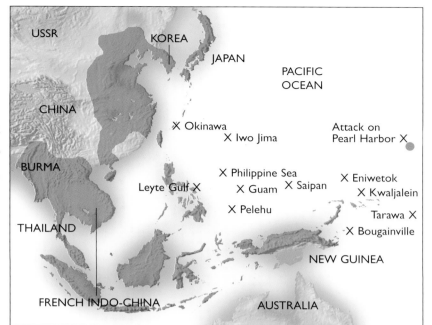

◁ *The war in the Pacific* began when Japan bombed Pearl Harbor, in 1941. A year later, it held all the orange areas on the map. The crosses mark the ensuing battles.

NUREMBERG TRIALS

After World War II, the Allies set up an international military court at Nuremberg in Germany to try the Nazi leaders. They were accused on four counts: conspiracy to make war, war crimes, crimes against peace, and crimes against humanity. Twelve were sentenced to death by hanging and six were sent to prison. Hermann Goering committed suicide before his sentence could be carried out and only two were acquitted. Lesser Nazi officials, such as concentration camp commanders, were also tried.

△ *The atomic bombs* that were dropped on Nagasaki (above) and Hiroshima totally devastated the two cities. Heat from the blast destroyed buildings in a 5-mile radius and over 155,000 people were killed in Hiroshima alone.

Others died through ill treatment as prisoners of war. On both sides there had also been millions of civilian casualties, either through bombing raids or through illness, cold, and hunger in cities such as Leningrad, which were besieged for many months. Probably the worst affected of all, however, were the Jews of occupied Europe. Hitler had been determined to wipe out the Jewish people and around six million died as a result of slave labor, torture, medical experiments, and gassing in concentration camps throughout Germany and Poland.

After the war, Soviet troops occupied most of eastern Germany and other Allied troops the west. Its devastated capital, Berlin, was divided among the Allied powers. In November 1945, leading Nazis were put on trial at Nuremberg before an international military court. They were tried for war crimes and crimes against humanity.

▽ *The Allied invasion of Normandy* began on June 6, 1944 (D-Day). Around 156,000 troops were landed in the largest seaborne attack ever mounted.

Indian Independence

At the start of the 20th century, India was the largest colonial territory in the world. It included Pakistan and Bangladesh, as well as India and had been ruled directly from Britain since 1858.

The people of India wanted independence not only for self-government but also to build up their industries again, instead of having to supply raw materials to Britain and buy back manufactured goods at high prices. In 1885 a political party, the Indian National Congress, was founded and began to campaign for reforms. At first it wanted India to remain part of Britain, but from 1917 onward, the National Congress began to campaign for Home Rule.

Britain saw India as the "jewel in the crown" of its empire and so was reluctant to let it go. Instead, mainly in gratitude for India's support during World War I, the British government passed a Government of India Act in 1919. This made some reforms, but most power remained with Britain. In the same year, British soldiers opened fire on a crowd at Amritsar protesting against British rule. Almost 400 people were killed and, as a result, the campaign for Indian independence began to grow.

By 1920 Mohandas Karamchand Gandhi had become the leader of the Indian National Congress and he launched a policy of non-cooperation with the British. This included encouraging Indians to boycott British goods, give up their jobs in local government, and refuse to obey any British authorities. Many blocked the streets by sitting down and refusing to move even if they were beaten by the police. Gandhi himself was arrested several times and sent to prison, where he continued his campaign of civil disobedience by going on hunger strike. His biggest protest against British rule in India was in 1930, when he led thousands of people on the Salt March to the coast. There they made salt from sea water in protest against the law that made everyone

◁ **Nehru (left) and Jinnah (right).** *Jawaharlal Nehru was India's first prime minister and ruled until his death in 1964. His daughter, Indira Gandhi, was India's first woman prime minister from 1966. Mohammed Ali Jinnah (1876–1948) was the first governor general of Pakistan.*

▷ **The partition of India** *was followed by a mass migration of Muslims from India to Pakistan and of Hindus from Pakistan to India. Many traveled on foot or by oxcart with all their possessions. More than one million people were killed as violence flared up between the two sides.*

buy heavily taxed salt from the state, even though they could make it very cheaply themselves.

In 1945, the British government finally agreed to India's independence within the British Commonwealth. One of the greatest problems to independence was religion. The majority of India's people were Hindus, but there were also large numbers of Muslims who did not want to live under Hindu rule. Violence often broke out between the two sides, so Mohammed Ali Jinnah began to campaign for a separate state for the Muslims. This was finally agreed by the British government. On August 14, 1947, two areas to the northeast and northwest of India became the independent country of Pakistan, with Jinnah as their governor general. The following day the rest of India gained its independence with Jawaharlal Nehru as prime minister. Immediately violence broke out as a result of this partition. Millions of people found themselves living in the "wrong" country – Muslims in India and Hindus in Pakistan – and so mass migrations began. As the people fled, atrocities were inflicted on both sides and hundreds of thousands of people were killed.

◁ *Mohandas Gandhi (1869–1948), also known as Mahatma, which means "Great Soul." He was a peace-loving man who enjoyed a simple life. The violence of partition led to his assassination at a peace rally in Delhi by a Hindu extremist.*

▷ *This map shows how India was divided. East Pakistan became Bangladesh in 1971. Burma (now Myanmar) and Ceylon (Sri Lanka) gained their independence in 1948.*

WEST PAKISTAN
Karachi
New Delhi
Dhaka
INDIA
EAST PAKISTAN
BURMA
Rangoon
Colombo   CEYLON

INDIAN INDEPENDENCE
1885 Indian National Congress (INC) founded.
1887 Gandhi goes to London to study law and works in South Africa from 1893.
1905 Foundation of the Muslim League in India.
1915 Gandhi returns to India and turns down leadership of the INC.
1919 Government of India Act passed.
1919 Almost 400 Indians are killed by the British army in massacre at Amritsar.

△ *Lord Mountbatten of Burma was the last viceroy (British ruler) of India. In 1947 he oversaw the transfer of power from Britain to India and Pakistan. He then remained in India as governor general until 1948.*

1920 Gandhi, now leader of the INC, launches non-cooperation with British.
1930 Gandhi leads the Salt March.
1934 Mohammed Ali Jinnah becomes president of the Indian Muslim League.
1935 Second Government of India Act.
1945 British government decides to grant independence to India.
1947 On August 14, northeast and northwest India become the independent state of Pakistan.
1947 On August 15, the rest of India becomes independent.

Israel and Palestine

The spiritual homeland of the Jews was in and around the ancient city of Jerusalem, but by the start of the 20th century most Jews lived elsewhere, especially in Europe, the USA, and Russia. Jerusalem itself was in a country called Palestine, which was part of the Ottoman empire. Most of its people were Arabs, but from the 1880s small numbers of Jews began to go back there and settle.

In the Balfour Declaration of 1917 Britain promised its support for the establishment of a Jewish homeland within Palestine. At this time the Ottoman empire was facing defeat in World War I and was about to be broken up. When this happened, the League of Nations gave Britain its mandate (permission) to rule over Palestine until the country was able to govern itself.

At first, only small numbers of Jews arrived in Palestine. After the Nazi party came to power in Germany in the 1930s, German Jews were persecuted, imprisoned or even killed. Their businesses were destroyed and their families terrorized. Those who could began to leave.

△ **Golda Meir** (1898–1978) was a member of Israel's parliament from 1949, foreign minister from 1956–1966 and prime minister from 1969 until 1974. Born in Russia, she was taken by her parents to live in the US as a child and moved to Palestine in 1921. She always hoped to solve the problems of Israel and Palestine by peaceful means, but under her leadership Israel was involved in the Six Day and Yom Kippur wars.

△ **Children in Palmyra, Syria.** Palmyra has been a Muslim city since 634, just two years after the death of Muhammad, the great prophet of Islam.

▷ **A kibbutz** in Israel in which all the land and property are owned or rented by the people who live there. All the work (usually farming) and meals are organized collectively.

Some went to other parts of Europe and the USA, but some started a new life in Palestine. As the numbers of Jewish immigrants increased, tension grew and fighting broke out. To keep the peace, Britain restricted the numbers of new settlers allowed in.

After World War II, many more Jews wanted to move to Palestine and Jewish terrorists (or Zionists) started to attack the British as well as the Arabs. Unable to solve the problem itself, Britain took the matter to the United Nations and in 1947 it was decided to split Palestine into two states, one Jewish and the other Arab. Jerusalem would become international, since it was equally sacred to Jews, Muslims and Christians. The Jews agreed to this, but the Arabs did not.

Britain gave up its mandate on May 14, 1948 and, on the same day, Jewish leader David Ben Gurion announced the founding of the state of Israel. The Arab League (Lebanon, Syria, Iraq, Transjordan, and Egypt) instantly declared war on Israel and attacked it. Israel quickly defeated them, taking Palestinian lands that increased Israel's territory by a quarter.

△ **Two of Jerusalem's holiest sites.** *The Dome of the Rock (top) is sacred to Muslims while nearby is the Wailing Wall (above), a very important site to the Jews.*

▷ **Israeli soldiers** *on patrol. Israel's refusal to acknowledge Palestinian claims to land and Arab refusal to recognize the state of Israel has led to decades of unrest.*

ISRAEL AND PALESTINE

1840 After brief rule by Egypt, Palestine becomes part of Ottoman empire once more.

1882 First Zionist settlement established in Palestine.

1917 The Balfour Declaration supports a Jewish homeland in Palestine.

1920 The Treaty of Sevres ends Ottoman empire.

1922 Britain is given the mandate for Palestine.

1929 First major conflict between Jews and Arabs.

1933 Persecution of the Jews begins in Germany.

1939 Britain agrees to restrict the number of Jews allowed to emigrate to Palestine.

△ **David Ben Gurion** *(1886–1973) was born in Poland and emigrated to Palestine in 1906. Known as the Father of the Nation, he was Israel's first prime minister and renowned for his magnetic personality and informal approach.*

1946 British headquarters in Jerusalem blown up.

1947 The United Nations votes to divide Palestine.

1948 On May 14 the state of Israel is founded and Arab League declares war.

1949 UN negotiated cease-fire leaves Israel with the area allotted to it in 1947.

The Cold War

△ *The Berlin Wall was built
right across the city in 1961.
The wall was built by the
Soviets to divide the eastern
part from the west and so
prevent people escaping from
the east. It was heavily guarded
on the East German side.*

**The United States of America and the
Soviet Union emerged from World
War II as the world's dominant
superpowers. Even though they
had fought together against the
Axis powers, they soon became
enemies in what was known as the Cold War.**

The Cold War started when the Soviet Union set up communist
governments in the countries of Eastern Europe liberated by the
Red Army. This effectively divided Europe by an "iron curtain." To
stop communism spreading to the West, the US-backed Marshall
Plan was set up to give financial aid to countries whose
economies had been ruined by the war.

One of the first conflicts was the blockade
of West Berlin in 1948. After the war
Germany was divided between the
Allies. The US, Britain, and France
controlled the western part of the
country, while the east was
controlled by the Soviet Union.
The capital city, Berlin, lay inside
Soviet-controlled territory, but
was also divided. The Soviets tried
to blockade West Berlin, forcing
the Allies to airlift in supplies. Five
months later, the blockade was
defeated and the following year
Germany was divided into West and East.

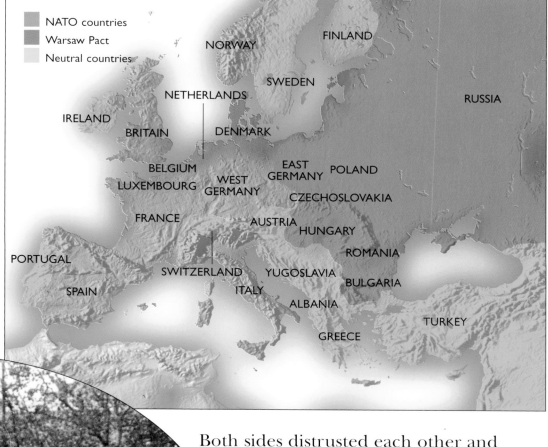

NATO countries
Warsaw Pact
Neutral countries

◁ **This map shows** how Europe was divided after World War II. The boundary between the two halves of Europe was first named the "iron curtain" by Winston Churchill. Few people were able to cross this divide.

NATO

The North Atlantic Treaty Organization (whose symbol is shown below) was set up on April 4, 1949, with its headquarters in Brussels, Belgium. It was a military alliance between several Western European countries, Canada, and the United States, against aggression from any outside nation. In 1955, the Soviet Union formed an alliance of communist states, the Warsaw Pact.

Both sides distrusted each other and expected an attack at any time. To protect against this, the countries of Western Europe and North America formed the North Atlantic Treaty Organization (NATO) in 1949. In response, the Soviet Union set up the Warsaw Pact, an alliance of the Eastern European states under Soviet control, in 1955.

Both sides also began developing and stockpiling nuclear weapons. This led to another crisis in 1962 when Cuban dictator Fidel Castro allowed the Soviet Union to build missile bases in Cuba that threatened the United States. President John F. Kennedy ordered the US Navy to blockade Cuba and eventually the Soviets agreed to withdraw. Both sides realized the danger of a nuclear war and the missiles were removed.

The USA and the Soviet Union encouraged many countries to take sides in the Cold War and, while they never fought against each other directly, the two superpowers became involved in many armed struggles in all parts of the world.

△ **Soviet tanks rolled into Budapest, Hungary,** in October 1956, and crushed a rebellion, which started when police opened fire on a student demonstration. The army joined the people in rebelling against Communist rule.

◁ **Soviet tanks entering Prague,** Czechoslovakia's capital, in August 1968. Earlier that year, in the "Prague Spring" a liberal government had introduced many reforms, which worried the Soviets.

▷ **Churchill, Roosevelt and Stalin** at the Yalta Conference 1945, when, along with France, Britain, the US, and the Soviet Union, decided to divide Germany.

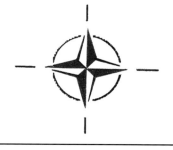

△ **In 1962 a crisis arose** when the Americans discovered Soviet plans to site rockets in Cuba. A clash of the superpowers was avoided only when Soviet ships carrying rockets turned back.

The Space Race

THE SPACE RACE

1957 Soviet Union launches the first artificial satellite, *Sputnik 1*. Laika the dog is the first animal in space.

1958 US launches its first satellite, *Explorer 1*.

1959 *Luna 2*, a Soviet space probe, reaches the Moon.

1961 Soviets launch first manned spacecraft, *Vostok I*. A month later, US launches its first manned spacecraft, *Mercury*.

1962 Launch of the first communications satellite by the US.

1963 Russian cosmonaut Valentina Tereshkova becomes the first woman in space.

1965 Russian cosmonaut Alexi Leonov becomes the first person to walk in space.

1969 US astronaut Neil Armstrong becomes the first person to land on the Moon.

1970 A Soviet spacecraft lands on Venus.

1971 A Soviet spacecraft lands on Mars.

1972 US makes its last Apollo Moon landing.

1975 Soviet and US spacecraft link up in space.

▽ *John F. Kennedy (1917–1963) was elected president of the US in 1960. The youngest man to hold the office, he took a firm stand against communism. His vision and vigor gave Americans the will to meet the challenges of a scientific age and his sudden assassination in Dallas, Texas, stunned the world.*

During the 1930s, scientists in Germany experimented with making rockets. The first ones were used to launch guided missiles during World War II. When the war ended, many of the scientists left Germany and continued their research either in the United States or in the Soviet Union.

The scientists realized that their technology might make it possible for people to travel in space one day and, as the Cold War worsened, the "space race" started. Both countries wanted to be the first to send a rocket into space.

In 1957 the Soviet Union launched *Sputnik 1*, the first artificial Earth satellite. It weighed about 185 pounds (84 kg) and took 96 minutes to orbit the Earth once at a maximum distance of 620 miles (942 km). The following year the US launched its first satellite *Explorer 1* and both sides started to spend vast amounts of money on space exploration.

The first person to orbit the Earth was Yuri Gagarin of the Soviet Union in 1961. This achievement prompted President John F. Kennedy to say that the United States would land a man on the Moon by 1970. This ambition was achieved when Neil Armstrong became the first person to walk on the Moon in 1969.

▷ **Sputnik 1** *was the first craft to go into space, launched on October 4, 1957. It traveled at 16,800 mph, transmitting a radio bleep that was picked up around the world. Three months later it burned up.*

△ **Laika the dog** on board Sputnik 2 *was the first living creature to go into space. She wore a special suit, but as no one knew how to return the satellite to Earth, she died in space.*

During the 1970s, Britain, China, France, India, and Japan all joined in the space race and started launching their own spacecraft. Many of these were satellites, used for weather forecasting and for communications. At the same time the United States and the Soviet Union continued to send craft deeper and deeper into space. Equipped with computers, these rival spacecraft were able to send back pictures and other information from planets as far away as Mars, Venus, Jupiter, Saturn, Uranus, and Neptune.

With the easing of the Cold War, both sides began to share their ideas and worked together on projects, such as building and maintaining an orbiting space station. Improvements in computer technology and communications on Earth have made it possible for the US spacecraft *Pathfinder* to land a robot explorer on Mars in 1997, which was controlled from Earth. The pictures it sent back were not only seen by scientists in their laboratories, but also by ordinary people at home watching television.

△ *The first space shuttle* lifted off in 1981. Launched like a rocket it lands back on Earth like a glider. In 1986 the Challenger shuttle exploded 73 seconds after takeoff. This disaster halted the shuttle program for over two years.

▽ *The* **Mir** *space station* was launched by the Soviet Union in 1986. Astronauts from the Soviet Union, the US, and other countries have visited Mir to carry out experiments. The longest time spent aboard is 365 days.

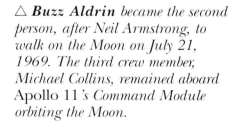

△ *Buzz Aldrin* became the second person, after Neil Armstrong, to walk on the Moon on July 21, 1969. The third crew member, Michael Collins, remained aboard Apollo 11's Command Module orbiting the Moon.

▷ **Pathfinder** landed on Mars in August 1997. It sent out a small Earth-controlled rover called Sojourner to take photographs and examine the planet's surface.

◁ *Yuri Gagarin* aboard Vostok 1 orbited the Earth for 89 minutes on April 12, 1961. He reached a height of about 200 miles above the Earth's surface.

143

African Independence

After World War II, many of the countries of Europe found it difficult to maintain their overseas colonies. In Africa, as elsewhere, some achieved independence peacefully, but others had to use violence to regain the right to govern themselves.

Most African countries gained their independence in the 1960s and 1970s. Once they were independent, these countries had to work out their own systems of government, law, education, and health services, which had previously been organized along European-style forms of government. They also had to run their own economies and their own armed forces.

What did not change at first, however, were the borders of the new countries. They remained as they had been set by the Europeans during the Scramble for Africa in the late 19th century. These borders did not reflect natural boundaries nor the ethnic groups of the peoples of Africa. This led inevitably to civil wars in several countries, notably in the Congo, Ethiopia, and Nigeria, as people from one area within a country tried to become independent and form a new country of their own.

POVERTY AND FAMINE

Since independence, famine has become a great problem in parts of Africa. In places where the land has been overfarmed for too long, the soil is no longer fertile and, if the rains fail, crops cannot grow. Famine on a massive scale is made worse by over-population and civil wars. The people caught in the disaster have to rely on aid or face starvation and disease.

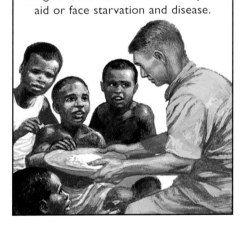

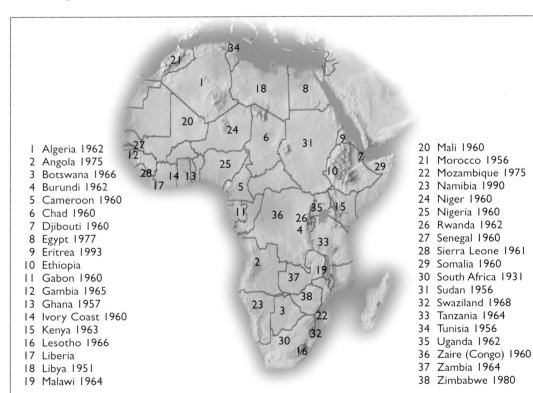

1 Algeria 1962	20 Mali 1960
2 Angola 1975	21 Morocco 1956
3 Botswana 1966	22 Mozambique 1975
4 Burundi 1962	23 Namibia 1990
5 Cameroon 1960	24 Niger 1960
6 Chad 1960	25 Nigeria 1960
7 Djibouti 1960	26 Rwanda 1962
8 Egypt 1977	27 Senegal 1960
9 Eritrea 1993	28 Sierra Leone 1961
10 Ethiopia	29 Somalia 1960
11 Gabon 1960	30 South Africa 1931
12 Gambia 1965	31 Sudan 1956
13 Ghana 1957	32 Swaziland 1968
14 Ivory Coast 1960	33 Tanzania 1964
15 Kenya 1963	34 Tunisia 1956
16 Lesotho 1966	35 Uganda 1962
17 Liberia	36 Zaire (Congo) 1960
18 Libya 1951	37 Zambia 1964
19 Malawi 1964	38 Zimbabwe 1980

◁ **Kenneth Kaunda** (born 1924) founded the militant Zambia African National Congress in what was Northern Rhodesia in 1958. He was imprisoned for his political activities until in 1964 he became the first president of Zambia.

△ **This map shows** European colonies in Africa, which mostly gained their independence in the 1960s and 1970s. Only Ethiopia and Liberia were never colonized.

1960   1970   1980   1990   2000

In other countries, such as Angola, Rwanda, and Burundi, civil wars broke out between rival ethnic groups, which wanted complete control of the whole country. In some countries the military overthrew the elected government, while others were ruled by dictators.

Problems also occurred in countries where the white settlers wanted to stay in control. This happened in Algeria, Rhodesia (now Zimbabwe), and South Africa and in each case cost many lives and much bitterness between the two groups. It was especially difficult in South Africa, where, from 1948 to 1990, the white government used a system known as Apartheid to keep blacks out of power by not giving them the right to vote. Once Apartheid was abolished, free elections were held and in 1994 Nelson Mandela became the first black president of South Africa.

△ *Ghanaian chiefs* waiting for the first session of parliament to begin. Ghana, formerly known as the Gold Coast, gained full independence from Britain in 1957.

▽ *Robert Mugabe* became prime minister of Zimbabwe in 1980. After independence, it took a long and bitter struggle for the black majority to gain power from whites.

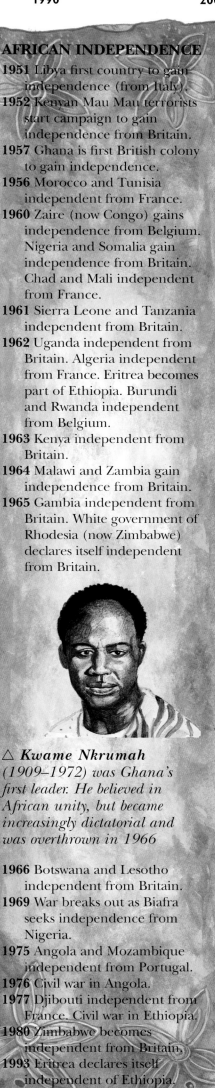

AFRICAN INDEPENDENCE

1951 Libya first country to gain independence (from Italy).
1952 Kenyan Mau Mau terrorists start campaign to gain independence from Britain.
1957 Ghana is first British colony to gain independence.
1956 Morocco and Tunisia independent from France.
1960 Zaire (now Congo) gains independence from Belgium. Nigeria and Somalia gain independence from Britain. Chad and Mali independent from France.
1961 Sierra Leone and Tanzania independent from Britain.
1962 Uganda independent from Britain. Algeria independent from France. Eritrea becomes part of Ethiopia. Burundi and Rwanda independent from Belgium.
1963 Kenya independent from Britain.
1964 Malawi and Zambia gain independence from Britain.
1965 Gambia independent from Britain. White government of Rhodesia (now Zimbabwe) declares itself independent from Britain.

△ *Kwame Nkrumah* (1909–1972) was Ghana's first leader. He believed in African unity, but became increasingly dictatorial and was overthrown in 1966

1966 Botswana and Lesotho independent from Britain.
1969 War breaks out as Biafra seeks independence from Nigeria.
1975 Angola and Mozambique independent from Portugal.
1976 Civil war in Angola.
1977 Djibouti independent from France. Civil war in Ethiopia.
1980 Zimbabwe becomes independent from Britain.
1993 Eritrea declares itself independent of Ethiopia.

145

A Social Revolution

At the start of the second half of the 20th century, many people throughout the world were still treated unequally because of their race, the color of their skin, their religion, or sex.

Black people were especially discriminated against in education, employment, housing, transportation, and health care. Many also had to use separate facilities in public places such as restaurants, beaches, restrooms, and theaters. With few or no civil rights, they could not even vote to try and change their situation. All they could do was protest and campaign, even though this often led to fines, imprisonment, or worse.

Some of the earliest protests were in the southern United States. They started in earnest in 1955 when Rosa Parks, an African American, was arrested for refusing to move from a seat reserved for whites on a bus in Montgomery, Alabama. This led to a boycott of the local bus service that lasted for over a year. It was followed by many more nonviolent protests, often inspired by Dr. Martin Luther King, a Baptist minister. The largest was a march to Washington, D.C., in 1963 to demand equal justice for everybody. More than 250,000 people took part and, in the following year, the US government passed the Civil Rights Act, which made discrimination illegal.

At the same time, the white minority government in South Africa was tightening up on its policy of Apartheid (the separation of whites and blacks). In 1960 the police opened fire on a group of unarmed protesters in Sharpeville, killing 69 of them. This brought an end to peaceful demonstrations and led to the formation of a guerrilla army called Umkhonto we Sizwe (Spear of the Nation). One of its most

important members was Nelson Mandela, but in 1962 he was arrested and sent to prison. The following year he was accused of plotting to overthrow the government and sentenced to life imprisonment. This action drew attention to what was happening in South Africa and people all over the world started to protest against it. By 1990 the government, led by F. W. de Klerk, knew it had to change its policy and on February 11, Mandela was released from prison. After long discussions, Apartheid was abolished and in 1994 South Africa held its first election in which all adults had the right to vote.

The struggle for black equality led others to protest against injustice. In the 1960s, women began to campaign for equal pay and job opportunities, better health care, and the right to have abortions. New laws were introduced to ban sex discrimination in employment. In the late 60s, gay men and women also began to campaign for equal rights. Since then, in many countries there have been protests about lack of government action on gay issues, which include sexual freedom and equal rights of marriage and parenthood.

△ **Solidarity** *was a trade union started in the shipyards of Gdansk, Poland, in 1980. It was formed to campaign for workers' rights and better conditions as well as freedom from communism.*

◁ **Black townships in South Africa** *were often disturbed by unrest and violence during the 1980s. Many people were killed or injured and vehicles and houses were set alight as a tide of protest arose against Apartheid.*

APARTHEID

Apartheid was a policy followed in South Africa from 1948 to 1990. The word means "apartness" and it was used to divide the country into separate areas for whites and blacks. There were different systems of education, employment, housing, and health care, with the black majority always receiving inferior treatment. While whites usually had good jobs and lived in comfort, the blacks did all the heavy and dirty work and lived in crowded townships outside the cities. Township houses were often very basic and lacked facilities such as electricity and running water.

◁ **Martin Luther King** *(1929–1968) was an outstanding speaker whose belief in the non-violent resistance to oppression won him the Nobel peace prize in 1964. His most famous speech included the words "I have a dream". In 1968 he was shot dead in Memphis.*

◁ **Nelson Mandela** *was born in 1918 and trained as a lawyer. He remained in prison from 1962 until 1990 . He was able to vote for the first time in April 1994, when the country held its first free elections. Mandela's party, the ANC, won with a large majority and he became president.*

147

The Vietnam War

THE VIETNAM WAR

1946 Start of the war between Ho Chi Minh's Vietnamese nationalists and French colonial troops.

1954 Vietnamese communists defeat the French at Dien Bien Phu. The country is divided into North Vietnam and South Vietnam.

1961 South Vietnamese ask for military advice from the US to combat Viet Cong guerrillas.

1963 South Vietnamese government is overthrown. Viet Cong increase their activities.

1964 War breaks out between North Vietnam (backed by the Soviets) and South Vietnam (backed by the US).

1965 The US sends combat troops to South Vietnam.

1966 Australian troops arrive in Vietnam to fight with the Americans. The first anti-war demonstrations take place in the US.

1967 The first efforts are made toward peace, but they fail. Antiwar demonstrations increase and spread to other countries.

1968 North Vietnamese and Viet Cong launch an attack known as the Tet offensive against the South. Some Americans begin to realize that the Viet Cong cannot be crushed and the war will go on for many years.

1969 US withdraws 25,000 of its 540,000 troops. The fighting, and the antiwar protests, continue.

1970 US Army invades Cambodia to support an anticommunist government and prevent supplies reaching North Vietnam.

1971 Fighting spreads to Laos.

1972 Peace talks start again.

1973 A cease-fire is agreed and the US withdraws its troops by the end of the year. The Vietnamese continue to fight.

1975 The communists take control of the whole of Vietnam.

1976 Vietnam is reunited under a communist government.

Vietnam, together with Cambodia and Laos, was part of the French colony of Indochina. It was occupied by the Japanese in World War II and during this time the Viet Minh league, led by the communist Ho Chi Minh, declared Vietnam independent.

After the war, France refused to recognize Ho Chi Minh's government and war broke out between the French and Vietnamese. This war ended in defeat for the French at the battle of Dien Bien Phu in 1954. An international agreement then divided Vietnam into communist North and noncommunist South.

Almost immediately civil war broke out between the two countries. From 1959, communist guerrillas in the South, known as the Viet Cong, were helped by North Vietnam. The US, worried about the spread of communism, sent military aid to help the South Vietnamese. As the conflict escalated, the US began sending troops to help the South from 1965. The Viet Cong's guerrilla tactics made it very difficult to defeat them. In an attempt to cut off their

△ **Ho Chi Minh** *(1892–1969) led Vietnam in its struggle for independence from France. As president of North Vietnam from 1954 he fought for a united Vietnam, achieved after his death.*

▽ **Most Vietnamese** *lived by farming, mostly growing rice in the fields around their villages. Many suffered greatly in the war as crops and villages were destroyed to flush out and kill the Viet Cong.*

▽ **Most of the war** *was fought in the jungles of South Vietnam. The Ho Chi Minh trail, from China through Laos into South Vietnam, was the Viet Cong's supply line from the North.*

CHINA

Hanoi

NORTH VIETNAM

LAOS

THAILAND

CAMBODIA

Saigon

SOUTH VIETNAM

supply lines, US planes began bombing North Vietnam. At the same time, whole villages in the south and vast areas of forest were sprayed with chemicals to destroy any Viet Cong hiding places.

By 1966, antiwar demonstrations had begun and in 1968, the Viet Cong's major Tet offensive on the South convinced Americans that the war could not be won. In 1969 the US began to withdraw its troops and a cease-fire was agreed in 1973. Fighting continued until 1975, when the North brought the South under its control.

◁ **Viet Cong soldiers** *used guerrilla warfare to defeat the enemy. One tactic was to dig a maze of secret tunnels. More than 16,000 soldiers lived underground, attacking US troops from their hiding places.*

△ **US soldiers** *were expecting to fight a traditional war, with large scale battles between two sides. They had to adapt to the Viet Cong's guerrilla tactics using small groups to mount surprise attacks.*

ANTIWAR DEMONSTRATIONS

The Vietnam War was the first to be widely covered on television. People throughout the world, but especially in the US, were able to see events as they happened. As growing numbers of troops were killed or injured and large parts of Vietnam destroyed, people took to the streets in protest. By 1967, the protests had spread beyond the US and the strength of antiwar feeling helped persuade President Nixon to withdraw from the war.

The Cultural Revolution

When Mao Zedong came to power in 1949, many Chinese could not read or write. Many also suffered from ill health and hunger. To try and make life better for everyone, the new government improved health care and provided schools in which adults as well as children could be taught.

For the first time, women were given equal rights with men. Large farms were taken from wealthy landowners and divided up among the peasants. New roads and railroads and power plants to generate electricity were built. But the problem of providing enough food for everyone remained. In 1958, Mao introduced the Great Leap Forward, to try and make each village self-sufficient, not only by growing its own food, but also by producing its own clothing and tools in small factories belonging to the whole village. The plan

▷ *In the Cultural Revolution schools and colleges were closed and teachers and students forced to work on the land. Opposition was brutally put down by the Red Guards.*

▽ *Tiananmen Square, Beijing full of students demonstrating for democracy in May 1989. The Chinese government sent in troops and tanks to clear the protesters and many people were killed.*

△ *This poster of a triumphant Mao appeared in 1949 when he first came to power. He took over a country where many could not read or write and civil war had left the country in financial disorder. Mao's initial reforms, called the Five Year Plan, helped to improve the economy.*

failed, because the government did not invest enough money in it, while bad weather led to poor harvests and even greater food shortages. Many people died of starvation and in 1959 Mao Zedong decided to retire.

Over the next seven years, Mao's successors tried to solve the economic problems caused by the Great Leap Forward. At the same time, tension grew between China and the Soviet Union. Mao thought the Soviet Union had lost its revolutionary spirit. Not wanting the same to happen to China, he swept back to power in 1966 and launched the Cultural Revolution. Its aim was to overthrow old traditional ideas and habits and rid the Communist party and the country of people who disagreed with Mao. Young people formed groups of Red Guards who criticized foreigners and their elders. Many artists, writers, and teachers were forced to leave their jobs and go to work on the land. Schools, universities, factories, and hospitals closed as older members of staff were forced out by students. Many people were killed and others were sent into exile for criticizing Mao.

When Mao died in 1976, the Cultural Revolution came to an end. His successor, Deng Xiaoping, began to open up China to trade and contact with the West.

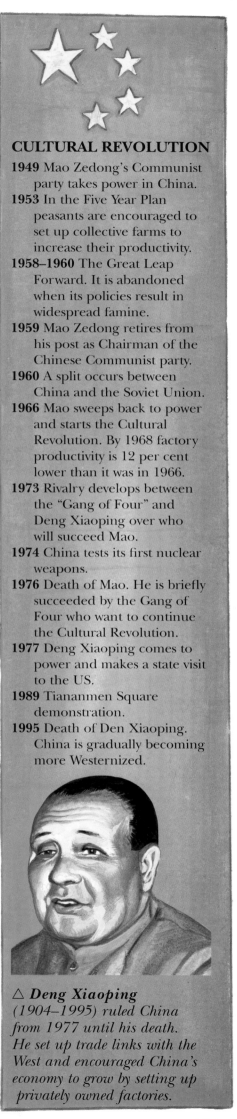

CULTURAL REVOLUTION

1949 Mao Zedong's Communist party takes power in China.

1953 In the Five Year Plan peasants are encouraged to set up collective farms to increase their productivity.

1958–1960 The Great Leap Forward. It is abandoned when its policies result in widespread famine.

1959 Mao Zedong retires from his post as Chairman of the Chinese Communist party.

1960 A split occurs between China and the Soviet Union.

1966 Mao sweeps back to power and starts the Cultural Revolution. By 1968 factory productivity is 12 per cent lower than it was in 1966.

1973 Rivalry develops between the "Gang of Four" and Deng Xiaoping over who will succeed Mao.

1974 China tests its first nuclear weapons.

1976 Death of Mao. He is briefly succeeded by the Gang of Four who want to continue the Cultural Revolution.

1977 Deng Xiaoping comes to power and makes a state visit to the US.

1989 Tiananmen Square demonstration.

1995 Death of Den Xiaoping. China is gradually becoming more Westernized.

△ *Deng Xiaoping (1904–1995) ruled China from 1977 until his death. He set up trade links with the West and encouraged China's economy to grow by setting up privately owned factories.*

151

Crisis in the Middle East

An uneasy peace followed the defeat of the Arab League by Israel in 1948. Jordan had captured Israeli land on the West Bank of the River Jordan, including much of Jerusalem. At the same time, Israel continued to encourage large numbers of Jews to migrate from Europe, Russia, and the United States. The Palestinian Arabs were pushed into separate communities within Israel and they began to campaign for a land of their own.

The next crisis came in 1956, when Egypt took control of the Suez Canal. This led to a war, with Egypt on one side and Britain and France, who had previously controlled the canal, on the other. Feeling threatened by this, Israel invaded the Sinai Peninsula and destroyed Egyptian bases there. The third war between Israelis and their Arab neighbors broke out on June 5, 1967 and lasted for six days. In this, Israel destroyed the Egyptian air force and also took control of the whole of Jerusalem, the West Bank, the Golan Heights, the Gaza Strip, and Sinai. A fourth war broke out in October 1973 when Egyptian forces attacked Israel across the Suez Canal and Syrian forces attacked on the Golan Heights. Israel managed to defeat both forces.

▷ **Beirut**, *the capital of Lebanon, large parts of which were destroyed by fighting which broke out in 1976. By the time peace returned in the mid-1990s, many people had been killed and injured on all sides.*

▽ **Ayatollah Khomeini** *(1900–1989) was a revolutionary religious leader of Iran. He came to power in 1979 after the Shah of Iran was overthrown. Under Khomeini, Iran became a strictly Muslim state.*

▽ *Saddam Hussein* (*born 1938*) *became dictator of Iraq in 1979 and the following year went to war with Iran. In 1990 he launched a war with Kuwait, but was heavily defeated by US-led troops. He managed to keep hold of power, but is deeply distrusted by the West.*

Three years later, fighting broke out in Lebanon, where many Palestinians lived in refugee camps. They joined forces with Lebanese Muslims who were in conflict with Lebanese Christians. Syrian and UN troops were also involved. In 1982, Israel invaded Lebanon to try and drive the Palestinians out, but failed.

From 1980 to 1988 another large-scale war broke out between Iraq and Iran, both of which were major oil-producing countries. Then in 1990 Iraqi troops invaded oil-rich Kuwait. UN forces freed Kuwait in 1991.

Since then, peace agreements have been signed between Israel and Egypt, Jordan, and Syria. Israel has granted limited Palestinian self-rule, but tension and conflict continue to disrupt the peace process.

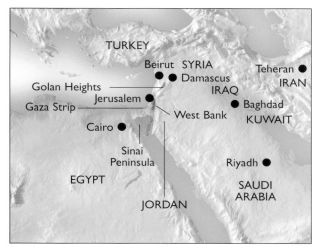

▽ *At peace talks* *in 1993, Israeli prime minister Yitzhak Rabin (left) and Yasser Arafat, leader of the Palestinian Liberation Organization (right) under the guidance of President Clinton (center), agreed in principle to Palestinian self-rule in Gaza and Jericho.*

MIDDLE EAST CRISIS

1956 Egypt takes control of the Suez Canal.
1964 Formation of the Palestinian Liberation Organization (PLO).
1967 Six Day War, between Israel and Egypt, Jordan and Syria, is won by Israel.
1973 The Yom Kippur War between Israel and Egypt and Syria.
1976 Fighting breaks out in Lebanon.
1979 Peace treaty between Israel and Egypt. Shah of Iran is overthrown and Islamic republican government set up.

◁ *Wars in the Middle East. The shaded area shows land taken by Israel in the Six Day War.*

1980–1988 Iran-Iraq War.
1982 Israel invades Lebanon.
1987 Violent fighting starts between Palestinians and Israeli troops in the West Bank and Gaza Strip.
1990–1991 In the Gulf War, Iraq invades Kuwait, but is repulsed by UN troops.
1993 Israeli prime minister Yitzhak Rabin, and PLO leader Yasser Arafat, meet in Washington.
1994 Israel and Jordan sign a peace agreement.
1995 Israel signs an agreement to extend self-rule to the Palestinians.

The End of the Cold War

▽ *Many symbols of communism were destroyed after the Soviet Union split up. Statues of past leaders and heroes, such as Lenin, were pulled down and dismantled for scrap metal. When the communists came to power in 1917, they had done a similar thing with symbols of czarist rule.*

By the beginning of the 1960s, the division between the Soviet Union and the United States was becoming less clear. China and the Soviet Union had split apart, while Western Europe, after recovering from the effects of World War II, was no longer as dependent on the United States. In spite of this, both the superpowers remained deeply suspicious of each other.

Tension between the two superpowers eased a little in the late 1960s. After a great deal of negotiation, known as the Strategic Arms Limitation Talks (SALT), two agreements were signed. This was an attempt to reduce the arms race, payment for which was ruining the economies of countries in Eastern Europe. The situation worsened after 1980, however, when Ronald Reagan became president. He was extremely anticommunist and increased military spending. One project began looking at the possibility of defending the United States from nuclear attack by building a defense system in space. At the same time, both superpowers tried to extend their influence in developing countries and continued to increase stockpiles of weapons.

Then, in 1985, the Soviets elected a new leader, Mikhail Gorbachev, as their general secretary. Unlike his predecessors, he tried to introduce political, social, and economic reforms. This lessened the tension

△ *The hated Berlin Wall was demolished in 1989 after the collapse of communism in East Germany. It had divided the city since 1961 and many had been shot trying to cross it. As the wall came down and the guards left, people from both sides chipped off pieces to take away as souvenirs.*

between the two superpowers once more. Two years later, Gorbachev and Reagan signed an agreement to ban all medium-range nuclear missiles.

Gorbachev's reforms in the Soviet Union had led to demands for free elections in the countries of Eastern Europe and by the end of 1989, communism had collapsed in Poland, Hungary, East Germany, Czechoslovakia, and Romania. In the following year, East and West Germany were reunited for the first time since 1945 and free elections were held in Bulgaria. In August 1991 an attempted coup in the Soviet Union led to the downfall of Gorbachev's government and the banning of the Communist party. By December the Soviet Union had been abolished and its former members split up into 15 independent nations. Its superpower status vanished as each nation tried to set up new systems of administration and rebuild their economies under private ownership. After more than 40 years, the Cold War had finally come to an end.

▷ **Czechoslovakians demonstrate** *in the capital Prague in 1989. Throughout that year, people in Eastern Europe began to demand greater democracy without fear of recriminations.*

▽ **The first McDonald's restaurant** *in Moscow. Gorbachev, realizing the Soviet economy was in a mess, began opening his country to Western enterprise. Despite the McDonald's reputation for quick service, long lines soon built up as so many people wanted to try the food.*

END OF THE COLD WAR

1967 The US, Britain, and the Soviet Union sign a treaty banning the use of nuclear weapons in outer space.

1969 President Johnson initiates the Strategic Arms Limitation Talks.

1972 The first SALT agreement is signed by US President Nixon, and Brezhnev of the Soviet Union.

1979 Second SALT agreement is signed by President Carter and Brezhnev.

1981 Ronald Reagan becomes president and increases military spending.

1985 Mikhail Gorbachev comes to power in the Soviet Union and starts to make reforms.

1989 Free elections are held in Poland. Communism collapses in Hungary, East Germany, Czechoslovakia, and Romania. The Berlin Wall is demolished.

1990 East and West Germany are reunited. Free elections are held in Bulgaria.

1991 A multiparty government is set up in Albania. The Soviet Union is abolished and replaced by 15 independent nations.

▽ **Mikhail Gorbachev (left) and Ronald Reagan (right)** *got on remarkably well together despite their different ideologies. In 1987, they signed a treaty banning all medium-range nuclear missiles.*

Global Awareness

FAMINE IN AFRICA

Although famine had long been a problem in many parts of Africa, television pictures of famine in Ethiopia in 1984 shocked the world. Money poured in to charities to help provide food and medicine. This only solved the problem in the short term. Now aid agencies realize they must support long-term projects that will help prevent famine in the future.

One of the greatest changes in the 20th century has been in the speed at which news and other information can travel around the world. Radio, television, and computers now make it possible to see or hear events all over the world as they take place.

This revolution in communications, together with faster and more convenient ways of traveling, has helped scientists and others to become aware of what is happening at a global level, rather than just in their own town or country.

One of the biggest concerns of the late 20th century has been for the environment. Until the 1960s, very few people believed that Earth was in danger. During the 1970s, however, pressure groups, such as Greenpeace and Friends of the Earth, were formed and started to campaign on many different environmental issues. These included the dumping of nuclear and toxic waste, the protection of endangered wildlife, and the destruction of the rain forests in Africa, Asia and South America. At the same time, scientists began to study the effects of pollution, especially the increasing amounts of carbon dioxide in the air. Carbon dioxide is a gas that comes from the burning of fossil fuels, such as coal and oil. These fuels are used to provide power for factories and transportation, as well as for heating homes, stores, and offices. At one time the amount of fossil fuel that was burned was much smaller and could be safely

△ **Recycling** *is one way in which the Earth's resources may be saved. Items such as paper, glass, metal and some plastics can be reused again and again. These items would otherwise be burned in incinerators or buried in landfill sites.*

▷ **Burning fossil fuels releases carbon dioxide** *into the atmosphere where it dissolves in rainwater, making acid rain that can destroy trees and kill fish.*

◁ ***Computers*** *linked to television, telephone, and satellite services now let people exchange or obtain information almost immediately. Tiny microchips have revolutionized home and work life.*

▽ ***The nuclear reactor at Chernobyl*** *in Ukraine exploded in 1986, releasing about 8 tons of radioactive material into the atmosphere. Traces of it spread as far as Italy, France, Scandinavia, and Britain. The incident turned many firmly against building more nuclear power stations.*

absorbed by trees and plants all over the world. Now the amount is much larger, but there are fewer trees as forests are cut down to make way for more farms. This means that the carbon dioxide stays in the air where it can trap the heat of the Sun and cause the temperature of the Earth to rise. In turn, the rising temperatures cause more land to turn to desert which leads to more frequent droughts. Carbon dioxide in the air also dissolves in rainwater, making acid rain that can destroy trees and kill fish.

Many governments have now taken action to try and limit the amount of carbon dioxide released into the air, by encouraging the use of public transportation instead of private cars, funding research into alternative sources of energy, such as solar power and wind power, and encouraging people to recycle items such as paper, glass, and metal. In parts of the developing world, many people's only chance of supporting their families or of making income is by cutting down the forests and selling the timber, then growing crops on the cleared land. Cutting down the forests may also be leading to climatic changes and to increased flooding and soil erosion.

GLOBAL AWARENESS

1962 Rachel Carson's *The Silent Spring* creates an awareness of the dangers of pollution.

1971 Founding of Greenpeace, the international organization concerned with protecting the environment.

1972 Government concern for the environment starts when the United States bans DDT, a powerful pesticide.

1976 US scientists voice the first fears about damage to the ozone layer. .

1980 Computers are now widely used in business and industry.

1985 In New Zealand, French agents blow up Greenpeace's ship *Rainbow Warrior,* which is protesting against nuclear testing in the Pacific. Live Aid concerts are organized in Britain and the US to help famine victims in Ethiopia.

1986 A serious explosion and fire at the nuclear power station at Chernobyl, Ukraine (then part of the Soviet Union) releases large amounts of radioactivity into the surrounding area.

1987 Scientists discover a hole in the ozone layer above the Antarctic.

1991 The world's population is estimated to be 5.3 billion. A gigantic tidal wave kills at least 100,000 people in Bangladesh.

1992 All nations send representatives to the Earth summit in Rio de Janeiro, Brazil, organized by the UN to discuss the future of the planet.

1995 A year of natural disasters. An avalanche in the Himalayas traps 5,000 people in their cars; at least 200 of them die. In the US a heatwave in June kills 1,000 people. In August flash floods in Morocco kill 200 people with 500 missing. In December 350 people die in a period of intense cold that spreads across Europe and Asia.

	1000–1050	1050–1100	1100–1150	1150–1200	1200–1250
POLITICS	**1016** Canute II of Denmark becomes King of England **1040** Macbeth murders Duncan of Scotland and becomes king **1042** Saxon Edward the Confessor becomes King of England	**1066** Harold II becomes King of England; he defeats an invasion from Norway, but is killed at the battle of Hastings and William of Normandy becomes king **1076** Pope Gregory VII excommunicates German emperor Henry IV	**1120** Heir of Henry I of England is drowned in the *White Ship* disaster **1135** Henry I dies; his nephew Stephen takes the throne; he is challenged by Henry's daughter Matilda and civil war breaks out	**1154** Henry Plantagenet becomes King of England as Henry II **1155** Pope Adrian IV "gives" Ireland to Henry II of England **1187** Muslim leader Saladin captures Jerusalem	**1206** Tribal chief Temujin is proclaimed Genghis Khan, ruler of Mongolia **1215** King John of England is forced to agree to Magna Carta **1228** Emperor Frederick of Germany leads the Sixth Crusade to Palestine
EXPLORATION	**1004–1013** Vikings try unsuccessfully to settle in Vinland, North America	**1096–1099** Members of the First Crusade travel to Turkey and Palestine	*c.* **1150** Rabbi Benjamin of Tudela, Spain, travels to Mesopotamia and Iran	*c.* **1154** Al-Idrisi's map muddles the Nile and the Niger rivers **1183–1187** Ibn Jubayr, a Spanish Moor, travels to Mecca, Baghdad and Damascus	**1245–1247** Franciscan friar John of Pian del Carpine visits Mongolia
TECHNOLOGY	**1035** Spinning wheels are in use in China *c.* **1050** Arabs introduce the decimal system into Spain *c.* **1050** Chinese begin printing books from movable type	**1066** Halley's Comet is seen, and is feared in Europe to portend evil **1100** Italians find out how to distill brandy from wine	**1107** Chinese use multi-color printing for paper money **1129** Flying buttresses are first used in building churches in Europe **1142–1154** Books on algebra and optics are translated from Arabic	**1150** The Chinese make the first rockets **1189** First European paper mill is built in Hérault, France	**1202** Italian Leonardo Fibonacci introduces 0 (zero) to Europe **1221** Chinese use bombs containing shrapnel
ARTS	*c.* **1050** Polyphonic (many voiced) singing is introduced in the Christian Church	**1067** Monte Cassino Monastery, Italy, is rebuilt **1078** Work begins to build the Tower of London	**1110** Earliest known miracle play is performed in England **1147** Geoffrey of Monmouth writes his *History of Britain*	**1151** Golden age of Buddhist art in Burma (now Myanmar) **1174** Bell tower of Pisa, Italy, is built and at once begins to lean	*c.* **1220** Italian poets develop the form of the sonnet **1225** *Sumer is icumin in* is the earliest known English round song
RELIGION	**1012** Persecution of heretics begins in Germany **1030** Norway is converted to Christianity **1042** Edward the Confessor begins to build Westminster Abbey	**1084** Carthusian order of monks is founded **1098** First Cistercian monastery is founded at Cîteaux, France	**1119** Military Order of Knights Templars is founded **1123** First Lateran Council in Rome forbids priests to marry	**1154** Adrian IV becomes the only English pope (Nicholas Breakspear) **1155** Carmelite Order of monks is founded in Palestine **1170** Archbishop Thomas à Becket is murdered in Canterbury Cathedral	**1215** Spanish priest Dominic founds the Dominican Order **1229** The Inquisition in Toulouse, France, forbids laymen to read the Bible **1233** Pope Gregory IX asks the Dominicans to carry out the Inquisition
DAILY LIFE	*c.* **1009** Persians introduce 7-day week to China, which had 10-day weeks	**1086** *Domesday Book* is first complete survey of England **1094** Gondolas come into use in Venice	**1124** Scotland has its first coins **1133** St. Bartholomew's Hospital, London, founded **1133** St. Barthlomew's Fair begins in London (closed 1855)	**1151** Game of chess is introduced into England **1189** Silver florins are first minted at Florence, Italy	**1230** Returning Crusaders bring disease of leprosy to Europe **1233** Coal mining at Newcastle, England, begins **1244** First competition for the Dunmow Flitch for married couples is held

1250–1300	1300–1350	1350–1400	1400–1450	1450–1500
1272 Edward I becomes King of England 1274 Kublai Khan, Emperor of China, tries to conquer Japan, but fails 1286 Margaret, the Maid of Norway, becomes Queen of Scotland, aged three; she dies in 1290	1301 Edward I of England creates his son Prince of Wales 1306 Robert Bruce is crowned King of Scotland 1337 Hundred Years War between England and France begins	1363 Mongol ruler Tamerlane begins the conquest of Asia 1368 Ming dynasty in China ousts the Mongol Yuan dynasty 1375 Truce halts Hundred Years War (until 1378)	1413 Henry V becomes King of England and claims large areas of France 1428–1430 Joan of Arc leads the French armies against England 1438 Inca rule begins in Peru	1453 Hundred Years War ends 1453 Turks capture Constantinople; end of the Byzantine empire 1455 Wars of the Roses break out in England; end with accession of Henry VII (Tudor) in 1485
1253–1254 Guillaume of Rubruquis, a French friar, travels to Mongolia 1271–1295 Venetian trader Marco Polo spends 24 years at the court of Kublai Khan in China	1325–1349 Moroccan explorer Ibn Battuta visits Mecca, India and China	c. 1352 Ibn Battuta explores African empires of Songhai and Mali 1391 Venetian brothers Niccolo and Antonio Zeno set off to Iceland and the Faeroe Islands	1420 João Zarco of Portugal discovers Madeira	1488 Bartolomeu Dias rounds Cape of Good Hope, at the tip of Africa 1492 Christopher Columbus explores the Caribbean 1498 Vasco da Gama makes the first sea voyage to India
1267 English scientist Roger Bacon proposes the use of spectacles c. 1290 Cable bridges are built over deep valleys in the Andes 1299 Florence, Italy, bans the use of Arabic numerals	c. 1310 First mechanical clocks are made in Europe 1327 Grand Canal in China, begun AD 70, is completed 1336 University of Paris insists that students study mathematics	c. 1380 Cast iron becomes generally used in Europe 1391 Geoffrey Chaucer of England writes on how to make and use an astrolabe c. 1400 Ethiopians start making a drink from wild coffee	1408 The Dutch use a windmill for pumping water c. 1440 Johannes Gutenberg of Germany begins printing with type	1454 Gutenberg produces the first printed Bible 1476 William Caxton prints the first book in English 1480 Italian artist Leonardo da Vinci designs a parachute
1257 Persian poet Saadi writes *The Fruit Garden* 1285 French composer Adam de la Halle writes comic opera *Le Jeu de Robin de Marion*	1325 Aztecs of Mexico build their capital city, Tenochtitlan 1341 Italian poet Petrarch is crowned as poet laureate in Rome 1348 Italian poet Giovanni Boccaccio begins writing the *Decameron* (to 1353)	1369 Geoffrey Chaucer writes *The Book of the Duchesse* 1375 First appearance of Robin Hood in English legends 1387–1400 Chaucer writes *The Canterbury Tales*	1414 German monk Thomas à Kempis writes *The Imitation of Christ* 1426 Netherlands becomes the center of music in Europe 1444 Cosimo de' Medici founds a library in Florence, Italy	1463 French poet François Villon sentenced to death for brawling, but escapes 1473 Sheet music printed from wood blocks is produced in Germany
1256 Order of Augustine Hermits, or Austin Friars, founded 1268–1271 Quarrels keep the papacy vacant until Gregory X is elected 1276 Popes Gregory X, Innocent V and Adrian V die in turn; John XXI succeeds them	1309 Pope Clement V moves his office from Rome to Avignon, France 1322 Pope John XXII bans the singing of counterpoint in churches 1349 Persecution of Jews breaks out in Germany	1377 Gregory XI returns the papacy to Rome 1378 Gregory dies: Great Schism begins when two popes are elected, one in Rome, one in France	1415 Bohemian reformer Jan Hus is burned at the stake for heresy 1417 End of the Great Schism: Martin V is elected pope in Rome	1453 St. Sophia Basilica, Constantinople, becomes a mosque 1484 Papal bull is issued against witchcraft and sorcery 1492 Roderigo Borgia becomes pope as Alexander VI
1278 In London, 278 Jews are hanged for clipping coins 1284 Legend of the Pied Piper of Hamelin begins; it may be founded on fact	1332 Bubonic plague is first heard of in India 1347–1351 The Black Death (bubonic plague) kills 75 million Europeans 1348 Edward III of England founds the Order of the Garter	1360 France issues its first francs 1373 English merchants are made to pay tunnage and poundage taxes	1416 Dutch fishermen begin using drift nets 1433 Holy Roman emperors adopt the double-eagle as an emblem c. 1450 Mocha in southern Arabia (now in Yemen) begins exporting coffee	1467 Scots parliament bans soccer and golf 1485 Yeomen of the Guard formed in England 1489 The symbols + and − come into general use

	1500–1520	1520–1540	1540–1560	1560–1580	1580–1600
POLITICS	**1509** Henry VIII becomes King of England, marries Catherine of Aragon **1517** Ottoman Turks conquer Egypt **1519** Charles I of Spain becomes Holy Roman emperor, uniting Austria and Spain	**1531** Protestants in the Holy Roman empire form a defensive alliance **1533** Henry VIII divorces his wife and marries Anne Boleyn **1536** England and Wales are united by the Act of Union	**1541** Ottoman Turks conquer Hungary **1553** Mary I, a Roman Catholic, becomes Queen of England **1558** Elizabeth I, a Protestant, succeeds Mary as Queen of England	**1562** Huguenots (French Protestants) begin emigrating to England **1567** Mary, Queen of Scots, abdicates after her husband's murder **1571** Christian fleet defeats a Turkish fleet at battle of Lepanto	**1581–1582** Livonian War Poles take Livonia and Russian access to sea **1587** Mary, Queen of Scots, imprisoned in England, is executed **1588** The Spanish Armada, an attempt to invade England, fails
EXPLORATION	**1502–1508** Ludovico de Varthema is the first Christian to visit Mecca **1519–1521** Hernando Cortés conquers Aztec empire in Mexico **1519–1522** Sebastian del Cano is the first captain to sail round the world	**1527–1536** Cabeza de Vaca explores southern North America **1531–1532** Francisco Pizarro explores Peru and conquers the Incas **1535** Jacques Cartier explores the St. Lawrence River for France	**1541** Spanish soldier Hernando de Soto discovers the Mississippi **1553–1554** Richard Chancellor opens up trade between England and Moscow, which he reaches by way of the White Sea	**1565** Spanish establish St. Augustine, Florida, the oldest city in the present-day United States **1577–1580** Francis Drake of England sails around the world	**1584** Sir Walter Raleigh begins colonization of Virginia **1596–1597** Dutch navigator Willem Barents dies trying to find the Northeast Passage
TECHNOLOGY	**1502** Peter Henlein of Germany makes the first pocket watch **1507** The name America is used on maps for the first time **1520** First turkeys are imported to Europe from America	**1523** Anthony Fitzherbert writes the first English manual on agriculture **1528** Michelangelo designs fortifications for the city of Florence, Italy **1530** Swiss physician Paracelsus writes book on medicine	**1543** Nicolas Copernicus declares that the Earth revolves around the Sun **1551** Leonard Digges invents the theodolite, used for surveying **1557** Julius Scaliger of Italy discovers the metal platinum	**1569** Gerhardus Mercator invents his projection for maps **1570** The camera obscura, or pinhole camera, is invented **1576** Danish astronomer Tycho Brahe begins sensational discoveries	**1589** William Lee in England invents a knitting machine **1592** Galileo of Italy invents a primitive thermometer **1600** William Gilbert of England proposes that the Earth is a giant magnet
ARTS	**1503** Leonardo da Vinci paints the *Mona Lisa* **1508–1512** Michelangelo paints the ceiling of the Sistine Chapel, Rome **1513** Niccolo Machiavelli writes *The Prince* on the theory of government	**1532** François Rabelais of France writes the comic book *Pantagruel* **1538** The first five-part madrigals are published	**1543** Benvenuto Cellini makes golden salt cellars for the King of France **1545** First ever book fair is held in Leipzig, Germany **1548** Building of the Pitti Palace, Florence, begins	**1570** Andrea Palladio writes influential work on architecture **1572** Luis de Camõens of Portugal writes his epic poem *Os Lusíados* **1576** First theater in England opens in London	**1587** Christopher Marlowe of England writes play *Tamburlaine the Great* **1590–1594** William Shakespeare of England begins writing his plays
RELIGION	**1507** Church begins selling indulgences to pay for St. Peter's Basilica, Rome **1517** Martin Luther begins the Reformation in Europe **1519** Ulrich Zwingli reforms the Church in Switzerland	**1526** Sweden converts to Protestantism **1534** English Church breaks from Rome, with the monarch as its head **1534** Ignatius Loyola of Spain founds the Jesuit order	**1545** Council of Trent begins the Counter Reformation **1549** Jesuit missions are sent to Brazil and Japan **1555** In England, persecution of protestants begins; many are burned	**1560** Scotland breaks with the Roman Catholic Church **1570** Pope Pius V excommunicates Queen Elizabeth of England **1572** Massacre of St. Bartholomew: French Protestants are killed	**1590–1592** Three popes die in a period of three months **1593** Attendance in church on Sundays is made compulsory in England
DAILY LIFE	**1504** First shillings are minted in England **1517** The first coffee is imported into Europe **1519** Hernando Cortés reintroduces horses to North America	**1525** Hops are introduced to England from France **1528** Severe outbreak of bubonic plague hits England **1531** Halley's Comet returns, causing great alarm	**1547** Fire destroys Moscow **1550** People begin playing billiards in Italy **1555** Tobacco is imported to Spain from America	**1560** Madrid becomes the capital of Spain **1565** The first potatoes arrive in Spain from America **1568** Bottled beer is first produced in London	**1582** Most Roman Catholic countries adopt new Gregorian calendar **1596** Tomatoes are introduced into Europe from America **1596** Sir John Harington of England invents the first water closet (lavatory)

1600–1620	1620–1640	1640–1660	1660–1680	1680–1700
1603 James VI of Scotland becomes King of England as James I, uniting crowns	**1624** Cardinal Richelieu becomes all-powerful in France	**1642** Civil War breaks out in England between King Charles I and Parliament	**1662** England sells city of Dunkirk to France	**1686** France annexes the island of Madagascar
1614 French Estates General (parliament) suspended until 1789	**1629** Charles I of England quarrels with Parliament, rules without it until 1640	**1649** Charles I is beheaded and England becomes a republic under Cromwell	**1664** England seizes New Netherland (now New York) from the Dutch	**1688–1689** Peaceful revolution in England drives the Catholic James II off the throne; Protestants William II and Mary II are offered the throne
1618–1648 Thirty Years War engulfs most of Europe	**1637** Manchu rulers of China turn Korea into a vassal state	**1660** Monarchy is restored under Charles II	**1676** King Philip War crushes Native Americans in Massachusetts	
1605 Samuel de Champlain of France explores Nova Scotia coast	**1613** Pedro Paez of Spain discovers source of the Blue Nile in Ethiopia	**1642** Abel Tasman of the Netherlands discovers New Zealand and Tasmania	**1673** Jacques Marquette and Louis Joliet of France explore the Mississippi	**1686** William Dampier of England explores northern coast of Australia
1615 Luis Vaez de Torres discovers strait between Australia and New Guinea	**1627** Thomas Herbert of England explores Persia (now Iran)	**1650** Franciscan missionaries explore the upper river Amazon	**1679** Louis de Hennepin and René Cavalier of France reach the Niagara Falls	**1689** Louis de Lahontain of France reaches the Great Salt Lake in Utah
1620 Pilgrim Fathers sail to America in *Mayflower* and found Plymouth Colony	**1637–1639** Pedro Teixeira of Portugal explores the river Amazon	**1651** Dutch pioneers begin to settle at the Cape of Good Hope		
1608 Hans Lippershey of the Netherlands invents the microscope	**1622** William Oughtred, English mathematician, invents the slide-rule	**1642** Blaise Pascal of France designs an adding machine	**1665** Isaac Newton of England develops calculus	**1682** Edmund Halley of England observes comet now named after him
1610 With a telescope Galileo of Italy discovers Jupiter's moons	**1624** Flemish chemist Jan van Helmont invents the word "gas"	**1642** Evangelista Torricelli of Italy invents the barometer	**1675** Greenwich Royal Observatory is founded in England	**1684** Robert Hooke of England invents the heliograph
1613 Galileo agrees with the theory that the Earth goes round the Sun	**1637** Pierre Fermat and René Descartes of France develop analytic geometry	**1650** Otto von Guericke of Germany invents an air pump	**1679** Denis Papin of France invents the pressure cooker	**1698** Thomas Savery of England invents the first steam pump
1605 Miguel de Cevantes of Spain writes the first part of *Don Quixote*	**1623** The *First Folio* prints most of Shakespeare's plays	**1642** Rembrandt van Rijn of the Netherlands paints *The Night Watch*	**1662** Work begins on Louis XIV's Palace of Versailles in France	**1688** Aphra Behn becomes first English woman novelist
1607 Composer Claudio Monteverdi is working in Mantua, Italy	**1624** Frans Hals of the Netherlands paints *The Laughing Cavalier*	**1652** Vienna opens its first opera house	**1667** The colonnaded square of St. Peter's, Rome, is completed	**1692** Henry Purcell of England composes opera *The Fairy Queen*
1611 Royal mosque at Isfahan, Persia (Iran) is built	**1633** John Milton of England writes poems *L'Allegro* and *Il Penseroso*	**1660** Samuel Pepys, English civil servant, begins his diary	**1677** John Dryden is England's leading poet	
1604 England's rulers clamp down on Roman Catholics and Puritans	**1633** The Catholic Church forces Galileo to say Sun revolves around Earth	**1645** Presbyterianism is made England's official religion	**1662** England forbids Nonconformist priests to preach	**1684** Increase Mather becomes a leading preacher in Massachusetts
1611 The Authorized Version of the Bible is published in Britain	**1634** First Oberammergau Passion Play is put on as thanks for avoiding the plague	**1648** George Fox founds the Society of Friends (Quakers)	**1678–1684** John Bunyan of England writes *The Pilgrim's Progress*	**1692** At witch trials in Salem, Massachusetts, 19 people are hanged
1616 Protestants in Bohemia are oppressed	**1637** Japan bans Christian missionaries	**1650** Archbishop James Ussher of Ireland says the Creation was in 4004 BC		**1699** Roman Catholic priests face life in jail in England
1607 Table forks come into use in England and France	**1625** England has its first fire engines and hackney coaches	**1644** Harvard College founded in Cambridge, Massachusetts	**1665** Plague ravages London, killing 68,596 people	**1683** Wild boars become extinct in Britain
1610 The first China tea is imported into Europe by the Dutch	**1626** The Dutch buy Manhattan Island from Native Americans for $24	**1654** Paris has its first mailboxes	**1666** Fire destroys most of London and ends the plague there	**1692** Lloyd's Coffee House, London, becomes marine insurance office
1619 First black slaves are employed in Virginia	**1630** The card game cribbage is invented	**1658** Sweden's state bank issues the first banknotes in Europe	**1677** Ice cream becomes popular in Paris	**1697** Fire destroys most of the Palace of Whitehall, London

	1700–1720	1720–1740	1740–1760	1760–1780	1780–1800
POLITICS	**1702** Anne, daughter of James II, succeeds to the English throne **1707** England and Scotland are united as Great Britain **1715** Stuart rebellion in Britain against new king, George I, fails	**1721** Robert Walpole is Britain's first prime minister (to 1742) **1727–1728** War between England and Spain over Gibraltar	**1745–1746** British Jacobite rebellion, led by Bonnie Prince Charlie, fails **1756** Seven Years War begins in Europe **1760** George III becomes British king (to 1820)	**1763** Seven Years War ends: Britain gains French lands in India and America **1775–1783** American War of Independence from Britain **1776** The 13 Colonies declare independence from Britain	**1789** The French Revolution begins **1789** George Washington elected as US president and US constitution takes effect **1800** Napoleon Bonapart assumes power in France
EXPLORATION	**1708** Alexander Selkirk, the original "Robinson Crusoe," is rescued from an island off the coast of Chile **1719** Bernard de la Harpe of France explores North American rivers	**1722** Jacob Roggeveen of the Netherlands discovers Easter Island and Samoa **1736** Anders Celsius leads French expedition to Lapland **1740** George Anson of Britain begins round the world voyage (to 1744)	**1741** Vitus Bering explores Alaskan coast for Russia **1748** American Pioneers cross the Cumberland Gap in the Appalachian Mountains	**1766** Louis de Bougainville of France discovers Tahiti and New Guinea **1768–1771** James Cook of Britain makes his first round the world voyage	**1790** George Vancouver England explores northwest coast of America **1793** Alexander Macken of Scotland explores northwest Canada **1795** In Africa, Mungo Park of Scotland explore the river Niger
TECHNOLOGY	**1707** Johann Böttger of Germany discovers how to make hard porcelain **1709** Abraham Darby of England begins using coke to smelt iron **1714** Gabriel Fahrenheit of Germany makes a mercury thermometer	**1733** John Kay of Britain invents the flying shuttle **1735** John Harrison of Britain builds first accurate chronometer **1737** Georg Brandt of Sweden discovers cobalt	**1742** Anders Celsius of Sweden invents the centigrade thermometer **1751** Carl Linnaeus of Sweden publishes his landmark book on botany **1752** American Benjamin Franklin invents the lightning conductor	**1769** James Watt of Scotland invents the steam condenser **1769** Nicolas Cugnot of France builds first steam road carriage **1773** First cast iron bridge built at Coalbrookdale, England	**1783** Montgolfier brothe of France make first hot-balloon ascent **1792** Claude Chappe of France invents the mechanical semaphore **1793** Eli Whitney of the United States invents the cotton gin
ARTS	**1709** Bartolommeo Cristofori of Italy invents the piano **1710** Building of St. Paul's Cathedral in London is completed **1719** Daniel Defoe writes first part of the story of *Robinson Crusoe*	**1721** J. S. Bach of Germany composes the *Brandenburg Concertos* **1735** Imperial ballet school in St. Petersburg, Russia, opens **1737** England begins censorship of plays	**1741** German George Frederick Handel composes *Messiah* in England **1747** Samuel Johnson of Britain begins work on his dictionary **1751–1772** French scholars compile the *Encyclopédie*	**1768** The Royal Academy of Arts is founded in London **1773** Johann von Goethe of Germany writes first version of *Faust* **1778** In Milan, Italy, La Scala Opera House opens	**1786** In Scotland Robert Burns publishes his first book of poems **1790** In Austria, Mozart composes the opera *Cosi Fan Tutte* **1793** Building of the Capitol in Washington, D.C., begins
RELIGION	**1716** Chinese emperor bans the teaching of Christianity **1719** Dunkards, German Baptist Brethren, settle in Pennsylvania	**1725–1770** Great Awakening series of religious revivals sweeps through British colonies in North America **1730** John and Charles Wesley establish the Methodist movement	**1759** Jesuits are expelled from Portugal and its colonies	**1766** Catherine the Great of Russia grants her people freedom of worship **1767** Jesuits are expelled from Spain **1776** Mystic Ann Lee forms the first Shaker colony in America	**1781** Religious tolerance proclaimed in Austria **1785** State of Virginia passes a statute of religio freedom **1790** Jews in France are granted civil liberties
DAILY LIFE	**1711** South Sea Company takes over £9 million of Britain's National Debt **1712** The last execution of a witch in England takes place **1720** South Sea Company crashes; thousands of people are ruined	**1722** Thomas Guy, British bookseller, helps found Guy's Hospital, London **1725** New York City gets its first newspaper, the *New York Gazette* **1727** Brazil sets up its first coffee plantation	**1752** Britain adopts the Gregorian calendar, dropping 11 days **1755** Earthquake kills 30,000 people in Lisbon	**1768** Publication of the *Encyclopaedia Britannica* in weekly parts begins **1770** Paris has its first public restaurant **1774** Rhode Island abolishes slavery	**1787** United States adop the Stars and Stripes flag **1792** Denmark abolishes the slave trade **1792** Scot William Murdoch is first person light his home with gas

1800–1820	1820–1840	1840–1860	1860–1880	1880–1900
1801 Act of Union unites Great Britain and Ireland **1803** USA buys Louisiana from France **1804** Napoleon becomes Emperor of France and is finally defeated in 1815	**1820** Missouri Compromise sets limits on slavery in the USA **1822** Brazil becomes independent of Portugal **1823** Monroe Doctrine announced, to oppose European intervention in the Americas	**1845** The United States annexes Texas **1848** Year of Revolutions: Austria, France, Germany, Italy, and Hungary **1853–1856** The Crimean War: Britain, France, and Turkey against Russia	**1861–1865** American Civil War: 11 states secede from the Union **1865** President Abraham Lincoln is assassinated as Civil War ends **1867** The United States buys Alaska from Russia for $7,200,000	**1881** President James Garfield of the USA is assassinated **1883** The scramble for European colonies in Africa starts **1898** Spanish-American War starts in Cuba
1803–1806 Lewis and Clark expedition finds a route to the Pacific from the east **1812** William Moorcroft of England explores Tibet **1822–1825** Denham Dixon and other Britons cross the Sahara	**1829** Charles Sturt finds the Murray River in Australia **1831** James Clark Ross of Britain reaches the North Magnetic Pole **1840–1841** Edward Eyre crosses the Nullarbor Plain of Australia	**1852–1856** David Livingstone of Scotland explores the Zambesi River **1854** Richard Burton explores East Africa, including Ethiopia **1858** John Speke and Richard Burton discover Lake Tanganyika	**1871** Henry Stanley is sent to look for Livingstone and finds him at Ujiji **1872** *HMS Challenger* begins a world survey of the oceans **1879** Nils Nordenskiöld of Sweden sails through the Northeast Passage	**1882** Adolphus Greely explores Greenland and the Arctic **1888–1892** Emin Pasha of Germany explores central Africa **1893** Fritjof Nansen of Norway tries to reach the North Pole, but fails
1807 Robert Fulton makes the first commercial steamboat trip in New York **1814** George Stephenson builds first successful steam locomotive **1816** René Laennec of France invents the stethoscope	**1825** First passenger railroad opens in northern England **1827** Joseph Niépce of France takes the world's first photograph **1834** Cyrus McCormick of the United States invents a reaping machine	**1844** Artist Samuel Morse of the USA demonstrates the use of the Morse Code **1847** James Simpson of Britain uses chloroform as an anesthetic **1860** Christopher Scholes of the USA invents a practical typewriter	**1873** Joseph Glidden of the USA invents barbed wire **1876** Alexander Graham Bell invents the telephone **1879** Electric lamp bulbs are invented	**1885** Karl Benz of Germany builds the first automobile **1895** Guglielmo Marconi of Italy invents wireless telegraphy **1900** Graf von Zeppelin (Germany) invents the rigid airship
1801 Joseph Haydn of Austria composes oratorio *The Seasons* **1813** Franz Schubert of Austria writes his first symphony **1814** Walter Scott writes his first novel, *Waverley*	**1822** Royal Academy of Music is founded in London **1835** Hans Christian Andersen publishes his first fairy tales	**1846** Adolphe Sax of Belgium invents the saxophone **1851** Herman Melville writes *Moby Dick* **1860** George Eliot (Mary Anne Evans) of Britain writes *The Mill on the Floss*	**1868** Louisa M. Alcott writes *Little Women* **1874** Impressionist movement in painting starts in Paris **1875** Gilbert and Sullivan produce their first light opera, *Trial by Jury*	**1883** Royal College of Music in London founded **1884** Mark Twain writes *Huckleberry Finn* **1895** Promenade Concerts begin in London
1804 British and Foreign Bible Society is formed in London **1808** Napoleon abolishes the Inquisition in Italy and Spain **1812** Restrictions on Nonconformists in England are relaxed	**1826** Jesuits are allowed to return to France **1827** John Nelson Darby founds the Plymouth Brethren **1830** Joseph Smith founds the Church of Latter-Day Saints (Mormons)	**1846** Mormons in the USA begin migrating to the Great Salt Lake, Utah **1853–1868** Johann Herzog writes *Encyclopedia of Protestant Theology* **1854** Pope Pius IX proclaims Immaculate Conception as dogma	**1865** William Booth founds the Salvation Army in Britain **1871** Charles Russell founds the Jehovah's Witnesses **1879** Mary Baker Eddy founds the Christian Science Church	**1890** James Frazer of Britain writes *The Golden Bough: A Study in Magic and Religion* **1896** Theodor Herzl of Austria proposes a Jewish state in Palestine
1807 Britain ends the slave trade **1814** British troops burn the White House and Capitol during war of 1812 **1815** Tambora Volcano in Indonesia erupts: 50,000 people are killed	**1825** Opening of Erie canal links New York City with Midwest **1830** Nat Turner leads unsuccessful slave revolt in Virginia **1840** Penny Postage and adhesive stamps are introduced	**1844** First co-operative society is formed in Rochdale, England **1851** The Great Exhibition is held in Hyde Park, London **1855** Britain abolishes stamp duty on newspapers	**1864** Louis Pasteur of France invents pasteurization **1871** Great Fire destroys Chicago **1874** Walter Wingfield invents Sphairistiké—now called lawn tennis	**1886** The Statue of Liberty is dedicated in New York Harbor **1900** The Labour Party is founded in Britain

	1900–1910	1910–1920	1920–1930	1930–1940	1940–1950
POLITICS	**1901** President William McKinley assassinated by an anarchist **1903** United States recognizes Panamanian independence and signs treaty to build a canal **1904–1905** Russo-Japanese War; Japan wins	**1911** China becomes a republic after 2,000 years under emperors **1914–1918** World War I: nearly 10 million soldiers die **1917** October Revolution in Russia: Lenin and the Bolsheviks seize power	**1922** Benito Mussolini forms a Fascist government in Italy **1924** Joseph Stalin becomes ruler of the Soviet Union **1924** Britain has its first Labour government	**1933** The Nazi leader Adolf Hitler becomes dictator of Germany **1936–1939** Spanish Civil War **1939** World War II begins as Germany and the Soviet Union invade Poland	**1941** The US enters World War II, following Japan's attack on Pearl Harbor **1945** World War II ends with German and Japanese surrender **1947–1951** Marshall plan pumps $12 billion into Europe for rebuilding
EXPLORATION	**1901–1903** Erich von Drygalski of Germany explores Antarctica **1907–1909** Ernest Shackleton of Britain nearly reaches South Pole **1909** Robert Peary of the USA reaches North Pole	**1911** Roald Amundsen of Norway leads first party to reach the South Pole **1911** Hiram Bingham discovers lost Inca city of Machu Picchu **1919** Alcock and Brown make first nonstop flight across the Atlantic	**1926** Richard Byrd and Floyd Bennett of the USA fly over the North Pole **1927** Charles Lindbergh makes first nonstop New York–Paris flight **1929** Richard Byrd flies over the South Pole	**1931** First submarine ventures under the Arctic Ocean ice **1932** Auguste Piccard ascends 28km in a stratospheric balloon	**1946–1947** Operation Highjump maps coast of Antarctica from the air **1947** Thor Heyerdahl of Norway sails the raft *Kon Tiki* from Peru to the Tuamoto Islands
TECHNOLOGY	**1903** In the USA, the Wright Brothers make the first powered flights **1907** Louis Lumière of France develops color photography **1908** The first Ford Model T car is sold	**1914** Official opening of the Panama canal **1917** Ernest Rutherford of Britain splits the atom **1919** First mass spectrograph machine is built	**1922** Insulin is first given to diabetics **1925** John Logie Baird invents a primitive form of television **1928** Alexander Fleming accidentally discovers penicillin	**1935** Radar is developed for use in detecting aircraft **1937** Frank Whittle builds the first jet aero engine **1940** Howard Florey develops penicillin as a working antibiotic	**1942** Magnetic recording tape is invented **1946** ENIAC, first fully electronic digital computer, is built **1948** Peter Goldmar invents the long-playing record
ARTS	**1901** Ragtime music becomes popular in America **1905** First regular cinema opens in Pittsburgh, Pennsylvania **1909** Sergei Diaghilev's Ballets Russes starts performing in Paris	**1914** Charlie Chaplin creates his film character in *The Tramp* **1916** Artists and poets start the Dadaist movement in Switzerland **1917** The Original Dixieland Jazz Band is formed in New York	**1926** A. A. Milne writes *Winnie the Pooh* **1927** Theremin, the first electronic musical instrument, is invented **1927** The *Jazz Singer*, pioneering feature-length "talking" film, opens	**1935** American George Gershwin writes *Porgy and Bess* **1937** First full-length cartoon film, *Snow White and the Seven Dwarfs* **1938** Radio play *War of the Worlds* causes panic in the United States	**1947** *The Diary of Anne Frank* is published **1949** George Orwell writes the satire *Nineteen Eighty-Four* **1950** United Nations building in New York City is completed
RELIGION	**1904** Germany partly lifts its ban on Jesuits **1909** First Jewish kibbutz is founded in Palestine	**1912** Church of Scotland issues a revised prayer book **1917** Balfour Declaration: Britain backs homeland for Jews in Palestine **1920** Joan of Arc is canonized (declared to be a saint)	**1924** Mahatma Gandhi fasts in protest at religious feuding in India **1929** Presbyterian Churches in Scotland unite	**1932** Methodist Churches in Britain reunite (split since 1797) **1933** All Protestant Churches in Germany unite **1937** Protestant parson Martin Niemöller is interned by Hitler	**1946** Pope Pius XII creates 32 new cardinals **1947** The Dead Sea Scrolls are discovered in caves at Qumran, Jordan **1948** The World Council of Churches is established
DAILY LIFE	**1902** Eruption of Mt. Pelée in Martinique kills 38,000 people **1903** The first teddy bears are made in Germany **1906** An earthquake destroys most of San Francisco; 3,000 people die	**1912** Liner *Titanic* sinks on her maiden voyage; more than 1,517 people drowned **1918** First airmail service is established in the United States **1919–1933** Prohibition outlaws alcoholic beverages in the USA	**1920** Women in the USA gain the vote **1929** Wall Street crash: biggest world economic crisis begins **1930** Youth Hostels Association founded	**1932–1934** Pontine Marshes in Italy are drained **1934** Dionne Quintuplets are born in Canada **1936** King Edward VIII abdicates to marry divorcee Wallis Simpson	**1946–1949** New suburbs built to accommodate returning US military personnel **1945** Bebop form of jazz comes into fashion **1947** First microwave oven go on sale

1950–1960	1960–1970	1970–1980	1980–1990	1990–2000
1956 Egypt's ruler Gamel Nasser seizes Suez Canal **1959** Alaska and Hawaii become 49th and 50th US states **1960** Seventeen African colonies gain independence	**1961** Communists build the Berlin Wall **1963** President John F. Kennedy is assassinated **1965–1973** The Vietnam War **1967** Six Day War between Israel and Arab nations	**1972** President Richard Nixon visits China to restore relations **1974** President Nixon resigns over Watergate scandal **1980** Marshal Tito, leader of Yugoslavia since 1953, dies	**1982** Argentina's invasion of the Falkland Islands fails **1983** US troops land in Grenada to depose Marxist regime **1989** Communist rule ends in East Germany; Berlin Wall is demolished	**1991** Collapse of the Soviet Union: republics become independent **1991** Breakup of Yugoslavia: civil war breaks out **1991** UN allies drive Iraq out of Kuwait
1957–1958 Vivien Fuchs of Britain makes first crossing of Antarctica **1958** US nuclear submarine *Trieste* travels under the North Polar ice **1960** A Bathyscaphe descends 35,700 feet into the Mariana Trench	**1961** Yuri Gagarin of the Soviet Union makes the first manned space flight **1968** US space craft *Apollo 8* first orbits the Moon **1969** Neil Armstrong of the USA is the first person to walk on the Moon	**1971** Space probes orbit Mars and send back photographs **1979–1989** Space probe *Voyager 2* flies past and photographs Jupiter, Saturn, Uranus, and Neptune	**1981** The first space shuttle, *Columbia*, orbits the Earth **1982** Soviet space probes land on Venus and send back color pictures **1984** Two US astronauts fly in space untethered to their spacecraft	**1993** Two Britons complete the first foot crossing of Antarctica **1997** US robot, controlled from Earth, explores surface of Mars
1956 Albert Sabin invents oral vaccine against polio **1957** Soviet Union launches the first Earth satellites, *Sputniks 1* and *2* **1959** St. Lawrence Seaway opened	**1967** Christiaan Barnard performs the first human heart transplant **1963** Theory of continental drift is proved by two British geophysicists **1969** First flight of the supersonic airliner *Concorde*	**1972** *Apollo 17* crew make last manned visit to the Moon **1978** Louise Brown, the first "test tube baby," is born **1980** Smallpox is eradicated worldwide	**1984** The first Apple Macintosh microcomputer goes on sale **1986** The Dutch complete their flood protection scheme after 33 years **1988** Undersea tunnel linking Honshu and Hokkaido, Japan, opens	**1993** Astronauts repair the Hubble Space Telescope (launched 1990) **1994** Channel Tunnel is completed at a cost of £10 billion
1950s Rock and Roll develops **1951** John Osborne's *Look Back in Anger* is staged in London **1960** New buildings completed in Brasilia, capital of Brazil	**1965** Op Art, based on optical illusions, becomes popular **1966** New Metropolitan Opera House opens in New York City **1968** Four Soviet writers are jailed for "dissidence"	**1971** *Fiddler on the Roof* closes after record New York run of 3,242 performances **1980** Former Beatle John Lennon is murdered in New York	**1983** Symphony written by Mozart aged nine is discovered **1985** Live Aid rock concert raises $60 million for African famine relief **1986** Wole Soyinka is the first black African to win the Nobel Prize for Literature	**1993** Missing treasure from Troy found in 1873 is rediscovered in Russia
1958 John XXIII becomes pope **1958** Supreme Religious Centre for World Jewry is opened in Jerusalem **1960** Swedish Lutheran Church admits women ministers	**1968** In Northern Ireland, Catholics and Protestants clash over civil rights **1969** Pope Paul VI removes 200 saints from the liturgical calendar **1970** Jewish and Roman Catholic leaders confer in Rome	**1978** Deaths of Pope Paul VI and his successor Pope John Paul I; succeeded by Pope John II, a Pole and fist non-Italian pope for 456 years	**1981** John Paul II becomes the first pope to visit Britain **1986** Desmond Tutu becomes the first black archbishop of Cape Town **1990** First Anglican women priests are ordained in Northern Ireland	**1992** Ten women become Anglican priests in Australia **1996** Strict Islamic law is imposed in Afghanistan
1953 Mount Everest is climbed for the first time **1954** Roger Bannister runs the mile in under four minutes **1958** First life peerages are created in Britain	**1967** Francis Chichester completes single-handed voyage around the world **1968** Martin Luther King and Robert Kennedy are assassinated **1970** Storms and floods kill 500,000 people in East Pakistan (Bangladesh)	**1976** Earthquakes shake China, Guatemala, Indonesia, Italy, the Philippines and Turkey: 780,000 people die **1976** Widespread parties and celebrations as the United States celebrates its Bicentennial	**1986** Space shuttle *Challenger* explodes, killing six astronauts **1987** World stock market crash on Black Monday **1989** World ban on ivory trading is imposed	**1992** Riots sweep through South-Central Los Angeles after four white policemen are acquitted of beating a black man **1997** Hong Kong is returned to China

IMPORTANT BATTLES

Hastings (1066) Duke William of Normandy defeated the Saxons under King Harold II and conquered England

Crécy (1346) Edward III of England defeated Philip VI of France, using archers to shoot his opponents

Agincourt (1415) Henry V of England defeated a much larger French army and captured Normandy

Orléans (1429) The French under Joan of Arc raised the siege of Orléans and began liberating France from England

Constantinople (1453) Ottoman Turks captured the city and ended the Byzantine (Eastern Roman) Empire

Lepanto (1571) A Christian fleet defeated a Turkish fleet in the Mediterranean and halted Muslim designs on Europe

Spanish Armada (1588) England fought off a Spanish attempt to invade and conquer it

Naseby (1645) Parliamentary forces defeated Charles I, leading to the end of the English Civil War

Blenheim (1704) During the War of the Spanish Succession, British and Austrian forces stopped a French and Bavarian attempt to capture Vienna

Poltava (1709) Peter the Great of Russia fought off an invasion by Charles XII of Sweden

Plassey (1757) An Anglo-Indian army defeated the Nawab of Bengal, beginning England's domination of India

Quebec (1759) British troops under James Wolfe defeated the French and secured Canada for Britain

Bunker Hill (1775) In the Revolutionary War, British troops drove the Americans from hills near Boston, Mass.

Brandywine Creek (1777) British troops forced American forces to retreat

Saratoga (1777) American troops surrounded a British army and forced it to surrender

Savannah (1778) Britain captured the port of Savannah from the Americans and gained control of Georgia

King's Mountain (1780) Americans surrounded and captured part of a British army

Yorktown (1781) A British army surrendered to a larger American force, ending the Revolutionary War

The Nile (1798) A British fleet shattered a French fleet in Abu Kir Bay, ending Napoleon's attempt to conquer Egypt

Trafalgar (1805) A British fleet defeated a Franco-Spanish fleet, ending Napoleon's hopes of invading England

Austerlitz (1805) Napoleon I of France defeated a combined force of Austrian and Russian soldiers

Leipzig (1813) Austrian, Prussian, Russian and Swedish armies defeated Napoleon I, leading to his abdication the following year

Waterloo (1815) A British, Belgian, and Dutch army supported by the Prussians defeated Napoleon I, ending his brief return to power in France

Fort Sumter (1861) In the opening battle of the Civil War, Confederate forces captured this fort in the harbour of Charleston, South Carolina

Merrimack and Monitor (1862) This inconclusive battle was the first between two ironclad warships

Gettysburg (1863) Union forces defeated the Confederates, marking a turning point in the Civil War

Vicksburg (1863) After a long siege Union forces captured this key city on the Mississippi River

Chickamauga (1863) At this town in Georgia the Confederates won their last major battle

Chattanooga (1863) A few weeks after Chickamauga Union forces won a decisive victory over the Confederates

Tsushima (1905) A Japanese fleet overwhelmed a Russian one, ending the Russo-Japanese War

Tannenberg (1914) At the start of World War I two Russian armies invaded East Prussia, but a German army under Paul von Hindenburg crushed them

Marne (1914) The French and British halted a German invasion of France at the start of World War I

1st Ypres (1914) A series of German attacks on this Belgian town were beaten back with heavy losses on each side

2nd Ypres (1915) The Germans attacked again with heavy shelling and chlorine gas, but gained only a little ground

Isonzo (1916–1917) This was a series of 11 inconclusive battles on the Italo-Austrian front

Verdun (1916) French forces under Philippe Pétain fought off a German attempt to take this strong point

Jutland (1916) This was the major naval battle of World War I; neither Germans nor British won

Brusilov Offensive (1916) A Russian attack led by General Alexei Brusilov nearly knocked Germany's Austrian allies out of the war

Somme (1916) A British and French attack was beaten back by German machine-gunners; total casualties for both sides were more than 1 million

3rd Ypres (1917) British and Canadian troops attacked to drive the Germans back, fighting in heavy rain and mud

Passchendaele (1917) This village was the furthest advance of 3rd Ypres; casualties of both sides totaled 500,000

4th Ypres (1918) This was part of a general German offensive, which died down after heavy fighting

Marne (1918) French, American, and British forces halted the last German attack of World War I

Britain (1940–1941) In World War II, German attempt to eliminate Britain's air force failed

The Atlantic (1940–1944) Germany narrowly lost the submarine war against Allied shipping

Pearl Harbor (1941) In a surprise air attack Japan knocked out the United States fleet at Hawaii

Coral Sea (1942) In the first all-air naval battle, Americans thwarted a Japanese attack on New Guinea

Stalingrad (1942–1943) The German siege of Stalingrad (now Volgograd, Russia) ended with the surrender of a German army of 100,000 men

El Alamein (1942) The British Eighth Army finally drove German and Italian forces out of Egypt

Midway (1942) An American fleet defeated a Japanese attempt to capture Midway Island in the Pacific

Normandy (1944) American and British troops landed in occupied France to begin the defeat of Germany; the largest ever seaborne attack

Leyte Gulf (1944) In the biggest naval battle of World War II, an American fleet thwarted a Japanese attempt to prevent the recapture of the Philippines

Ardennes Bulge (1944–1945) A final German attempt to counter the Allied invasion failed

Hiroshima/Nagasaki (1945) Two US atomic bombs on these cities knocked Japan out of World War II

Falklands (1982) A British seaborne assault recaptured the Falkland Islands following an Argentine invasion

Desert Storm (1991) An American, British and Arab attack ended Iraq's invasion of Kuwait

NOTABLE PEOPLE OF THE LAST 1000 YEARS

Roald Amundsen (1872–1928), a Norwegian explorer, was the first to navigate the north-west passage around Canada in 1906. In 1911 he was the first to reach the South Pole, beating his English rival Robert Scott

Mustafa Kemal Atatürk (1881–1938), the founder of modern Turkey. A fine soldier, he served in the Ottoman army in World War I and drove the Greeks out of Turkey in 1922. With the fall of the Ottoman Empire, the Turkish Republic was proclaimed. Kemal, who was given the name Atatürk (meaning "Father of the Turks"), was its first president, and virtual dictator, from 1923 to his death. He modernized the country with a number of sweeping reforms, introducing new laws and giving women the vote

Jane Austen (1775–1817) was an English novelist whose six great novels, including *Emma*, *Pride and Prejudice* and *Sense and Sensibility*, comment on the society and manners of her time. Her ability to create a range of living characters with both imagination and wit have made her books as popular today as when they were first published

Lucretia Borgia (1480–1519) was the daughter of Pope Alexander VI. Her father wanted his many illegitimate children to be rich and powerful and Lucretia married four times to further his ambitions. Her court at Ferrara in Italy was a center for artists, poets, and scholars

Brian Boru (died 1014), king of Munster, he made himself High King over all Ireland in 1002. He spent much of his reign making sure of his position against discontented lords and Viking settlers. In 1014, Brian was killed after defeating the Vikings at the battle of Clontarf near Dublin

Robert the Bruce (1274–1329) was the Scottish national leader against English kings Edward I and II. Crowned king of Scotland in 1306, after years of struggle he defeated the English at Bannockburn in 1314, securing independence for Scotland

Al Capone (1895–1947), born in Italy, in the 1920s he became one of the US's most notorious gang leaders. He controlled Chicago's underworld and bootleg (illegal) alcohol during Prohibition (a period when alcohol was illegal in the US). Under his orders, many people were shot in gang warfare. In 1931 he was jailed for tax evasion

Samuel de Champlain (1567–1635) is called the Father of Canada. The son of a French naval captain he dedicated his life to creating a French empire in Canada, or "New France." In 1593 he was part of an expedition that explored the St Lawrence River. He returned in 1608 to found a trading station, which was to become Quebec, the first city in Canada

Charlie Chaplin (1889–1977) was known as the Little Tramp. He was the first international screen star. Born in London, he went to the US in 1910. He made 35 films in his first year in Hollywood, and he went on to make such films as *The Kid*, *The Gold Rush*, and *The Great Dictator*

El Cid (c.1035–1099), from an Arabic word meaning "lord", was the name given to Spanish knight Rodrigo Díaz de Vivar. He led raids into Moorish (Muslim) territory in Spain, but also fought against the Christian king. Myth has made him a national hero of Spain

Davy Crockett (1786–1836) was a Tennessee-born frontiersman and twice elected US congressman. He joined the Texas rebels fighting against Mexican rule and was one of the 200 rebels who died defending the Alamo against 4,000 Mexican troops

Marie Curie (1867–1934) is often thought of as the first great woman scientist. Born in Poland, she studied in Paris, where she met her husband, Pierre Curie, a professor of physics. Together they discovered radium and won the 1903 Nobel Prize for Physics. In 1911, Madame Curie also won the Nobel Prize for Chemistry

Charles Darwin (1809–1882) was an English naturalist and pioneer of experimental biology. After his voyage around the world on the *Beagle* in the 1830s, he spent over 20 years building up evidence for his theory of evolution, before publishing it in *The Origin of Species* (1859)

Charles Dickens (1812–1870) was a popular, extremely successful English novelist, whose enormous output includes some of the most vivid stories in English literature. One of his best-known, *A Christmas Carol*, has directly influenced the way we celebrate Christmas

Albert Einstein (1879–1955) was a Swiss-born mathematical physicist. He published his famous theory of relativity in 1915 and won the Nobel Prize for Physics in 1921. He was driven by the Nazis to flee to the US, where his work led to the development of the atomic bomb

Eleanor of Aquitaine (1122–1204) married the king of France in 1138. The marriage was annulled (dissolved) and in 1152 she married Henry of Anjou, becoming queen of England in 1154. With her rich duchy of Aquitaine, the English king ruled more than half of France. Her eldest son was Richard I, known as the Lionhearted.

Elizabeth I (1533–1603), daughter of Henry VIII, succeeded her sister Mary as queen of England in 1558. Intelligent, politically able, but personally vain, her long reign was one of stability and a golden age for England. Known as the Virgin Queen, she never married

Haile Selassie (1891–1975) was the last emperor of Ethiopia from 1930 to 1974. He worked to modernize the country. When Italy occupied Ethiopia from 1936 to 1941 he fled to England. Before taking the title Haile Selassie ("Light of the Trinity") he was known as Ras (Prince) Tafari. Many Caribbean people of African origin saw him as a symbol of hope and named themselves Rastafarians after him. Since the 1970s, reggae music inspired by Rastafarian ideas of a better life, has spread their ideas worldwide

Henry Ford (1863–1947) was a US industrialist who pioneered the mass-production of inexpensive automobiles. In 1903, he founded the Ford motor company in Detroit and introduced the Model T, "a motor car for the great multitude" in 1908

Ernesto "Che" Guevara (1928–1967) was a revolutionary hero. Born in Argentina, he helped guerilla leader Fidel Castro overthrow the dictatorship in Cuba in 1959. He was killed while leading a band of guerillas against the US-trained Bolivian army

Ivan IV (the Terrible) (1530–1584) crowned himself the first czar of Russia in 1547. He made a series of reforms, but his first wife's death in 1560 seemed to derange his mind. He introduced a reign of terror that devastated the country. He married six more times and, in a fit of rage, killed his eldest son

Ned Kelly (1855–1880) was a notorious Australian outlaw who led a gang of bushrangers (bandits). He often wore home-made armour as protection. The Kelly Gang roamed the country, staging hold-ups and bank robberies. Some people saw them as heroes fighting the rich to help the poor. Ned Kelly was finally captured and hanged

Omar Khayyam (c.1050–c.1123) was a Persian mathematician and royal astronomer, who devised a new calendar. He also wrote a famous sequence of poems called *The Rubaiyat.*

Mary Kingsley (1862–1900) was an English explorer who travelled the rivers of West Africa by canoe, bringing back insects, reptiles and fish to England. Her books about Africa became very popular

Flora Macdonald (1722–1790) was a Scottish heroine who saved the life of Charles Stuart (Bonnie Prince Charlie) after his defeat at Culloden in1746. She disguised him as her maid so that Charles could flee from Scotland to France

Michelangelo Buonarroti (1475–1564) was an Italian painter, sculptor and poet. Like Leonardo da Vinci, he studied anatomy, but became obsessed with the problem of representing the human body. His many famous works include the ceiling of the Sistine Chapel in St. Peter's Rome and his statue of *David* in Florence

Alfred Nobel (1833–1896) was a Swedish inventor and philanthropist. He discovered dynamite and built up a fortune from the manufacture of explosives. He left his fortune as a fund for annual prizes for those who had contributed most to the benefit of mankind in the fields of physics, chemistry, medicine, literature, and peace

Vaslav Nijinsky (1892–1950) is considered to be one of the greatest ballet dancers of all time. He was a member of the Russian Ballet Company under the direction of Sergei Diaghilev, which took Paris and London by storm before World War I

Jesse Owens (1913–1980) was a black US athlete who won four gold medals at the Berlin Olympics, Germany in 1936. His triumph infuriated Adolf Hitler, who refused to congratulate him

Louis Pasteur (1822–1895) was a French chemist whose research on fermentation led to the scientific study of bacteria. He investigated infectious diseases and their prevention and in 1888 he set up the Pasteur Institute in Paris. His work influenced many later scientists, including Joseph Lister.

Eva "Evita" Perón (1919–1952) was the flamboyant wife of Juan Perón, president of Argentina. A radio actress, she was hugely popular with workers and the poor. She began reforms in education and won the right to vote for Argentinian women. Her death at the age of 33 greatly diminished support for her husband

Pablo Picasso (1881–1973) was a Spanish painter who settled in Paris in 1903. He founded Cubism and greatly influenced contemporary art. He also produced many sculptures and ceramics, and designed costumes and sets for the ballet

Pocahontas (c.1595–1617) was a young Native American woman who saved Captain John Smith, leader of the Jamestown colony, Virginia, from death at the hands of her people. In 1612 she was held hostage by the English to force her father to make peace. A year later she married John Rolfe and went to England with him

Rembrandt van Rijn (1606–1609) was a Dutch painter and engraver whose enormous output is characterized by bold realism, vitality and simplicity. He produced landscapes, portraits, large groups, etchings and drawings, as well as many self-portraits charting his path to lonely old age

Franklin Delano Roosevelt (1882–1945) became US president in 1933 and held office until his death. A distant cousin of Theodore Roosevelt, he was stricken by polio in 1921, which left him in a wheelchair. He introduced the New Deal to boost industry and alleviate the hardship of mass unemployment during the Depression

Theodore Roosevelt (1858–1919) was president of the US from 1901–1909. Brilliant, flamboyant, and energetic, he was immensely popular. Teddy bears get their name from him after he refused to shoot a bear cub on a hunting trip. His mediation in 1905 at the end of the Russo-Japanese War earned him the Nobel Peace Prize

Shaka (1787–1828) was a great Zulu warrior king who was renowned for his military skills. He became leader of the Zulu nation in South Africa in 1816 and introduced new weapons and battle skills to the army. His army rapidly took cóntrol of a large area of land, but constant fighting with their neighbours led to the *mfecane* or "time of troubles"

William Shakespeare (1564–1616), England's greatest poet and dramatist, he came to London at the height of the Elizabethan golden age, becoming involved with the Globe theatre as an actor and playwright. In his 38 plays he showed a mastery of language, understanding of character, dramatic perception and skill that has never been surpassed

Sitting Bull (died 1890) was a Native American shaman (medicine man) and Sioux chief. He led a group at the Battle of Little Bighorn in 1876 when General George Custer and his men were trapped and killed. Sitting Bull fled to Canada with his people, but later surrendered to US troops

Joseph Stalin (1879–1953) born Joseph Djugashvili, he later changed his name to Stalin, which means "man of steel." Leader of the Russian people for nearly 30 years, he took control after the death of Vladimir Lenin, ousting his rival Leon Trotsky in 1928. He launched a series of five-year plans to expand farming and industry under state control. He also instituted a wave of terror (1935–1938) to remove all possible enemies. More than ten million people were sent to labour camps or executed

Abel Tasman (1603–1659) was a Dutch explorer. He was sent by Anthony Van Deimen, governor-general of the Dutch East India Company in Indonesia, to lead an expedition to find a shorter route to South America. He was the first European to set food in Tasmania (which he called Van Diemen Land) and New Zealand in 1642. He went on to reach Tonga and Fiji

Toussaint L'Overture (1743–1803), born a slave, Pierre Toussaint-Breda (known as L'Overture), led a rebellion in French-held Santo Domingo (Haiti). In 1795 the French government gave him control of most of the island. Toussaint abolished slavery and declared the island independent in 1801. Napoleon sent a force to reimpose French authority and in 1803 Toussaint was captured and taken to France where he died in prison

Harriet Tubman (1821–1913) was also an escaped slave who, during the Civil War made numerous trips through Southern territory to help 300 slaves escape to the North. She also spied for the Union (Northern) Army

PRIME MINISTERS OF AUSTRALIA

Name and Party	Held office
Edmund Barton (Protectionist)	1901–1903
Alfred Deakin (Protectionist)	1903–1904
John C. Watson (Labor)	1904
George H. Reid (Free trade)	1904–1905
Alfred Deakin (Protectionist)	1905–1908
Andrew Fisher (Labor)	1908–1909
Alfred Deakin (Fusion)	1909–1910
Andrew Fisher (Labor)	1910–1913
Joseph Cook (Liberal)	1913–1914
Andrew Fisher (Labor)	1914–1915
William H. Hughes (Labor)	1915–1917
William H. Hughes (Nationalist)	1917–1923
Stanley M. Bruce (Nationalist)	1923–1929
James Scullin (Labor)	1929–1932
Joseph A. Lyons (United)	1932–1939
Earle Page (Country)	1939
Robert G. Menzies (United)	1939–1941
Arthur Fadden (Country)	1941
John Curtin (Labor)	1941–1945
Francis M. Forde (Labor)	1945
Ben Chifley (Labor)	1945–1949
Robert G. Menzies (Liberal)	1949–1966
Harold E. Holt (Liberal)	1966–1967
John McEwen (Country)	1967–1968
John G. Gorton (Liberal)	1968–1971
William McMahon (Liberal)	1971–1972
Gough Whitlam (Labor)	1972–1975
Malcolm Fraser (Liberal)	1975–1983
Robert Hawke (Labor)	1983–1991
Paul Keating (Labor)	1991–1996
John Howard (Liberal-National coalition)	1996–

20TH CENTURY BRITISH PRIME MINISTERS

Marquess of Salisbury (Conservative)	1895–1902
Arthur Balfour (Conservative)	1902–1905
Sir Henry Campbell-Bannerman (Liberal)	1905–1908
Herbert Asquith (Liberal)	1908–1915
Herbert Asquith (Coalition)	1915–1916
David Lloyd-George (Coalition)	1916–1922
Andrew Bonar-Law (Conservative)	1922–1923
Stanley Baldwin (Conservative)	1923–1924
James Ramsay MacDonald (Labour)	1924
Stanley Baldwin (Conservative)	1924–1929
James Ramsay MacDonald (Labour)	1929–1931
James Ramsay MacDonald (Coalition)	1931–1935
Stanley Baldwin (Coalition)	1935–1937
Neville Chamberlain (Coalition)	1937–1940
Winston S. Churchill (Coalition)	1940–1945
Winston S. Churchill (Conservative)	1945
Clement Attlee (Labour)	1945–1951
Sir Winston S. Churchill (Conservative)	1951–1955
Sir Anthony Eden (Conservative)	1955–1957
Harold Macmillan (Conservative)	1957–1963
Sir Alec Douglas-Home (Conservative)	1963–1964
Harold Wilson (Labour)	1964–1970
Edward Heath (Conservative)	1970–1974
Harold Wilson (Labour)	1974–1976
James Callaghan (Labour)	1976–1979
Margaret Thatcher (Conservative)	1979–1990
John Major (Conservative)	1990–1997
Anthony Blair (Labour)	1997–

CANADIAN PRIME MINISTERS

Sir John MacDonald (Conservative)	1867–1873
Alexander Mackenzie (Liberal)	1873–1878
Sir John MacDonald (Conservative)	1878–1891
Sir John Abbott (Conservative)	1819–1892
Sir John Thompson (Conservative)	1892–1894
Sir Mackenzie Bowell (Conservative)	1894–1896
Sir Charles Tupper (Conservative)	1896
Sir Wilfred Laurier (Liberal)	1896–1911
Sir Robert L. Borden (Conservative)	1911–1917
Sir Robert L. Borden (Unionist)	1917–1920
Arthur Meighen (Unionist)	1920–1921

W. L. Mackenzie King (Liberal)	1921–1926
Arthur Meighen (Conservative)	1926
W. L. Mackenzie King (Liberal)	1926–1930
Richard B. Bennett (Conservative)	1930–1935
W. L. Mackenzie King (Liberal)	1935–1948
Louis S. St Laurent (Liberal)	1948–1957
John C. Diefenbaker (Progressive Conservative)	1957–1963
Lester B. Pearson (Liberal)	1963–1968
Pierre E. Trudeau (Liberal)	1968–1979
Charles J. Clark (Progressive Conservative)	1979–1980
Pierre E. Trudeau (Liberal)	1980–1984
John E. Turner (Liberal)	1984
Brian Mulroney (Progressive Conservative)	1984–1994
Kim Campbell (Progressive Conservative)	1994
Jean Chrétien (Liberal)	1994–

PRESIDENTS OF FRANCE SINCE 1947

Fourth Republic

Vincent Auriol (Socialist)	1947–1953
René Coty (Republican)	1953–1958

Fifth Republic

Charles de Gaulle (Gaullist)	1959–1969
Georges Pompidou (Gaullist)	1969–1974
Valéry Giscard d'Estaing (Independent Republican)	1974–1981
François Mitterand (Socialist)	1981–1995
Jacques Chirac (Conservative)	1995–

CHANCELLORS OF GERMANY SINCE 1949

(West Germany to 1990, united Germany from then)

Konrad Adenauer (Christian Democratic Union)	1949–1963
Ludwig Erhard (Christian Democratic Union)	1963–1966
Kurt Kiesinger (Christian Democratic Union)	1966–1969
Willy Brandt (Social Democrat)	1969–1974
Helmut Schmidt (Social Democrat)	1974–1982
Helmut Kohl (Christian Democratic Union)	1982–

PRIME MINISTERS OF INDIA SINCE 1950

Jawaharlal Nehru (Congress)	1950–1964
Lal Bahardur Shashtri (Congress)	1964–1966
Indira Gandhi (Congress)	1966–1977
Morarji Desai (Janata)	1977–1979
Indira Gandhi (Congress-I)	1979–1984
Rajiv Gandhi (Congress)	1984–1991
Narasimha Rao (Congress)	1991–1996
Atal Vajpayee (BJP)	1996
Deve Gowda (United Front Coalition)	1996
Inder Kumar Gujral (United Front Coalition)	1996–

NEW ZEALAND PRIME MINISTERS

Richard Seddon (Liberal)	1893–1906
William Hall-Jones (Liberal)	1906
Sir Joseph Ward (Liberal)	1906–1912
Thomas Mackenzie	1912
William F. Massey (Reform)	1912–1925
Francis Bell (Reform)	1925
Gordon Coates (Reform)	1925–1928
Sir Joseph Ward (United)	1928–1930
George Forbes (Coalition)	1930–1935
Michael J. Savage (Labour)	1935–1940
Peter Fraser (Labour)	1940–1949
Sidney J. Holland (National)	1949–1957
Keith Holyoake (National)	1957
Walter Nash (Labour)	1957–1960
Keith Holyoake (National)	1960–1972
Sir John Marshall (National)	1972
Norman Kirk (Labour)	1972–1974
Wallace Rowling (Labour)	1974–1975
Robert Muldoon (National)	1975–1984

David Lange (Labour)	1984–1989
Geoffrey Palmer (Labour)	1989–1990
Michael K. Moore (Labour)	1990
James Bolger (National)	1990–1996
James Bolger (Coalition)	1996–

SOUTH AFRICAN LEADERS

(Prime Ministers up to 1984, thereafter Presidents)

Louis Botha (South African Party)	1910–1919
Jan Smuts (South African Party)	1919–1924
James Hertzog (Pact Coalition)	1924–1939
Jan Smuts (United Party)	1939–1948
Daniel Malan (National)	1948–1954
J. G. Strijdom (National)	1954–1958
D. H. Verwoerd (National)	1958–1966
B. J. Vorster (National)	1966–1978
P. W. Botha (National)	1978–1989
F. W. de Klerk (National)	1989–1994
Nelson Mandela (African National Congress)	1994–

PRESIDENTS OF THE UNITED STATES

George Washington (no party)	1789–1797
John Adams (Federalist)	1797–1801
Thomas Jefferson (Democratic-Republican)	1801–1809
James Madison (Democratic-Republican)	1809–1817
James Monroe (Democratic-Republican)	1817–1825
John Quincy Adams (Democratic-Republican)	1825–1829
Andrew Jackson (Democrat)	1829–1837
Martin Van Buren (Democrat)	1837–1841
William H. Harrison (Whig)	1841
John Tyler (Whig)	1841–1845
James K. Polk (Democrat)	1845–1849
Zachary Taylor (Whig)	1849–1850
Millard Fillmore (Whig)	1850–1853
Franklin Pierce (Democrat)	1853–1857
James Buchanan (Democrat)	1857–1861
Abraham Lincoln (Republican) *	1861–1865
Andrew Johnson (National Union)	1865–1869
Ulysses S. Grant (Republican)	1869–1877
Rutherford B. Hayes (Republican)	1877–1881
James A. Garfield (Republican) *	1881
Chester A. Arthur (Republican)	1881–1885
Grover Cleveland (Democrat)	1885–1889
Benjamin Harrison (Republican)	1889–1893
Grover Cleveland (Democrat)	1893–1897
William McKinley (Republican)*	1897–1901
Theodore Roosevelt (Republican)	1901–1909
William H. Taft (Republican)	1909–1913
Woodrow Wilson (Democrat)	1913–1921
Warren G. Harding (Republican)	1921–1923
Calvin Coolidge (Republican)	1923–1929
Herbert C. Hoover (Republican)	1929–1933
Franklin D. Roosevelt (Democrat)	1933–1945
Harry S. Truman (Democrat)	1945–1953
Dwight D. Eisenhower (Republican)	1953–1961
John F. Kennedy (Democrat)*	1961–1963
Lyndon B. Johnson (Democrat)	1963–1969
Richard M. Nixon (Republican)	1969–1974
Gerald R. Ford (Republican)	1974–1977
Jimmy Carter (Democrat)	1977–1981
Ronald Reagan (Republican)	1981–1989
George Bush (Republican)	1989–1994
William Clinton (Democrat)	1994–

* Assassinated

SECRETARIES-GENERAL OF THE UNITED NATIONS

Trygve Lie (Norway)	1946–1953
Dag Hammarskjöld (Sweden)	1953–1961
U Thant (Burma)	1961–1971
Kurt Waldheim (Austria)	1972–1982
Javier Pérez de Cuéllar (Peru)	1982–1991
Boutros Boutros-Ghali (Egypt)	1991–1997
Kofi Annan (Ghana)	1997–

BELGIAN MONARCHS

Leopold I	1831–1865
Leopold II	1865–1907
Albert I	1909–1934
Leopold III	1934–1951
Baudouin	1951–1993
Albert II	1993–

BRITISH RULERS

RULERS OF ENGLAND

Saxons

Egbert	827–839
Ethelwulf	839–858
Ethelbald	858–860
Ethelbert	860–866
Ethelred I	866–871
Alfred the Great	871–899
Edward the Elder	899–924
Athelstan	924–939
Edmund	939–946
Edred	946–955
Edwy	955–959
Edgar	959–975
Edward the Martyr	975–978
Ethelred II (the Redeless)	978–1016
Edmund Ironside	1016

Danes

Canute	1016–1035
Harold I (Harefoot)	1035–1040
Hardicanute	1040–1042

Saxons

Edward the Confessor	1042–1066
Harold II	1066

House of Normandy

William I (the Conqueror)	1066–1087
William II (Rufus)	1087–1100
Henry I (Beauclerk)	1100–1135
Stephen	1135–1154

House of Plantagenet

Henry II	1154–1189
Richard I (Coeur-de-Lion)	1189–1199
John (Lackland)	1199–1216
Henry III	1216–1272
Edward I (The Hammer of the Scots)	1272–1307
Edward II	1307–1327
Edward III	1327–1377
Richard II	1377–1399

House of Lancaster

Henry IV	1399–1413
Henry V	1413–1422
Henry VI	1422–1461

House of York

Edward IV	1461–1483
Edward V	1483
Richard III	1483–1485

House of Tudor

Henry VII	1485–1509
Henry VIII	1509–1547
Edward VI	1547–1553
Jane	1553
Mary I	1553–1558
Elizabeth I	1558–1603

RULERS OF SCOTLAND

Malcolm II	1005–1034
Duncan I	1034–1040
Macbeth	1040–1057
Malcolm III (Canmore)	1057–1093
Donald Bane	1093–1094
Duncan II	1094
Donald Bane	1094–1097
Edgar	1097–1107
Alexander I	1107–1124
David I	1124–1153
Malcolm IV	1153–1165
William (the Lion)	1165–1214
Alexander II	1214–1249
Alexander III	1249–1286
Margaret (the Maid of Norway)	1286–1290
Interregnum	1290–1292
John Balliol	1292–1296
Interregnum	1296–1306
Robert I (Bruce)	1306–1329
David II	1329–1371

House of Stuart

Robert II	1371–1390
Robert III	1390–1406
James I	1406–1437
James II	1437–1460
James III	1460–1488
James IV	1488–1513
James V	1513–1542
Mary, Queen of Scots	1542–1567
James VI	1567–1625

RULERS OF GREAT BRITAIN

House of Stuart

James I and VI	1603–1625
Charles I	1625–1649

Commonwealth

Oliver Cromwell (chairman, Council of State)	1649–1653
Oliver Cromwell (Lord Protector)	1653–1658
Richard Cromwell, (Lord Protector)	1658–1659

House of Stuart

Charles II	1660–1685
James II and VII	1685–1688
William III (joint ruler with Mary)	1689–1702
Mary II	1689–1694
Anne	1702–1714

House of Hanover

George I	1714–1727
George II	1727–1760
George III	1760–1820
George IV (Prince Regent 1811–1820)	1820–1830
William IV	1830–1837
Victoria	1837–1901

House of Saxe-Coburg-Gotha

Edward VII	1901–1910

House of Windsor

George V	1910–1936
Edward VIII	1936
George VI	1936–1952
Elizabeth II	1952–

DANISH MONARCHS SINCE 1808

Frederik VI	1808–1839
Christian VIII	1839–1848
Frederik VII	1848–1863
Christian IX	1863–1906
Frederik VIII	1906–1912
Christian X	1912–1947
Frederik IX	1947–1972
Margrethe II	1972–

FRENCH KINGS SINCE 987

(Before this date the kings of France were rulers of various lands, and some of them were German emperors.)

Hugh Capet	987–996
Robert II	996–1031
Henri I	1031–1060
Philippe I	1060–1108
Louis VI (the Fat)	1108–1137
Louis VII (the Young)	1137–1180
Philippe II	1180–1223
Louis VIII	1223–1226
Louis IX (St Louis)	1226–1270
Philippe III (the Bold)	1270–1285
Philippe IV (the Fair)	1285–1314
Louis X	1314–1316
Jean I	1316
Philippe V	1316–1322
Charles IV	1322–1328
Philippe VI	1328–1350
Jean II	1350–1364
Charles V	1364–1380
Charles VI	1380–1422
Charles VII	1422–1461
Louis XI	1461–1483
Charles VIII	1483–1498
Louis XII	1498–1515
François I	1515–1547
Henri II	1547–1559
François II	1559–1560
Charles IX	1560–1574
Henri III	1574–1589
Henri IV	1589–1610
Louis XIII	1610–1643
Louis XIV	1643–1715
Louis XV	1715–1774
Louis XVI	1774–1792
The First Republic	1792–1804
Napoleon I (Emperor)	1804–1814
Louis XVIII	1814–1824
Charles X	1824–1830
Louis Philippe	1830–1848
The Second Republic	1848–1852
Napoleon III (Emperor)	1852–1870
The Third Republic	1870–1940
(Vichy Régime	1940–1945)
The Fourth Republic	1944–1958
The Fifth Republic	1958–

MONARCHS OF THE NETHERLANDS

Willem I	1815–1840
Willem II	1840–1849
Willem III	1849–1890
Wilhelmina	1890–1948
Juliana	1948–1980
Beatrix	1980–

Kingdom of the Netherlands became independent in 1815

NORWEGIAN MONARCHS SINCE 1905

Haakon VII	1905–1951
Olav V	1951–1991
Harald V	1991–

Danish kings ruled Norway from 1450, and Swedish kings from 1814

SPANISH RULERS SINCE 1874

Alfonso XII	1874–1885
Maria Cristina	1885–1886
Alfonso XIII	1886–1931
Republic	1931–1947
Francisco Franco, Caudillo and Chief of State	1936–1975
Juan Carlos	1975–

SWEDISH RULERS SINCE 1818

Carl XIV Johan (Jean-Baptiste Bernadotte)	1818–1844
Oscar I	1844–1859
Carl XV	1859–1872
Oscar II	1872–1907
Gustav V	1907–1973
Carl XVI Gustav	1973–

Jean-Baptiste Bernadotte was one of Emperor Napoleon I's marshals, and was adopted as heir by the childless King Carl XIII

Index

Page numbers in bold refer to main entries. Italic numbers refer to the illustrations and their captions.

171

Humayun, Emperor 50, 51
Hume, David 77
Hundred Years' War
(1338-1453) **30-31**
Hungary
Agricultural Revolution
79
Austro-Hungarian
Empire 81
collapse of communism
155
Mongols invade 23
Ottoman Empire 48
Soviet invasion 140
World War II 130, 131
Huron, Lake 63
Hussein, Saddam *153*

I

Ibn Battuta 25, *25*
Ibrahim Lodi, Sultan of
Delhi 51
Iceland 10, 12
Ieyasu, Tokugawa 31,
58-59
Illinois 102
Incas 33, **38-39**, 43
India
British Empire 71, *98*, 99,
100
cotton 92
Dutch traders 61
explorers 33, 40, 41, 43,
53
independence **136-137**
Mongols invade 25
Mughal Empire **50-51**
space race 143
Indian Mutiny
(1857-1858) 99, 101
Indian National Congress
(INC) 136, 137
Indian Ocean 33, 41
Indiana 102
Indochina 99, 148
Indonesia *60*, 98, 133
Industrial Revolution 9,
92-93
Ingolf 10
Inquisition 42
Internet 113
Iran *152*, 153
see also Persian Empire
Iraq
Arab-Israeli wars 139
Mongols conquer 25
Saddam Hussein *153*
war with Iran 153
Ireland
Black Death 26
emigration 103
Home Rule 112, **122-123**
potato famine 101, *101*
Vikings 10, 12, 13
Year of Revolutions 95
Irish Citizen Army 122
Irish Free State 122, 123,
123
Irish Republican Army
(IRA) 123
Irish Republican
Brotherhood 122
Irish Socialist and
Republican party 122
Irish Volunteers 122
"iron curtain" 140, *141*
Isandhlwana *110*
Islam and Muslims
in Africa 28, 29
Crusades **18-19**
in India *136*, 137
in Spain 42, 43
Isle of Man 12

Isle of Wight 65
Ismail I, Shah 49
Isonzo, battle of (1916-
1917) 166
Israel **138-139**
Arab-Israeli wars **152-153**
Istanbul *13*, 48
see also Constantinople
Italy
city-states 21
colonies 112
European Union 154
Fascists 112, 126, 127
Napoleonic Wars 88-89
Renaissance 33, 34
Scramble for Africa 110
unification 70, 95, **108-
109**
World War I 116, 117,
119
World War II 130, 131,
134
Ivan IV, Czar 167
Ivan V, Czar 72
Iwo Jima 134

J

Jackson, General,
"Stonewall" *104*
Jahangir, Emperor 51
Jamaica 66, 90
James I, King of England
33, *62*, 65
Jamestown 62
Jansz, Willem 55
Janzoon, Willem 86, *87*
Japan
explorers 40
Mongols attack 25
Russo-Japanese War
(1904-1905) 121, 166
Tokugawa period **58-59**
war with China 129, *129*
warlords **30-31**, 58
World War I 117
World War II 112, 130,
131, 132, *132*, 133, 134,
134, 135, 166
jarls 11
Jarrow Crusade 125, *125*
Java 61
Jericho *153*
Jerusalem 138, 139, *139*
Arab-Israeli wars 152
Crusades 18, 19
Dome of the Rock *139*
Israel and 138, 139
Wailing Wall *139*
Jesuits 46, 47, 53, 74
Jews
Arab-Israeli wars 152
expelled from Spain 43
Israel and Palestine
138-139
Nazi persecution *9*, 127,
138, 139
Spanish Inquisition 42
World War II 135
Jiangxi 128, *128*, 129
Jinnah, Mohammed Ali
136, 137
Joan of Arc *30*, 31, 166
John, King of England
17
John I, King of Portugal
43
John of Austria, Don 49
Johnson, Lyndon B. 155
Johnson, Samuel 76, 77
Joliet, Louis 63
Jordan 152, 153
Jordan, River 152
Jorvik 10, 13, *13*

Joseph II, Emperor of
Austria 81
jousting *15*
Jutland, battle of (1916)
119, 166

K

Kabuki drama *58*
Kaifeng 24
Kanem-Bornu 28, *29*, 44-
45, *45*
Kangxi, Emperor of China
74
Kano 28
Kant, Immanuel 76, 77
Karakorum 23
Kaunda, Kenneth *144*
Kaupang 10
Kelly, Ned 167
Kennedy, John F. 141, 142,
142
Kenya
British Empire 110
early inhabitants 29
independence 145
Kerensky, Alexander 120
khans 22
Khayyam, Omar 167
Khomeini, Ayatollah *152*
Khwarezm Empire 23
kibbutz *138*
Kilwa 28, 29
King, Martin Luther 146,
146
Kingdom of the Two
Sicilies *108*, 109
King's Mountain, battle of
(1780) 166
kings
absolute monarchs 80
castles 14
feudal system 16, *16*
Kingsley, Mary 167
knights
castles 14
feudal system 16, 17, *17*
jousting *15*
Knights Hospitalers 19
Knights of St. John 49
Knights Templar 19
Knox, John 46
Kongo 44
Korea 23
see also North Korea;
South Korea
Korean War (1950-1953)
140
Koumbi Saleh 28
Kowloon 98
Krak des Chevaliers 14, *18*
Kublai Khan **24-25**, *30*
kumiss 22
Kuomintang 128-129, *128*
Kuwait 153, *153*
Kyoto 59

L

La Salle 63
Lagos 101
Laika 142, *142*
Lalibela, Emperor of
Ethiopia 28, *44*
Laos
in Indochina 99
Vietnam War 148, 149
Latin language 47
Latvia 130
Lavoisier, Antoine 76, *77*
Lavoisier, Marie Anne *77*
Lawrence, T.E. *118*
laws
Code Napoleon *88*, 89

Viking *11*
League of Nations 119,
138
Lebanon 139, *152*, 153
Lee, General Robert E.
104, 105
Legion of Honour *88*
Leif Eriksson 10
Leipzig, battle of (1813)
91, 166
Lenin, Vladimir 120, *120*,
121, *154*, 167
Leningrad, siege of
(1941-1944) *132*, 135
see also St. Petersburg
Leonardo da Vinci *9*, 34,
34, 35
Leonov, Alexi 142
Leopold II, King of the
Belgians 110
Lepanto, battle of (1571)
33, 43, 49, *49*, 166
Lesotho 145
Lexington *82*
Lexington, battle of
(1775) 82
Liberia 96, 97, 110
Libya
independence 145
in Kanem-Bornu 44
World War II 132
Lincoln, Abraham 104,
105, *105*
Linnaeus, Carl 76, *76*
literature, Renaissance 34
Lithuania 130
Little Bighorn, battle of
(1876) 106, 107, 167
Little Rock, Arkansas 146
Live Aid 157
Livingstone, David 96, 97,
97
Livonia 72
Lloyd-George, David *118*
Locke, John 76
London
in Middle Ages 21
World War II 131
London Bridge 21
Long March (1934-1935)
128, 129, *129*
"The Long Walk" 106
Longfellow, Henry
Wadsworth *82*
longships, Viking 12
lords, feudal system 17
Lorraine 109
Louis IX, King of France
19
Louis XIII, King of France
57, 68
Louis XIV, King of France
33, 63, **68-69**
Louis XVI, King of France
84-85, *85*
Louis Philippe, King of
France 95
Louisiana 63, 102
Louisiana Purchase 103
Low Countries 60
Loyola, Ignatius 46
Lubeck 21
Luddites 93
Luftwaffe 131
Luther, Martin 33, 46-47,
47
Luxembourg 60, 154
Lvov, Prince George 120

M

Macao 43, 53
MacDonald, Flora 167

Machiavelli, Niccolo 35
Machu Picchu 39
Madeira Islands 41
Madrid 80
Magellan, Ferdinand 33,
41, *41*, 55
Magna Carta 17
Malacca 99
Malawi 145
Malay peninsula 99
Malaya 99, 133
Mali 96, 110, 145
Mali Empire 28, *29*, 44
Malindi 28
Malta
British Empire 101
Turks attack 49
Mamelukes 28, 49
Manchu Empire 33, 128,
129
Manchuria 74, 121
Manchus **74-75**
Mandela, Nelson 145, 146,
147, *147*
Mandingo Empire 44
Manhattan Island 63
Mansa Musa, King of Mali
28-29, *28*
Mantua 88
Mao Zedong 128-129, *129*,
150-151
Maoris 55
Captain Cook and *86*
European settlers and 87
stockades *54*
Treaty of Waitangi 86
war canoes 55
Marathas 51
Maria Theresa, Empress of
Austria 80-81, *80*, 85
Marie Antoinette, Queen
of France *85*
Marie Louise, Empress 89
Marie-Therese, Queen of
France 68
Marne, battle of the (1914
& 1916) 116, 166
Marquette, Jacques 63
Mars (planet) 142, 143,
143
Marshall Plan 140
Marston Moor, battle of
(1644) 65
Marx, Karl 95, 120
Marxism 121
Mary I, Queen of England
46
Mary II, Queen of
England 33, 61
masks, Inca *39*
Massachusetts 62, 63
Matabele 110
Mau Mau 145
Mauritius 101
Mayflower 33, 62
Mazarin, Jules 68
Mecca
Mansa Musa's pilgrimage
to 28, *28*
Medici, Lorenzo de 35
Medici, Marie de' *57*
medicine, Enlightenment
76
medieval period *see* Middle
Ages
Mediterranean
Ottoman Empire 48, 49
Suez Canal 110
Vikings 10
Meir, Golda *138*
merchants
caravans 24, 28
feudal system *16*
Middle Ages 17

174

Acknowledgments

**The publishers wish to thank the following artists who
have contributed to this book:**

Martin Camm, Richard Hook, Rob Jakeway, John James,
Shane Marsh, Roger Payne, Mark Peppé, Eric Rowe,
Peter Sarson, Roger Smith, Michael Welply and Michael
White.

**The publishers wish to thank the following for supplying
photographs for this book:**

Page 9 (CR) AFF/AFS Amsterdam, the Netherlands,
  (BR) Mary Evans Picture Library; 16-17 (C)
  Giraudon/Bridgeman Art Library; 21 (CT) AKG
  London; 28-29 (C) ET Archive; 34-35 (C) Mary Evans
  Picture Libary; 35 (CB) ET Archive; 39 (BL) AKG
  London; 42-43 (CB) AKG London; 43 (CB) AKG
  London; 45 (CR) Robert Harding Picture Library; 46
  (CL) AKG London; 46-47 (BC) ET Archive; 48 (CR)
  AKG London; 49 (BR) ET Archive; 50-51 (TC) AKG
  London; 55 (C) Bridgeman Art Library; 60 (BL) AKG
  London; 61 (TR) AKG London; 76 (C) ET Archive; 77
  (BR) ET Archive; 78 (BR) ET Archive; 82-83 (CB) AKG
  London; 83 (CR) AKG London; 88-89 (C) ET Archive;
  92 (B) AKG London; 93 (B) AKG London; 98 (TL) ILN,
  (BL) ET Archive; 98-99 (C) ET Archive; 99 (CB) ILN;
  100 (TR) ILN; 101 (C) ILN; 105 (C) ILN; 105 (C) ILN;
  107 (TC) AKG London; 108 (TL) ILN; 110 (BL) ILN;
  111 (TR) ILN; 114 (TR) ILN; 115 (CR) ILN; 116-117 (C)
  ILN; 117 (CL) ILN; 118-119 (B) ILN; 119 (C) ILN; 120-
  121 (C) ILN; 121 (CR) ILN; 124-125 (C) Corbis; 126
  (TL), (CL) ILN; 127 (CR) ILN; 129 (CL) ILN; 131 (C)
  ILN; 132 (BL) ET Archive, (TR) ILN; 133 (TC), (CR)
  ILN; 134 (CL), (CR) ILN; 134-135 (CT) ILN; 135 (CR)
  ILN; 136 (TR) ILN; 137 (CR) ILN; 140-141 (C) Rex
  Features; 141 (BC) ILN, (BR) Rex Features; 143 (BR)
  The Stock Market; 144 (BL) Rex Features; 145 (BR) Rex
  Features; 147 (CR) Rex Features, (CL) Panos Pictures;
  149 (CL), (CR) Rex Features; 150 (BL) ET Archive; 150-
  151 (BC) Panos Pictures; 152-153 (CB) Panos Pictures;
  153 (TL) Rex Features; 155 (C), (BR) Rex Features,
  (BL) Panos Pictures; 156 (CL) The Stock Market, (TL)
  Panos Pictures; 156-157 (C) Rex Features.

All other photographs from Miles Kelly Archives.

SALISBURY
Emily Parker of Lakeville prepares for dress rehearsal with her mates at Terre Lefferts's Arts in Motion studio. The ballet piece the girls will perform is set to Johann Strauss the Younger's "Blue Danube."
Photo by Anne Day

Connecticut 24/7 is the sequel to *The New York Times* bestseller *America 24/7* shot by tens of thousands of digital photographers across America over the course of a single week. We would like to thank the following sponsors, the wonderful people of Connecticut, and the talented photojournalists who made this book possible.

snapfish

WEBWARE

Google

DIGITAL POND

Compliments
John Barnett
wholesalebks@sbcglobal.net
Wallingford, CT

DK

LONDON, NEW YORK, MUNICH, MELBOURNE, and DELHI

Created by Rick Smolan and David Elliot Cohen

24/7 Media, LLC
PO Box 1189
Sausalito, CA 94966-1189
www.america24-7.com

First Edition, 2004
04 05 06 07 08 10 9 8 7 6 5 4 3 2 1

Published in the United States by
DK Publishing, Inc.
375 Hudson Street
New York, NY 10014

DK Publishing, Inc. offers special discounts for bulk purchases for sales promo-
tions or premiums. Specific, large-quantity needs can be met with special editions, personalized covers, excerpts of existing guides, and corporate imprints.
For more information, contact:

Special Markets Department
DK Publishing, Inc.
375 Hudson Street
New York, NY 10014
Fax: 212-689-5254

Cataloging-in-Publication data is available
from the Library of Congress
ISBN 0-7566-0046-4

Printed in the UK by Butler & Tanner Limited

First printing, October 2004

WOODBRIDGE
Cool morning air lifts the fog on a water
hazard near the 11th hole at Woodbridge
Country Club—one of 94 country clubs in
Connecticut.
Photo by Michael J. Ivins

CONNECTICUT 24/7

24 Hours. 7 Days.
Extraordinary Images of
One Week in Connecticut.

Created by Rick Smolan and David Elliot Cohen

DK Publishing

About the America 24/7 Project

A hundred years hence, historians may pose questions such as: What was America like at the beginning of the third millennium? How did life change after 9/11 and the ensuing war on terrorism? How was America affected by its corporate scandals and the high-tech boom and bust? Could Americans still express themselves freely?

To address these questions, we created *America 24/7*, the largest collaborative photography event in history. We invited Americans to tell their stories with digital pictures. We asked them to shoot a visual memoir of their lives, families, and communities.

During one week in May 2003, more than 25,000 professionals and amateurs shot more than a million pictures. These images, sent to us via the Internet, compose a panoramic yet highly intimate view of Americans in celebration and sadness; in action and contemplation; at work, home, and school. The best of these photographs, more than 6,000, are collected in 51 volumes that make up the *America 24/7* series: the landmark national volume *America 24/7*, published to critical acclaim in 2003, and the 50 state books published in 2004.

Our decision to make *America 24/7* an all-digital project was prompted by the fact that in 2003 digital camera sales overtook film camera sales. This technological evolution allowed us to extend the project to a huge pool of photographers. We were thrilled by the response to our challenge and moved by the insight offered into American life. Sometimes, the amateurs outshot the pros—even the Pulitzer Prize winners.

The exuberant democracy of images visible throughout these books is a revelation. The message that emerges is that now, more than ever, America is a supersized idea. A dreamspace, where individuals and families from around the world are free to govern themselves, worship, read, and speak as they wish. Within its wide margins, the polyglot American nation manages to encompass an inexplicably complex yet workable whole. The pictures in this book are dedicated to that idea.

—*Rick Smolan and David Elliot Cohen*

American nightlight: More than a quarter
of a billion people trace a nation with incandes-
cence in this composite satellite photograph.
Photo by Craig Mayhew & Robert Simmon, NASA
Goddard Flight Center/Visions of Tomorrow

A Nice Place to Live

By Tom Condon

Take a right out of New York City, or a left as you leave Boston, and soon you'll be in Connecticut. You won't necessarily know you're in a new state but for the helpful "Welcome to Connecticut" road signs. The Connecticut landscape, a pleasant but unspectacular array of low hills and valleys with a placid waterfront on Long Island Sound, doesn't trumpet any particular distinction.

The "big cities" you pass—Bridgeport, New Haven, and Hartford—are tiny by the standards of New York or Boston, yet our cities manage to have their share of the same urban troubles that bedevil larger ones.

Nor does Connecticut possess any major national tourist attractions, at least it didn't until two Indian tribes, thought to be extinct, magically sprang back to life and opened huge gambling casinos. We had one major league sports franchise (a hockey team) but it moved to that hotbed of hockey, North Carolina.

So it would be easy to assume Connecticut was a boring, undifferentiated suburb and keep driving; some do. Corporate leaders say they have trouble getting people to move to Connecticut. But there is a saving grace. Once workers are here, they don't want to leave. They discover it's a nice place to live.

In most years, the state has the highest per capita income in the country and the best-performing public schools. It has a fine collection of colleges, more than a dozen Fortune 500 companies, and a remarkable array of museums, theaters, and historical sites.

One reason for Connecticut's success is an ancient value that somehow

SIMSBURY
As glimpsed from a bluff on Metacomet Ridge, the Farmington River Valley wears its morning mist lightly.
Photo by Jonathan Olson

stays with us—good old Yankee ingenuity. We are the spiritual descendants of the Yankee peddlers who were so clever that they sold wooden nutmegs to unsuspecting rubes. Of course, the Department of Consumer Protection would get right on those rascals today, but that wily spirit lives. The Nutmeg State admires its inventors: Eli Whitney, Sam Colt, Charles Goodyear, Igor Sikorsky, and countless others. Connecticut folks claim to have invented the hamburger and the corkscrew. Think of us at your next barbecue.

Money isn't disrespected here, but wit is admired as much as wealth. Mark Twain, who wrote most of his major works in Hartford, the state's capital, is much quoted today, and his wonderful home is a must-see. It is perhaps telling that the most popular radio talk show host in Connecticut today, Colin McEnroe, is not a ranting, ideological wing nut. He is, however, brilliantly funny.

We have many unpaid comedians as well, even a few unintentional ones, some of whom are in city and state government (or were, until the indictments). But we also have some stellar public servants. New Haven Mayor John DeStefano, Jr., who has led a renaissance in his city, is actually taking down a sports arena—heresy in most cities—to replace it with a new home for the famed Long Wharf Theater.

As long as enough people run our cities and companies with the creative quality we call Yankee ingenuity, as long as wit is honored, whether in the plays of Arthur Miller, the cartoons of Gary Trudeau, or the conversation at the corner barbershop, there will be reason to stop in Connecticut.

New London native TOM CONDON *is an editor and columnist at* The Hartford Courant, *Connecticut's largest—and the nation's oldest—newspaper.*

STORRS
Tucked into the rocky soils of northeastern
Connecticut, this 1770 farmhouse on Codfish
Falls Road attracts its share of shutterbugs.
The owners say they're used to drivers slow-
ing down for the classic New England view.
Photo by Brett Mickelson

WATERBURY
The fast and the studious: Students from Yeshiva Gedolah in Waterbury rally participants at the Tour of Connecticut, a three-day, three-stage pro bicycle race running 220 miles from New Haven to Danbury. The yeshiva bochers hail from New York City.
Photo by Bob Falcetti

NEW LONDON
U.S. Coast Guard cadets stand at attention for a rehearsal march before commencement ceremonies. Students spent the weekend shining boots and practicing salutes as they prepared for the arrival of the keynote speaker: President George W. Bush.
Photo by Sean D. Elliot, The Day

LAKEVILLE
The average American child watches three hours of television per day, but Charlotte Day-Reiss, 11, prefers the company of books. Her parents, both journalists, report that Charlotte devours five books a week during the summer months.
Photo by Anne Day

Hearth & Home

MERIDEN
Glissade, chassé, sauté, and plié. Meghan
St. Amand and Kayleigh Crocetto visualize
the steps to their dance routine, the Paquita
waltz, while waiting for their cue to enter
stage left. The 100-dancer ballet, presented
by the Middlesex Dance Center, is titled
"From New York, with Love," and is comprised of dance tributes to the music, culture, and people of the Big Apple.
Photo by Cloe Poisson, The Hartford Courant

NEW HAVEN
Ryan Casolino checks the temperature out-doors before heading to the tub indoors.
Photo by Peter Casolino

WESTPORT
No boys allowed: Before her siblings come home from school, 5-year-old Camilla Meyer-Bosse retreats to her attic playroom for time alone with Madeline and Barbie.
Photos by Catherine Karnow

WESTPORT
Between preschool and ballet class, Camilla and her friends pad around on the front porch.

WATERTOWN

M-e-t-a-m-o-r-p-h-o-s-i-s. Maggie Luddy, Julie Audibert, Katie Falcetti, and Marisa Valenti show what happens to a tadpole in nine months—or about the time it takes to navigate a school year at Mother Goose Pre-school. The drawings were abetted by teacher and wildlife specialist Elizabeth Parisot.

Photo by Bob Falcetti

DERBY
"*Yo quiero* Taco Bell." No, not really. What 2-year-old Papa *really* wants is to go cruising around town with James Huertas, his best buddy. If, however, someone were to offer the Chihuahua a taco, he would not turn it down.
Photo by Peter Casolino

WESTPORT

A posse of Norfolk terriers gets ready to hit the ground running at a local dog park. The 15-year-old patriarch, Ralph (rear), his consort Hana (second from right), and young 'uns Reggie, Rex, Rosie, and Ruby belong to kennel owner Mel Goldman. He also runs Jet-A-Pet transport service. Door-to-door delivery of a terrier to, say, Paris, with attendant paperwork, costs $1,919.
Photo by Pamela Einarsen

SHARON

Did someone say Milkbone? West Highland white terriers Lucky and Lady, along with dachshund Bambi, have the run of their house and garden.
Photo by Anne Day

FAIRFIELD

Mary Bullard Rousseau's photograph of four generations of her family was taken in 1914 in the same spot: the sitting room of her grandmother, Sarah Adams MacWhorter Sturges. Rousseau bought the 30-room homestead, Sturges Cottage, decades ago from the family estate and began restoring it. She could afford to, she adds. "My husband was in Fritos."

Photo by Christian Abraham, Connecticut Post

NEWTON
Stephanie Paproski cossets her rooster George. On cold nights, the pampered bird migrates from the barn to the porch, where his plaintive scratching usually prompts Stephanie to let him in.
Photo by Wendy Carlson

WESTPORT

It's a weekday morning in Westport. The butter tub is empty, pastries disappear, and *The Times* remains unread. Max Meyer-Bosse and dad Hilmar quietly share the breakfast table.

Photo by Catherine Karnow

WESTPORT

Coty and Ryan Grosso (top of photo) do a round of math homework with neighborhood friends Carson and Connor Einarsen. Then they get to play.

Photo by Pamela Einarsen

Nick "Batso" Maccharoli shows no signs of slowing down with age. A custom-car maker, tattoo canvas, and martial artist, the septuagenarian recently appeared on the HBO prison drama *Oz*. "I like to freak people out," he says.
Photo by Peter Casolino

WESTON

After walking the dog, feeding the cat, reading the newspaper, and nibbling on a leisurely breakfast, Realtor Jerry Ward ties his tie. He takes his time. Unlike most of his Manhattan commuter neighbors, Ward lives just four miles from his office.

Photo by Rikki Ward

SALISBURY

Susan Rand cherishes good weather. A professional landscape painter, she works mostly with oils and outside in the hills and fields of northwestern Connecticut, whenever the view isn't buried in snow.

Photos by Anne Day

SHARON

Fashion designer and writer Carolyne Roehm prepares for a party in the ultra-spacious pantry of her home, Weatherstone. The historic mansion, home to Connecticut governor John Cotton Smith during the War of 1812, nearly burned to the ground in 1999. Roehm's party will showcase the restored house and benefit the town's historical society and volunteer fire department.

WESTPORT

11 p.m.: Ryan Grosso (center) celebrates her 12th birthday with seven best friends and her sister at a sleepover in the family room. Makeup sessions, videos, and discussions of important events keep the girls going 'til 2 a.m.

Photo by Pamela Einarsen

NEW MILFORD

Three-year-olds Maria del Carmen (Carmelita) and Maria Guadelupe (Lupita) Andrade Solis are dicephalus conjoined twins who share internal organs. The Veracruz, Mexico, natives came to New Milford in 2001 to undergo surgical separation, but doctors determined that it would be too risky. The sisters receive medical and financial assistance from Healing the Children, a local charity.

Photos by Wendy Carlson

NEW MILFORD

Carmelita and Lupita have the same lime-green colored toothbrushes but they know whose is whose. When their mother Norma (right) and sister Abigail (left) mix them up, the girls get upset.

NEW MILFORD

With the help of intense physical therapy, the twins are learning to walk. Because their weight is distributed above their waistline and they have only two legs to support themselves, the sisters get around with lots of teamwork. "Sometimes Lupita wants to go one way, and Carmelita the other," says their mother. "Lupita usually gets her way because her personality is stronger."

NORWALK

Alexina Martinez (right) vogues in her taffeta gown sewn especially for her cousin's *quinceañera*, or coming-of-age party. The details of the event are of special interest to Alexina who will be having her own sweet fifteen celebration in five short years.
Photo by Rikki Ward

The year 2003 marked a turning point in the history of photography: It was the first year that digital cameras outsold film cameras. To celebrate this unprecedented sea change, the *America 24/7* project invited amateur photographers—along with students and professionals—to shoot and, via the Internet, submit digital images. Think of it as audience participation. Their visions of community are interspersed with the professional frames throughout this book. On the following four pages, however, we present a gallery produced exclusively by amateur photographers.

ANSONIA Her first bubbles: Maddie Payne warily eyes floating spheres that disappear in an instant. *Photo by Bill Payne*

MIDDLEBURY On a Sunday morning, siblings Sierra and West Sutherland poke around the edge of Lake Elise. The lake is part of a donated open space called the Middlebury Land Trust. *Photo by Kristie Sutherland*

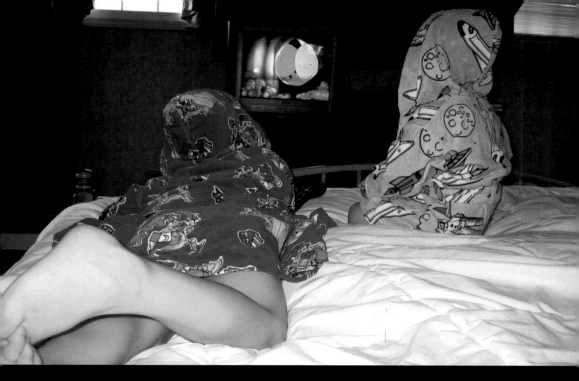

EASTON At 7:03 a.m., freshly showered Jay and John Montano watch a TiVo recording of *Caillou*, while mom showers uninterrupted. ***Photo by Christine Montano***

EAST HAMPTON Early risers Gretchen and Elizabeth Dusza from Manchester went on a drive with their parents to see a covered bridge. Seen. Played. Done. ***Photo by Michael Dusza***

05 12 2003 18:47

MERIDEN Driving home from work in the central Connecticut town of Meriden, photographer Mike Raymond was thrilled to see such a perfect rainbow. *Photo by Mike Raymond*

NEW MILFORD Reflections by Robert. At Elephant's Trunk flea market, held on Sundays on Route 7 in western Connecticut, treasures include old windows refurbished as new mirrors. *Photo by David Kyle*

STAMFORD Local legend has it that Captain Kidd dropped anchor in Stamford Harbor and hid treasure in town. None has been found, so far. *Photo by Susan Emmetsberger*

STONY CREEK A hammock outside a turn-of-the-century Victorian in the waterfront village of Stony Creek beckons Creekers with an open invitation to relax. *Photo by Nina Smith*

WATERBURY

"It's part of our culture," says Urim Belica, explaining his tattoo of an eagle superimposed on the Albanian flag. Belica and his relatives own Rocky's Pizza, decorated with images of their homeland. Belica plans to add a poster of the man he credits with keeping Albania united as one country: Woodrow Wilson.
Photo by Bob Falcetti

Hard At Work

FAIRFIELD COUNTY
Your stylist called. Most commuters on the 5:18 p.m. Metro-North train from Grand Central Station are too grumpy and tired to do much. But this man worked the whole ride. About 36,000 commuters make the daily round trip from Connecticut to New York.
Photo by George Ruhe

STRATFORD

At the Sikorsky Helicopter factory, airframe assembler Henry Lepri attaches the canopy to the mainframe of a Navy Seahawk. The Vietnam veteran started working at the factory 24 years ago. "I enjoy working on helicopters," he says. "I saw them come to rescue guys in 'Nam. I know what they're capable of doing in wartime and peacetime."

Photos by Peter Casolino

STRATFORD

Aeronautical engineer Igor Sikorsky patented his rotor-propelled, vertical-flight craft design plans in 1931. Eleven years and many crashes later, he delivered a successful model. Today, Sikorsky Aircrafts supplies the U.S. military, firefighters, and private companies with Black Hawks, S-76s, and Firehawks to name a few.

NEW HAVEN

Spanky sits quietly at Officer Ray Crowley's feet during morning roll call at the New Haven Police Station. Officers are briefed on the previous night's activities, pick up messages, and take care of administrative matters. Spanky, though, is waiting for breakfast.

NEW HAVEN

Spanky and Officer Crowley, a bomb technician, patrol New Haven's Government Center. Their beat also includes the city's train station and airport. Officer Crowley tests Spanky's nose each day, planting explosive packets for the dog to find. When he succeeds, he gets rewarded with kibble. With a 98 percent accuracy rate, Spanky gets plenty of treats.

GREENWICH
Fleur Biot's day at White Birch Farm starts at 5 a.m. The Belgian groom and trainer (left) leads some 55 polo ponies on their morning exercise run. The grooms and ponies migrate north to Greenwich in early May after the winter season in Palm Beach, Florida.
Photo by Andrew Douglas Sullivan

LYME

At Beaver Brook Farm, a herd of cheese makers fill up on succulent spring grass. Most of the 500 sheep are East Freesians, known for their excellent milk. Thai exchange student Warinthorn Maneerot is working at the farm to learn cheese making, a skill she'll take back to Thailand, where there was no demand for it—until McDonalds arrived in 1985.

Photo by Jonathan Olson

MIDDLEFIELD

A 700-pound feeder heifer cowtows to buyers at the Middlesex Livestock Auction. New England farmers flock to Connecticut's last remaining livestock auction every Monday to buy and sell cows, sheep, goats, pigs, and rabbits.

Photo by Cloe Poisson, The Hartford Courant

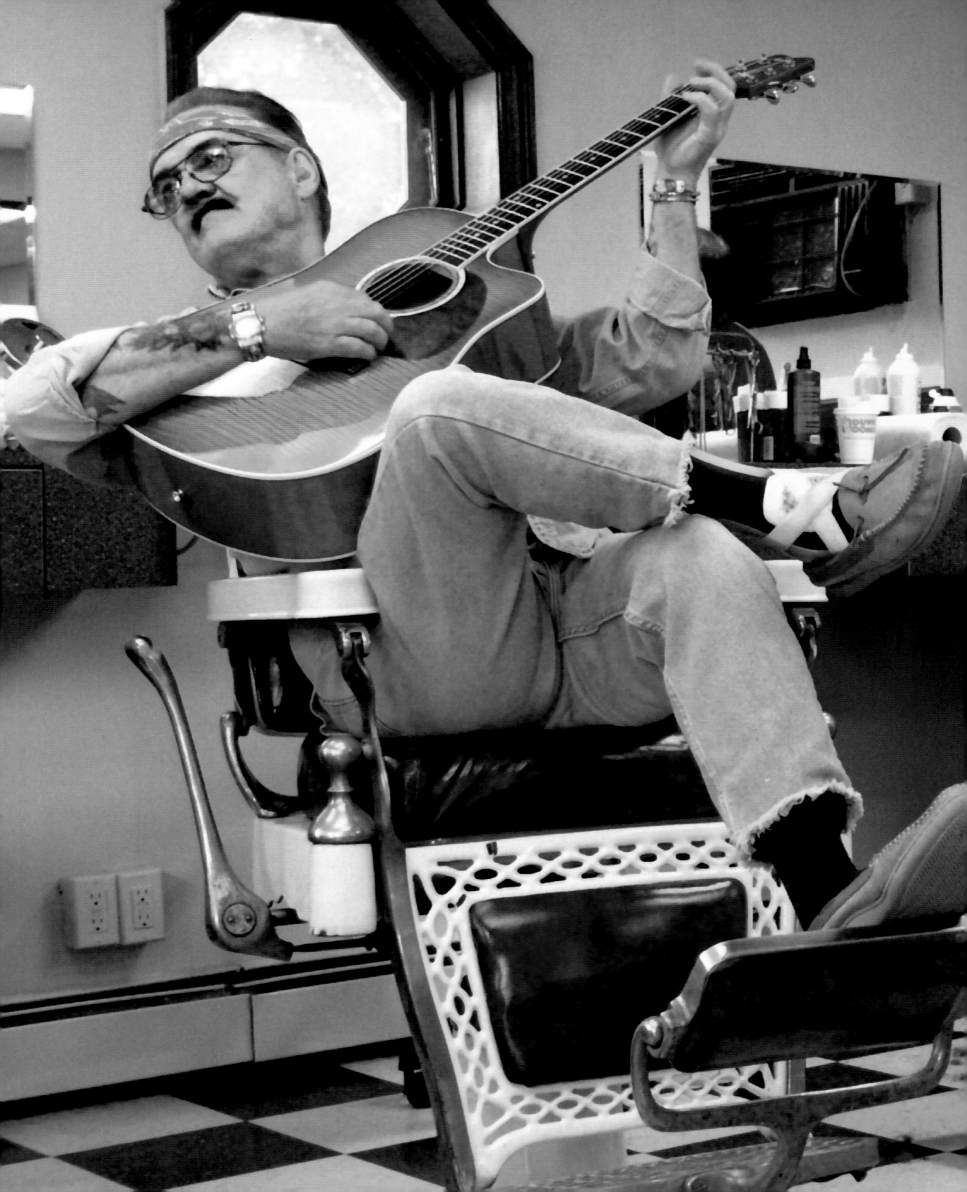

STAMFORD

"I play soft music, cuz it's a quiet place," says "Country Willie" Pulver. The place is Esquire Haircutters, owned by Mike Pelucci (working at right) who arranges to have music for his customers almost daily. Pulver, a former housepainter, comes by on Saturdays to play tunes by the Everly Brothers, among others.
Photo by Andrew Douglas Sullivan

Photographer Robert Lisak captures the moment
as 2-year-old Jacob Kogan breaks ground for the
Yale-New Haven Shoreline Medical Center. Jacob's
grandfather is a Yale doctor on the project. The
$13 million facility, slated to open in 2004, will
have an emergency room and provide health education and outpatient surgery.
Photos by Peter Casolino

NEW HAVEN

At Yale Field, Rich Withington, keeper of the scoreboard, watches a game between the New Haven Ravens and the Akron (Ohio) Aeros, two minor league baseball teams. Withington is paid minimum wage, but he doesn't mind—a true fan, he'd watch the games with or without pay.

SHARON
At a fundraising cocktail party at an historic mansion, college student and volunteer Leliane Aquino serves hors d'oeuvres.
Photo by Anne Day

GREENWICH

Cristine Vitola and Stephanie Lindley, dressed in the tea-serving outfits of the Royal Tea Company catering service, confer between serving and clearing at a job in the Belle Haven section of Greenwich. "Catering got me through nursing school," says Vitola, who also works at the Hospital of Saint Raphael in New Haven.
Photo by Andrew Douglas Sullivan

YALE
At the Yale Peabody Museum, preparator Marilyn Fox and intern David Mayer use feather dusters and a vacuum to clean a stegosaurus fossil exhibit. The dinosaur skeleton is just one of the museum's 55,000 catalogued vertebrate paleontology specimens. The big-boned guy is on permanent display in Peabody's Great Hall.
Photo by Peter Casolino

WATERBURY

Pizza parlor co-owner Urim Belica (left) was born in Waterbury, but his parents came from Albanian Macedonia. An estimated 10,000 Albanian Americans live in the greater Waterbury area. Those who came since the 1960s did so because of the blossoming Albanian colony. The earlier draw? A booming brass industry.

Photo by Bob Falcetti

STONINGTON

Dave Angrisani, 28, has worked at the Stonington Town Dock for 10 years, sorting fresh fish by type or size, depending on what his employers want. Today, the order is for cod. "It's a good living," Angrisani says. "But I think the heyday is over."

Photo by Tim Martin, The Day

NEW HAVEN

At Yale University, postdoctoral pharmacology associate Yongcheng Wang works on a cure for Alzheimer's. Wang isolated crystal material from the amyloid precursor protein (a protein linked to the neurodegeneration of Alzheimer's), got the molecular data X-rayed and computerized, and became the first person to *see* APP crystals. "Very exciting," Wang recalls.

Photo by Michael J. Ivins

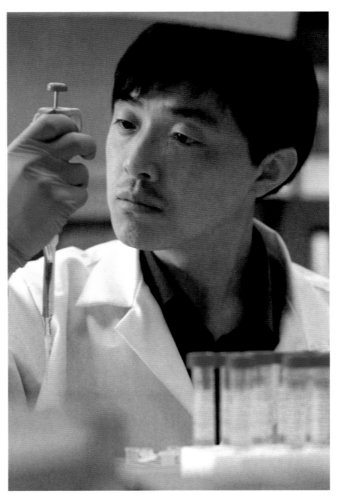

GROTON
Gail Eichenlaub is usually too busy to talk on the phone at the Hess gas station on Route 12. Beach-goers and tourists stop in for gas and snacks on their way to the seaside towns on Fisher Island Sound. Eichenlaub pulled the best duty this week: Sunday night, after the weekenders have gone home.
Photo by C.M. Glover, outtosee.com

NEW HAVEN
Nick Cretella has been a street hawker for the *New Haven Register* longer than he can remember. He works a traffic island bordering East Haven and New Haven at the entrance to Interstate 95 South.
Photo by Peter Casolino

NEW HAVEN
Dancing in the Streets: Members of the drill team Mob Squad shimmy their way down Dixwell Avenue during the Freddie Fixer Parade. In its 40th year, the annual event began as a neighborhood cleanup campaign and evolved into a celebration of the city's sizeable African-American community.
Photo by Peter Casolino

STAMFORD
Alex Gutierrez, 17, executes an ollie off a concrete platform, while Daniel López, 15, prepares for his flight. The ollie, involving a jump with both feet controlling the board, is named for Alan "Ollie" Gelfand. He's credited with inventing it 25 years ago—well before these skateboarders were born.
Photo by Andrew Douglas Sullivan

HARTFORD

Caribbean Cricket Club player Omar Mullings winds up for a fast bowl during a Sunday afternoon match against the West Indies Cricket Club. The fast pitcher from Jamaica likes the game's slow pace. "It's a way to hang out and relax with friends," he says. "And it reminds me of home."

Photo by Marc-Yves Regis II, The Hartford Courant

WATERBURY

Hector Maldonado breaks through defense moves by Ramon Gonzales and Jonathan Torres to turn a right hook into a score. They're in South End, Waterbury's traditional location for new communities—the latest being Puerto Rican.

Photo by Bob Falcetti

After watching his sister's soccer club practice at
Trotta Field, George Day-Reiss tries to quench his
thirst—without quenching his shirt. Mission not
accomplished.
Photo by Anne Day

WATERFORD

Waterford High's softball squad circles up for luck before every game. But the ritual didn't lead to victory. The team suffered a loss to Eastern Connecticut Conference rival Montville High.
Photo by Sean D. Elliot, The Day

WESTPORT

Postpartum obsession: Members of the Saugatuck Rowing Club rev up for a sprint during one of their daily morning practices. All eight women joined the highly competitive team after having children. "I wanted to return to serious exercise with other people who have the same intensity level," says Tanah Kalb (first rower) who competed with the Connecticut College crew as an undergraduate.

Photo by Catherine Karnow

At the annual fundraiser for the Greenwich Adult Day Care, held at a private waterfront home, models show off dresses while guests drink afternoon tea. The menu includes almond chicken sandwiches, Mrs. Pettigrew's Lemon Loaf, chocolate toffee trifle, and specially brewed Darjeeling tea.
Photos by Andrew Douglas Sullivan

GREENWICH

In addition to watching a fashion show, the 250 guests bid in a silent auction for items donated by local merchants. The town has so many fundraisers that the adult day care, which was established in 1977, decided to organize an event targeted solely to women.

GREENWICH

Guests leave the 1902 home of Susan Bevan and Anthony Daddino, who've hosted several fundraisers. By afternoon's end, the adult day care, which provides recreation, social services, and health care to impaired or isolated adults, including a day center for people with dementia, had $50,000 more to work with.

TORRINGTON

Students of the Nutmeg Ballet grand jeté across the studio. Opened in 1970 by Connecticut-native Sharon Dante, the company is known for its seasonal performances of classics such as *Nutcracker* and *Coppelia*. Dante and her instructors follow the Russian Vaganova method, breaking down each dance move into minute detail.
Photo by Anne Day

SALISBURY

Students at the Arts in Motion studio limber up before a dress rehearsal choreographed by the school's founder and director, Terre Lefferts. If the girls manifest the talent and dedication, they will one day join Syzygy, the studio's ensemble for teens and young adults. Syzygy, from the Greek, means celestial bodies yoked together by gravity.
Photo by Anne Day

MERIDEN

Dancers with the Middlesex Dance Center's Junior Ensemble assume the fourth position as they prepare to bourrée onto the stage during a performance to "A Little Night Music."
Photo by Cloe Poisson, The Hartford Courant

MERIDEN
Before performing her tap number, "Twelfth Street Rag," at the Middlesex Dance Center's recital rehearsal, Molly Dudko (right) secures her tap shoe.
Photo by Cloe Poisson, The Hartford Courant

NEW HAVEN

Chillin' in a customized car, revelers watch the annual Freddie Fixer Parade on Dixwell Avenue. In 1962, members of New Haven's African-American community invented a mascot, Freddie the Fixer, to encourage folks to clean up and fix up their neighborhoods. A year later, the first paraders marched down Dixwell Avenue with one bass drum. Eventually, the name was shortened to "Freddie Fixer."

Photos by Peter Casolino

NEW HAVEN

The ladies are in the hizzle! The parade is a churning mix of bands, floats, and food booths. It's also a great place for parade-goers to show off their mad style.

NEW HAVEN

Rap artist Eve might not really be at the Freddie Fixer Parade, but for five bucks, Tillian Taylor will take your picture next to a portrait of the singer. Edmond "B*Wak" Comfort painted these murals on bedsheets expressly for the parade.

NEW HAVEN

After cruising the parade on her bike, Nicole Rudolph of the all-female motorcycle club Elm City Angels touches up using a handy mirror.

HARTFORD

Alejandrina Navarro, her husband Secundino de Jesus, and Sara Santiago show up every day at the Hispanic Senior Center to play bingo. The seniors pay $10 a month to the center, which serves up a warm lunch and good company.
Photo by Patrick Raycraft

UNCASVILLE

Dealer takes all. Gamblers at the Mohegan Sun Casino's craps table have, at best, a 16 percent chance of winning. That is good news for the 1,500-member Mohegan tribe that owns the casino. Last year, the tribe's slot machines and table games brought in $1.12 billion, 15 percent of which went to the state in exchange for exclusive gaming rights.

Photo by Sean D. Elliot, The Day

WATERFORD

The end of the line: The #47 Sportsman waits for a tow after crashing at the Waterford Speedbowl NASCAR Dodge Weekly Series. One of three NASCAR tracks in Connecticut, the Speedbowl is known for its short 3/8-mile track that forces drivers to compete in tight quarters.
Photo by C.M. Glover, outtosee.com

A fleet of Etchells Class racing sloops do some close-hauled maneuvering just before the start of a race in Duck Island Roads. The three-crew boats, designed by naval architect Skip Etchells in the 1940s, are known for their speed, handling, and affordability.

Photo by Jonathan Olson

HARTFORD
Grace Wright leads members of the Cultural
Dance Troupe of the West Indies through a
Trinidadian folk dance. West Indian immi-
grants came to Connecticut during World
War I to work in the state's tobacco fields.
Over the years, their families followed and
Hartford is now home to 45,000 of them,
making it one of the largest West Indian en-
claves in the country.
Photo by Marc-Yves Regis II,
The Hartford Courant

NEW HAVEN

New Haven Ravens fans make their way up the Yale Field bleachers with baseball-watching essentials—hotdogs and sodas—in hand. The field's first ball game, in 1928, pitted the Yale Bulldogs against the Eastern League New Haven Professionals. The Bulldogs got shut out, and the Double-A New Haven Ravens likewise lost to the Akron, Ohio, Aeros, 5–3.
Photos by Peter Casolino

HAMMONASSET BEACH STATE PARK

At the Sound Winds Kite Festival charity event, Jesse Barto lets sail "Martin Lester's Legs." The resident of Millbrook, New York, traveled to the park to take part in the fundraiser for Middlesex Hospital's Cancer Center. And who is Martin Lester? The designer of Barto's kite.

KENT
Old Glory: After the terrorist attacks of September 11, 2001, the Sabia family used their Main Street colonial as a canvas for demonstrating their all-American pride.
Photo by Anne Day

Reason To Believe

FAIRFIELD
Reesa Antony and Matt Ryzewski wait for the baccalaureate mass to begin on the Bellarmine Lawn at Fairfield University, a private Jesuit school known for its community service projects. Volunteering with organizations like the Boys and Girls Club, Habitat for Humanity, or The Salvation Army Soup Kitchen is a freshman requirement.
Photo by Jean Santopatre,
Fairfield University

ASHFORD

Bryan Tawney and daughter Olivia take a breather after do-si-doing at the Hole in the Wall Gang Camp's square dance. The 5-year-old, who was diagnosed with leukemia in 2002, spent Mother's Day weekend with her family at the retreat for children with life-threatening diseases. "It was great to be around so many people facing the same struggles," says her dad.
Photos by Catherine Karnow

ASHFORD

Who said this would be fun? Amy Yeske has second thoughts as she prepares to whiz down the zipline at the Hole in the Wall Gang outdoor climbing course. The camp was built with funds donated by Paul Newman and the Kingdom of Saudi Arabia and is free for acutely ill children and their families.

NORWALK

A persistent cloud front finally breaks above the Grace Baptist Church in South Norwalk. Blue skies were a welcome respite for residents who toughed out an unusually wet and snowy spring and winter. Meteorologists hypothesize an on-going El Niño weather system in the Pacific was responsible for the Northeast's unremitting storms.

Photo by Rikki Ward

KENT

Founded by an Episcopalian minister in 1906, the Kent School still requires students to incorporate worship into their everyday routine. All students attend a mandatory Episcopal service at the chapel on Tuesdays and Thursdays, but Catholic, Jewish, and Muslim students are excused from Sunday morning sermons.
Photo by Wendy Carlson

NORWICH
Dennis Mercieri (center) leads a procession of priests, bishops, deacons, and cardinals down the aisle of the Cathedral of St. Patrick. More than 1,700 spectators gathered to see the installation of Michael R. Cote, the new bishop of the Diocese of Norwich. Cote takes over the reigns of a diocese rocked by allegations of priestly misconduct.
Photo by Sean D. Elliot, The Day

NORWICH
Bishop Cote prepares to serve communion. The former auxiliary bishop in Portland, Maine, he succeeds retired Bishop Daniel Hart (background).

MYSTIC
Most of the time, congregants sing the praises of Jesus, but today, the parishioners at Potter's House Church of God dedicate their songs and prayers to Pastor Bruno Spada. The special service marks Pastor Appreciation Day.
Photo by Dan Hunt

FAIRFIELD

Before taking the job of assistant chaplain with the Fairfield University Campus Ministry, Gregg Grovenburg explored the world. He taught Caribbean literature and religion in Belize, completed his Jesuit training in Ireland, and earned a graduate degree in theology in London. Finally, the globetrotter was ready to put down roots when he moved to Connecticut in 1999.

Photo by Jean Santopatre, Fairfield University

STAMFORD

After homework, play, dinner, and bath, Curtis Guinyard, Jr. says bedtime prayers with his mother, Tracy Jones, a customer service representative and receptionist at the *Advocate/Greenwich Times*. Curtis recites "Now I lay me down to sleep," while mom gives thanks for her miracle child. Curtis followed two failed pregnancies.
Photo by Andrew Douglas Sullivan

NORWICH

Overachievers Sandy Ma and Marissa Charles, seventh-graders at Saint Bernard Academy, earn community service extra credit handing out programs at the installation ceremonies for the new bishop of Norwich, Michael R. Cote.
Photo by Sean D. Elliot, The Day

SALISBURY

Zen and the art of being a 7-year-old: George Day-Reiss isn't sure when he first got in touch with his Buddha nature. Still, whenever the urge overcomes him, as it has on his neighbor's diving board, he just goes with the flow.
Photo by Anne Day

WATERBURY

Zeqir Berisha, aka Ziggy the Flagman, estimates he walks four hours a day waving the flag to promote patriotism in his adopted country. Berisha was born in Kosova and came to the U.S. in 1969, where he worked in construction until retirement several years ago. When he waves his flag, "I feel like I fly with the eagle," he says.

Photo by Bob Falcetti

WESTPORT

Activists bring their anti-Bush message to commuters on the Post Road Bridge. The bridge itself stirred controversy in 2003 when a lawmaker proposed renaming it after Westport activist and United Nations supporter Ruth Steinkaus-Cohen. Opponents of the renaming focused on the U.N. and its refusal to endorse the American-led invasion of Iraq. In May, the bridge was renamed the Ruth Steinkraus-Cohen Bridge.

Photo by Rikki Ward

MYSTIC
The country's oldest bascule drawbridge, built in 1924, connects Mystic to West Mystic. A bascule bridge opens by sinking a counterpoise that lifts the roadway into the air. The antique bridge opens at a quarter past each hour for sailboats traveling on the Mystic River.
Photo by Dan Hunt

Our Town

THE BLUE H

SALISBURY
Grace Lancto helps mom with the morning feed at their family home in northwestern Connecticut. The goats, sheep, and chickens are more pets than livestock, although the Lanctos do gather and eat the hens' eggs. The family moved to the 35-acre spread to escape the stress of New York City living.
Photo by Anne Day

SHARON

In the spring, the Weatherstone estate comes alive with flora. All 60 acres are landscaped under the guidance of owner Carolyne Roehm, a bestselling author of gardening books.
Photo by Anne Day

BETHANY

Geraniums share ledge space with the books at Whitlock Farm Booksellers. The building, a converted turkey barn, and another barn up the hill, hold 40,000 volumes, all used.

Photo by Michael J. Ivins

NEW HAVEN

New Haven—founded in 1637 and laid out on a nine-square grid—has long endured classic "town and gown" frictions. In the post–World War II period, the city's downtown deteriorated while Yale University's cloistered campus (to the right) prospered and expanded. One effort aimed at sprucing up Elm City is a Green and Clean initiative to make the Puritans' original village green (center) look its greenest.

Photo by Michael J. Ivins

WESTPORT
Shadow play: Visual identity specialist Jerry Kuyper has been erecting his finely balanced rock sculptures for 20 years. His day job is spent at the computer, designing logos for corporate clients; his hobby allows him outdoor and tactile refreshment.
Photo by Pamela Einarsen

HARTFORD
When Alphanso "Chippy" Edwards opened his restaurant, Chippy's, 20 years ago, he was one of only a few African-American business owners in Hartford. Today, his domain also includes the Laundromat next door, which is handy when it comes time to wash the tablecloths.
Photo by Marc-Yves Regis II,
The Hartford Courant

STAMFORD

The Most Worshipful Prince Hall Grand Lodge of Free and Accepted Masons (St. John's Lodge #14) is the oldest African-American organization in Stamford. Lodge Master Charles Paris (center) is proud that his branch of the largest charitable fraternal organization in the world (five million members strong) provides college scholarships for dozens of low-income students each year.

Photo by Andrew Douglas Sullivan

BRIDGEPORT

Say "ahoy!" To become a member of the Black Rock Yacht Club, candidates must convince three current members to endorse their application, pass an interview and evaluation in a social setting, and receive the approval of the yacht club's board.

Photo by Jean Santopatre, Fairfield University

KENT

Between crew practice, drama rehearsal, dressage, and advanced placement courses looking at the Homeric Epic and Constitutional Law, Kent School juniors find time to chill out in their dorm room. The private boarding high school provides a classical liberal arts education for a price tag of $33,000 a year.

Photo by Wendy Carlson

WATERBURY
Local basketball players pause and pose between pickup games at Rivera-Hughes Park. Left to right, Waterbury's finest: Hector Maldonado, Benny Soriano, Ramon Gonzalez, Timothy Herbert, Carlos Campos, and Jonathan Torres.
Photo by Bob Falcetti

NORWALK
Tianna Roy's broken wrist and fractured ulna were no big deal compared to her early childhood traumas. The fraternal twin was born prematurely at 4 months and spent 16 weeks on life support. After suffering from a collapsed lung and sustaining an eye injury, the resilient premie rallied and grew into an indomitable 10-year-old.
Photo by Rikki Ward

HARTFORD

Three months after a devastating fire killed 16 Greenwood Health Center residents, life is slowly getting back to normal. Hartford Mayor Eddie Perez has been friends with many of the residents for years and dropped by during National Nursing Home Week for a picnic in the central courtyard.

Photo by Patrick Raycraft

KENT

Fab four: Kent School students go to great lengths to challenge the dress code. Male students must don blue blazers, dress shirts, and ties during classes and meals, but the school doesn't prohibit loud colors or garish designs, hence, the prep school-cum-beach bum look of Matt Andrews, Adam Friedman, McComb Dunwoody, and Ben Coulter.

Photo by Wendy Carlson

BRIDGEPORT
City Hall was once the stomping grounds of P.T.
Barnum, the city's most famous mayor and cre-
ator of the Greatest Show on Earth.
Photo by Jean Santopatre, Fairfield University

NEW LONDON

Cadet Third Class Beth Newton is one of 255 female students enrolled in the U.S. Coast Guard Academy. The school began admitting women in 1980, and now 30 percent of its students are female.

Photo by Sean D. Elliot, The Day

BRIDGEPORT

Living classroom: Students at the Bridgeport Regional Vocational Aquaculture High School, a science magnet school, catch and dissect fish during a marine biology class. The school includes a pathology lab, a 56-foot research vessel, a propulsion and electronics lab, and a meteorology classroom. The subjects students study include boat building, marine ecology, and small engine repair.

Photo by Jean Santopatre, Fairfield University

NOANK

In calm waters just off New York's Montauk Point Lighthouse, the Noank-based charter fishing boat *Mataura* looks for fluke fish.

Photo by Dan Hunt

GROTON

The 360-foot, 6,927-ton USS *Toledo* a fast attack submarine, returns to the Navy Submarine Base at New London for routine maintenance after a six-month deployment in the Persian Gulf. The $900 million leviathan, built by General Dynamics Electric Boat in Groton, is equipped with torpedoes, Tomahawk cruise missiles, and mines.

Photo by Sean D. Elliot, The Day

OAKVILLE
Despite lots of competition and scant parking, spirits are high as Joyce Powell of Waterbury gets an extra lift from granddaughter Kimberly Hendrickson, 11. They have been working in their family's week-old venture, Roscello's Italian deli. The family plans to re-name it Sorrento Pizza & Deli.
Photo by Bob Falcetti

WEST HARTFORD
"Jazz is therapy for my soul," says Theresa Wright, front woman for the Distinguished Gentlemen jazz band. The mom of four works as a hairdresser and receptionist when she's not crooning old jazz standards like "Route 66," "The A-Train," and "East of the Sun." "I do what I can to bring home the dollars," she says. "But singing is what I love."
Photo by Marc-Yves Regis II, The Hartford Courant

BRIDGEPORT

"The Green Room is down to earth," says Jeff Gaines of his favorite bar in Bridgeport. "It's the kind of place where anybody could feel comfortable. That's hard to find in Fairfield County." The low-key watering hole is decorated with thrift store furniture and serves Brooklyn Lager on tap.
Photo by Jean Santopatre, Fairfield University

NOANK
The locals take it for granted, but Ford's Lobsters got its fifteen minutes of fame when it co-starred in *Mystic Pizza*, (1988) with the then-unknown actress Julia Roberts.
Photo by C.M. Glover, outtosee.com

How It Worked

The week of May 12-18, 2003, more than 25,000 professional and amateur photographers spread out across the nation to shoot over a million digital photographs with the goal of capturing the essence of daily life in America.

The professional photographers were equipped with Adobe Photoshop and Adobe Album software, Olympus C-5050 digital cameras, and Lexar Media's high-speed compact flash cards.

The 1,000 professional contract photographers plus another 5,000 stringers and students sent their images via FTP (file transfer protocol) directly to the *America 24/7* website. Meanwhile, thousands of amateur photographers uploaded their images to Snapfish's servers.

At *America 24/7*'s Mission Control headquarters, located at CNET in San Francisco, dozens of picture editors from the nation's most prestigious publications culled the images down to 25,000 of the very best, using Photo Mechanic by Camera Bits. These photos were transferred into Webware's ActiveMedia Digital Asset Management (DAM) system, which served as a central image library and enabled the designers to track, search, distribute, and reformat the images for the creation of the 51 books, foreign language editions, web and magazine syndication, posters, and exhibitions.

Once in the DAM, images were optimized (and in some cases resampled to increase image resolution) using Adobe Photoshop. Adobe InDesign and Adobe InCopy were used to design and produce the 51 books, which were edited and reviewed in multiple locations around the world in the form of Adobe Acrobat PDFs. Epson Stylus printers were used for photo proofing and to produce large-format images for exhibitions. The companies providing support for the *America 24/7* project offer many of the essential components for anyone building a digital darkroom. We encourage you to read more on the following pages about their respective roles in making *America 24/7* possible.

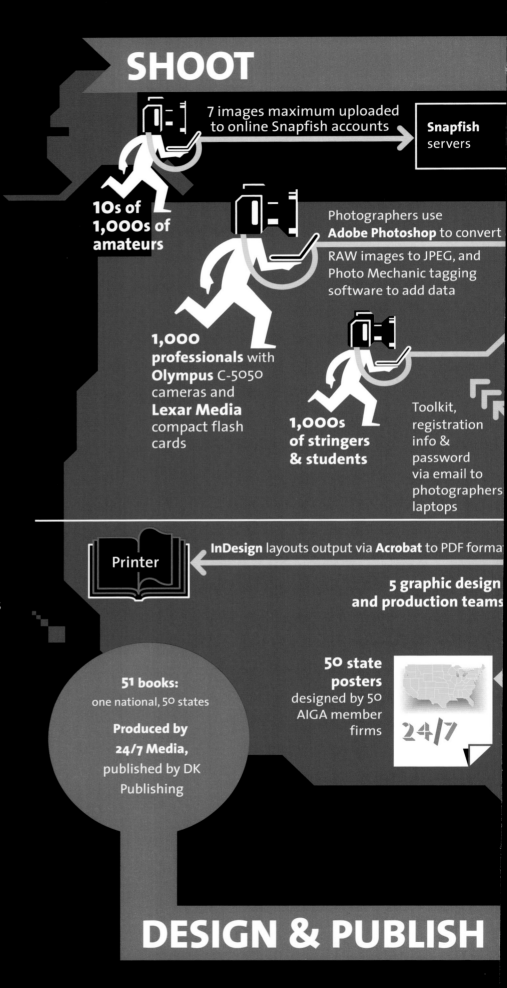

SHOOT

7 images maximum uploaded to online Snapfish accounts → **Snapfish** servers

10s of 1,000s of amateurs

Photographers use **Adobe Photoshop** to convert RAW images to JPEG, and Photo Mechanic tagging software to add data

1,000 professionals with **Olympus** C-5050 cameras and **Lexar Media** compact flash cards

1,000s of stringers & students

Toolkit, registration info & password via email to photographers laptops

Printer ← **InDesign** layouts output via **Acrobat** to PDF format

5 graphic design and production teams

51 books: one national, 50 states

Produced by 24/7 Media, published by DK Publishing

50 state posters designed by 50 AIGA member firms

24/7

DESIGN & PUBLISH

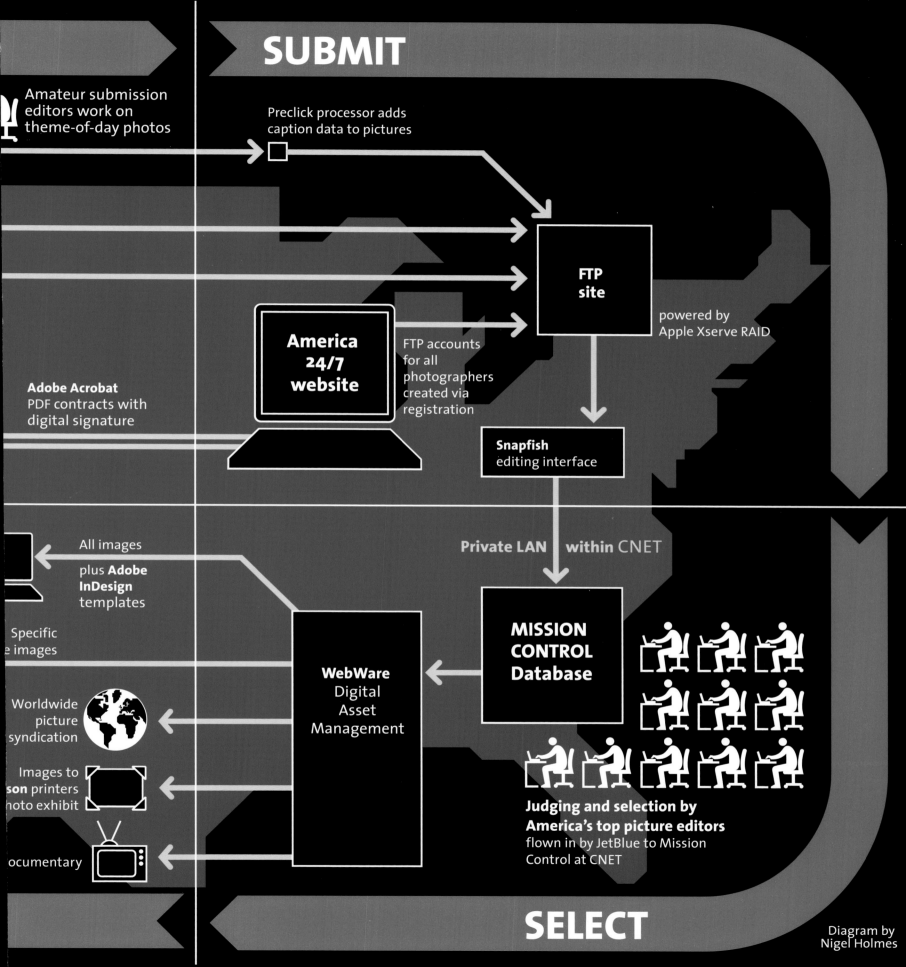

About Our Sponsors

America 24/7 gave digital photographers of all levels the opportunity to share their visions of what it means to live in the United States. This project was made possible by a digital photography revolution that is dramatically changing and improving picture-taking for professionals and amateurs alike. And an Adobe product, Photoshop®, has been at the center of this sea change.

Adobe's products reflect our customers' passion for the creative process, be it the photographer, graphic designer, layout artist, or printer. Adobe is the Publishing and Imaging Software Partner for *America 24/7* and products such as Adobe InDesign®, Photoshop, Acrobat®, and Illustrator® were used to produce this stunning book in a matter of weeks. We hope that our software has helped do justice to the mythic images, contributed by well-known photographers and the inspired hobbyist.

Adobe is proud to be a lead sponsor of *America 24/7*, a project that celebrates the vibrancy of the American spirit: the same spirit that helped found Adobe and inspires our employees and customers to deliver the very best.

Bruce Chizen
President and CEO
Adobe Systems Incorporated

Olympus, a global technology leader in designing precision healthcare solutions and innovative consumer electronics, is proud to be the official digital camera sponsor of *America 24/7*. The opportunity to introduce Americans from coast to coast to the thrill, excitement, and possibility of digital photography makes the vision behind this book a perfect fit for Olympus, a leader in digital cameras since 1996.

For most people, the essence of digital photography is best grasped through firsthand experience with the technology, which is precisely what *America 24/7* is about. We understand that direct experience is the pathway to inspiration, and welcome opportunities like this sponsorship to bring the power of the digital experience into the lives of people everywhere. To Olympus, *America 24/7* offers a platform to help realize a core mission: to deliver and make accessible the power of the digital experience to millions of American photographers, amateurs, and professionals alike.

The 1,000 professional photographers contracted to shoot on the America 24/7 project were all equipped with Olympus C-5050 digital cameras. Like all Olympus products, the C-5050 is offered by a company well known for designing, manufacturing, and servicing products used by professionals to perform their work, every day. Olympus is a customer-centric company committed to working one-to-one with a diverse group of professionals. From biomedical researchers who use our clinical microscopes, to doctors who perform life-saving procedures with our endoscopes, to professional photographers who use cameras in their daily work, Olympus is a trusted brand.

The digital imaging technology involved with *America 24/7* has enabled the soul of America to be visually conveyed, not just by professional observers, but by the American public who participated in this project—the very people who collectively breath life into this country's existence each day.

We are proud to be enabling so many photographers to capture the pictures on these pages that tell the story of who we are as a nation. From sea to shining sea, digital imagery allows us to connect to one another in ways we never dreamed possible.

At Olympus, our ideas have proliferated as rapidly as technology has evolved. We have channeled these visions into breakthrough products and solutions to meet the demands of our changing world-products like microscopes, endoscopes, and digital voice recorders, supported by the highly regarded training, educational, and consulting services we offer our customers.

Today, 83 years after we introduced our first microscope, we remain as young, as curious, and as committed as ever.

Lexar Media has grown from the digital photography revolution, which is why we are proud to have supplied the digital memory cards used in the America 24/7 project. Lexar Media's high-performance memory cards utilize our unique and patented controller coupled with high-speed flash memory from Samsung, the world's largest flash memory supplier. This powerful combination brings out the ultimate performance of any digital camera.

Photographers who demand the most from their equipment choose our products for their advanced features like write speeds up to 40X, Write Acceleration technology for enabled cameras, and Image Rescue, which recovers previously deleted or lost images. Leading camera manufacturers bundle Lexar Media digital memory cards with their cameras because they value its performance and reliability.

Lexar Media is at the forefront of digital photography as it transforms picture-taking worldwide, and we will continue to be a leader with new and innovative solutions for professionals and amateurs alike.

Snapfish, which developed the technology behind the *America 24/7* amateur photo event, is a leading online photo service, with more than 5 million members and 100 million photos posted online. Snapfish enables both film and digital camera owners to share, print, and store their most important photo memories, at prices that cannot be equaled. Digital camera users upload photos into a password-protected online album for free. Users can also order film-quality prints on professional photographic paper for as low as 25¢. Film camera users get a full set of prints, plus online sharing and storage, for just $2.99 per roll.

Founded in 1995, eBay created a powerful platform for the sale of goods and services by a passionate community of individuals and businesses. On any given day, there are millions of items across thousands of categories for sale on eBay. eBay enables trade on a local, national and international basis with customized sites in markets around the world.

Through an array of services, such as its payment solution provider PayPal, eBay is enabling global e-commerce for an ever-growing online community.

JetBlue Airways is proud to be *America 24/7's* preferred carrier, flying photographers, photo editors, and organizers across the United States.

Winner of Condé Nast Traveler's Readers' Choice Awards for Best Domestic Airline 2002, JetBlue provides friendly service and low fares for travelers in 22 cities in nine states across America.

On behalf of JetBlue's 5,000 crew members, we're excited to be involved in this remarkable project, and for the opportunity to serve American travelers each and every day, coast to coast, 24/7.

DIGITAL POND

Digital Pond has been a leading creator of large graphic displays for museums, corporations, trade shows, retail environments and fine art since 1992.

We were proud to bring together our creative, print and display capabilities to produce signage and displays for mission control, critical retouching for numerous key images for the book, and art galleries for the New York Public Library and Bryant Park.

The Pond's team and SplashPic® Online service enabled us to nimbly design, produce and install over 200 large graphic panels in two NYC locations within the truly "24/7" production schedule of less than ten days.

WebWare Corporation is pleased to be a major sponsor of the America 24/7 project. We take pride in being part of a groundbreaking adventure that is stretching the boundaries—and the imagination—in digital photography, digital asset management, publishing, news, and global events.

Our ActiveMedia Enterprise™ digital asset management software is the "nerve center" of *America 24/7*, the central repository for managing, sharing, and collaborating on the project's photographs. From photo editors and book publishers to 24/7's media relations and marketing personnel, ActiveMedia provides the application support that links all facets of the project team to the content worldwide.

WebWare helps Global 2000 firms securely manage, reuse, and distribute media assets locally or globally. Its suite of ActiveMedia software products provide powerful media services platforms for integrating rich media into content management systems marketing and communication portals; web publishing systems; and e-commerce portals.

Google's mission is to organize the world's information and make it universally accessible and useful.

With our focus on plucking just the right answer from an ocean of data, we were naturally drawn to the America 24/7 project. The book you hold is a compendium of images of American life distilled from thousands of photographs and infinite possibilities. Are you looking for emotion? Narrative? Shadows? Light? It's all here, thanks to a multitude of photographers and writers creating links between you, the reader, and a sea of wonderful stories. We celebrate the connections that constitute the human experience and are pleased to help engender them. And we're pleased to have been a small part of this project, which captures the results of that interaction so vividly, so dynamically, and so dramatically.

Special thanks to additional contributors: FileMaker, Apple, Camera Bits, LaCie, Now Software, Preclick, Outpost Digital, Xerox, Microsoft, WoodWing Software, net-linx Publishing Solutions, and Radical Media. The Savoy Hotel, San Francisco; The Pan Pacific, San Francisco; Four Seasons Hotel, San Francisco; and The Queen Anne Hotel. Photography editing facilities were generously hosted by CNET Networks, Inc.

Participating Photographers

Coordinator: Stephanie Heisler, *The Hartford Courant*

Christian Abraham, *Connecticut Post*
Wendy Carlson
Peter Casolino
Anne Day
Michael Dusza
Pamela Einarsen
Sean D. Elliot, *The Day*
Susan Emmetsberger
Bob Falcetti
C.M. Glover, outtosee.com
Dan Hunt
Michael J. Ivins
John Kane, Silver Sun Studio
Catherine Karnow
David Kyle

Tim Martin, *The Day*
Brett Mickelson
Christine Montano
Jonathan Olson
William H. Payne IV
Cloe Poisson, *The Hartford Courant*
Patrick Raycraft
Mike Raymond
Marc-Yves Regis II, *The Hartford Courant*
George Ruhe
Jean Santopatre, Fairfield University
Nina Smith
Andrew Douglas Sullivan
Kristie Sutherland
Rikki Ward

Thumbnail Picture Credits

Credits for thumbnail photographs are listed by the page number and are in order from left to right.

18 Catherine Karnow
Catherine Karnow
Catherine Karnow
Catherine Karnow
Catherine Karnow
Catherine Karnow
Catherine Karnow

22 Anne Day
Peter Casolino
Rikki Ward
Peter Casolino
Pamela Einarsen
Peter Casolino
Pamela Einarsen

23 Rikki Ward
Pamela Einarsen
E.B. Ruark
Rikki Ward
Anne Day
Peter Casolino
Bob Falcetti

27 Anne Day
Catherine Karnow
Pamela Einarsen
Anne Day
Pamela Einarsen
Catherine Karnow
Jean Santopatre, Fairfield University

28 Peter Casolino
Rikki Ward
Anne Day
Christian Abraham, *Connecticut Post*
Peter Casolino
Rikki Ward
Brett Mickelson

29 Anne Day
Wendy Carlson
Rikki Ward
Rikki Ward

Anne Day
Peter Casolino
Wendy Carlson

30 Anne Day
Anne Day
Anne Day
Anne Day
Dan Hunt
Anne Day
Anne Day

31 Anne Day
Jonathan Olson
Dan Hunt
Anne Day
Anne Day
Pamela Einarsen
Patrick Raycraft

34 Christian Abraham, *Connecticut Post*
Anne Day
Wendy Carlson
Marc-Yves Regis II, *The Hartford Courant*
Pamela Einarsen
Wendy Carlson
Marc-Yves Regis II, *The Hartford Courant*

35 Patrick Raycraft
Wendy Carlson
Marc-Yves Regis II, *The Hartford Courant*
Bob Falcetti
Wendy Carlson
Rikki Ward
Wendy Carlson

46 Anne Day
Anne Day
Anne Day
Peter Casolino

Pamela Einarsen
Christian Abraham, *Connecticut Post*
Anne Day

47 Dan Hunt
Anne Day
Peter Casolino
Anne Day
Peter Casolino
Pamela Einarsen
Peter Casolino

48 C.M. Glover, outtosee.com
Peter Casolino
Peter Casolino
Peter Casolino
Dan Hunt
Peter Casolino
Peter Casolino

49 George Ruhe
Peter Casolino
Peter Casolino
Rikki Ward
Peter Casolino
Bob Falcetti
George Ruhe

52 Christian Abraham, *Connecticut Post*
Jonathan Olson
Cloe Poisson, *The Hartford Courant*
Jonathan Olson
Cloe Poisson, *The Hartford Courant*
Jonathan Olson
Cloe Poisson, *The Hartford Courant*

53 Jonathan Olson
Jonathan Olson
Cloe Poisson, *The Hartford Courant*
Jonathan Olson
Jonathan Olson
Anne Day
Jonathan Olson

56 Christian Abraham, *Connecticut Post*
Christian Abraham, *Connecticut Post*
Andrew Douglas Sullivan
Peter Casolino
Jonathan Olson
George Ruhe
Michael J. Ivins

57 Christian Abraham, *Connecticut Post*
Andrew Douglas Sullivan
Peter Casolino
Dan Hunt
Rikki Ward
Peter Casolino
E.B. Ruark

58 Anne Day
Anne Day
Anne Day
Anne Day
Brett Mickelson
Bob Falcetti
Christian Abraham, *Connecticut Post*

59 Anne Day
Anne Day
Anne Day
Pamela Einarsen
Andrew Douglas Sullivan
Christian Abraham, *Connecticut Post*
Anne Day

62 Jean Santopatre, Fairfield University
Patrick Raycraft
Bob Falcetti
Michael J. Ivins
Marc-Yves Regis II, *The Hartford Courant*
Dan Hunt
Tim Martin, *The Day*

63 Peter Casolino
Tim Martin, *The Day*
Tim Martin, *The Day*
Dan Hunt
Michael J. Ivins
Susan Magnano
Michael J. Ivins

64 John Kane, Silver Sun Studio
Anne Day
E.B. Ruark
John Kane, Silver Sun Studio
C.M. Glover, outtosee.com
Jonathan Olson
Bob Falcetti

65 C.M. Glover, outtosee.com
Peter Casolino
C.M. Glover, outtosee.com
Peter Casolino
Peter Casolino
Rikki Ward
John Waiveris

71 Bob Falcetti
Marc-Yves Regis II, *The Hartford Courant*
Dan Hunt
Marc-Yves Regis II, *The Hartford Courant*
Bob Falcetti
Marc-Yves Regis II, *The Hartford Courant*
Bob Falcetti

72 Anne Day
Anne Day
Anne Day
Peter Casolino
Anne Day
Christian Abraham, *Connecticut Post*
Andrew Douglas Sullivan

73 Jean Santopatre, Fairfield University
Anne Day
Sean D. Elliot, *The Day*
Peter Casolino
Anne Day
Jean Santopatre, Fairfield University
Christian Abraham, *Connecticut Post*

76 Andrew Douglas Sullivan
Anne Day
Andrew Douglas Sullivan
Andrew Douglas Sullivan
Andrew Douglas Sullivan
Andrew Douglas Sullivan
Anne Day

77 Andrew Douglas Sullivan
Andrew Douglas Sullivan
Andrew Douglas Sullivan
Andrew Douglas Sullivan
Andrew Douglas Sullivan
Jean Santopatre, Fairfield University
Anne Day

78 Anne Day
Anne Day
Cloe Poisson, *The Hartford Courant*
Anne Day
Cloe Poisson, *The Hartford Courant*
Andrew Douglas Sullivan
Anne Day

79 Andrew Douglas Sullivan
Anne Day
Anne Day
Cloe Poisson, *The Hartford Courant*
Andrew Douglas Sullivan
Marc-Yves Regis II,
The Hartford Courant
John Kane, Silver Sun Studio

82 Peter Casolino
Peter Casolino
George Ruhe
Marc-Yves Regis II,
The Hartford Courant
Peter Casolino
Peter Casolino
George Ruhe

83 Bob Falcetti
Peter Casolino
Bob Falcetti
Marc-Yves Regis II,
The Hartford Courant
Peter Casolino
Marc-Yves Regis II,
The Hartford Courant
Peter Casolino

84 Rikki Ward
Christian Abraham, *Connecticut Post*
Patrick Raycraft
Christian Abraham, *Connecticut Post*
Bob Falcetti
Sean D. Elliot, *The Day*
Christian Abraham, *Connecticut Post*

85 Andrew Douglas Sullivan
Sean D. Elliot, *The Day*
Susan Magnano
Sean D. Elliot, *The Day*
Susan Magnano
Rikki Ward
Jean Santopatre, Fairfield University

86 Christian Abraham,
Connecticut Post
C.M. Glover, outtosee.com

Jonathan Olson
C.M. Glover, outtosee.com
Dan Hunt
C.M. Glover, outtosee.com
Wendy Carlson

87 Jonathan Olson
C.M. Glover, outtosee.com
Jonathan Olson
Christian Abraham, *Connecticut Post*
Jonathan Olson
C.M. Glover, outtosee.com
Jonathan Olson

90 Peter Casolino
Peter Casolino
Bob Falcetti
Bob Falcetti
Peter Casolino
Bob Falcetti
Bob Falcetti

96 Catherine Karnow
Catherine Karnow
Catherine Karnow
Cloe Poisson, *The Hartford Courant*
Catherine Karnow
Catherine Karnow
Cloe Poisson, *The Hartford Courant*

98 Brett Mickelson
Jean Santopatre, Fairfield University
Rikki Ward
Wendy Carlson
Jean Santopatre, Fairfield University
Brett Mickelson
Jonathan Olson

99 Jean Santopatre,
Fairfield University
Brett Mickelson
Wendy Carlson
Jean Santopatre, Fairfield University
Jonathan Olson
Jean Santopatre, Fairfield University
Jean Santopatre, Fairfield University

102 Sean D. Elliot, *The Day*
Anne Day
Anne Day
Dan Hunt
Sean D. Elliot, *The Day*
Jean Santopatre, Fairfield University
Anne Day

103 Susan Magnano
Jonathan Olson
Jean Santopatre, Fairfield University
Anne Day
Sean D. Elliot, *The Day*
Terrance J. Lush
Sean D. Elliot, *The Day*

104 Anne Day
Andrew Douglas Sullivan
Terrance J. Lush
Brett Mickelson
Sean D. Elliot, *The Day*
Pamela Einarsen
Dan Hunt

105 Jean Santopatre,
Fairfield University
Jonathan Olson
Peter Casolino
Peter Casolino
Anne Day
Rikki Ward
Jean Santopatre, Fairfield University

107 George Ruhe
Bob Falcetti
Rikki Ward
Anne Day
Rikki Ward
Bob Falcetti
Rikki Ward

112 Jonathan Olson
Anne Day
Anne Day
Rikki Ward
Anne Day
Anne Day
Michael J. Ivins

113 Wendy Carlson
Michael J. Ivins
Anne Day
Jonathan Olson
Anne Day
Anne Day
Anne Day

120 Brett Mickelson
Andrew Douglas Sullivan
E.B. Ruark
Andrew Douglas Sullivan
Jean Santopatre, Fairfield University
Brett Mickelson
Rikki Ward

121 Rikki Ward
Jean Santopatre, Fairfield University
Jean Santopatre, Fairfield University
Brett Mickelson
Peter Casolino
Dan Hunt
Jean Santopatre, Fairfield University

122 Rikki Ward
Rikki Ward
Wendy Carlson
Anne Day
John Kane, Silver Sun Studio
Sean D. Elliot, *The Day*
Rikki Ward

123 Patrick Raycraft
Anne Day
Jean Santopatre, Fairfield University
Wendy Carlson
Bob Falcetti
Wendy Carlson
Rikki Ward

124 Anne Day
Rikki Ward
John Kane, Silver Sun Studio
Anne Day
Anne Day
Peter Casolino
Jean Santopatre, Fairfield University

125 Patrick Raycraft
John Kane, Silver Sun Studio
Anne Day
Rikki Ward
Patrick Raycraft
Anne Day
Christian Abraham, *Connecticut Post*

128 John Kane, Silver Sun Studio
Sean D. Elliot, *The Day*
Anne Day
Jean Santopatre, Fairfield University
Anne Day
Andrew Douglas Sullivan
Andrew Douglas Sullivan

129 Patrick Raycraft
Brett Mickelson
Terrance J. Lush
Sean D. Elliot, *The Day*
Patrick Raycraft
Brett Mickelson
Sean D. Elliot, *The Day*

130 Dan Hunt
Jean Santopatre, Fairfield University
Susan Magnano
Gavin Shapiro
Dan Hunt
Sean D. Elliot, *The Day*
Dan Hunt

131 Sean D. Elliot, *The Day*
Dan Hunt
Sean D. Elliot, *The Day*
Dan Hunt
Sean D. Elliot, *The Day*
Jean Santopatre, Fairfield University
Michael J. Ivins

134 Cloe Poisson,
The Hartford Courant
C.M. Glover, outtosee.com
Marc-Yves Regis II,
The Hartford Courant
Michael J. Ivins
Marc-Yves Regis II,
The Hartford Courant
Rikki Ward
Marc-Yves Regis II,
The Hartford Courant

135 Anne Day
Rikki Ward
Jean Santopatre, Fairfield University
Rikki Ward
Jean Santopatre, Fairfield University
Marc-Yves Regis II,
The Hartford Courant
Rikki Ward

Staff

The *America 24/7* series was imagined years ago by our friend Oscar Dystel, a publishing legend whose vision and enthusiasm have been a source of great inspiration.

We also wish to express our gratitude to our truly visionary publisher, DK.

Rick Smolan, Project Director
David Elliot Cohen, Project Director

Administrative
Katya Able, Operations Director
Gina Privitere, Communications Director
Chuck Gathard, Technology Director
Kim Shannon, Photographer Relations Director
Erin O'Connor, Photographer Relations Intern
Leslie Hunter, Partnership Director
Annie Polk, Publicity Manager
John McAlester, Website Manager
Alex Notides, Office Manager
C. Thomas Hardin, State Photography Coordinator

Design
Brad Zucroff, Creative Director
Karen Mullarkey, Photography Director
Judy Zimola, Production Manager
David Simoni, Production Designer
Mary Dias, Production Designer
Heidi Madison, Associate Picture Editor
Don McCartney, Production Designer
Diane Dempsey Murray, Production Designer
Jan Rogers, Associate Picture Editor
Bill Shore, Production Designer and Image Artist
Larry Nighswander, Senior Picture Editor
Bill Marr, Sarah Leen, Senior Picture Editors
Peter Truskier, Workflow Consultant
Jim Birkenseer, Workflow Consultant

Editorial
Maggie Canon, Managing Editor
Curt Sanburn, Senior Editor
Teresa L. Trego, Production Editor
Lea Aschkenas, Writer
Olivia Boler, Writer
Korey Capozza, Writer
Beverly Hanly, Writer
Bridgett Novak, Writer
Alison Owings, Writer
Fred Raker, Writer
Joe Wolff, Writer
Elise O'Keefe, Copy Chief
Daisy Hernández, Copy Editor
Jennifer Wolfe, Copy Editor

Infographic Design
Nigel Holmes

Literary Agent
Carol Mann, The Carol Mann Agency

Legal Counsel
Barry Reder, Coblentz, Patch, Duffy & Bass, LLP
Phil Feldman, Coblentz, Patch, Duffy & Bass, LLP
Gabe Perle, Ohlandt, Greeley, Ruggiero & Perle, LLP
Jon Hart, Dow, Lohnes & Albertson, PLLC
Mike Hays, Dow, Lohnes & Albertson, PLLC
Stephen Pollen, Warshaw Burstein, Cohen, Schlesinger & Kuh, LLP
Rick Pappas

Accounting and Finance
Rita Dulebohn, Accountant
Robert Powers, Calegari, Morris & Co. Accountants
Eugene Blumberg, Blumberg & Associates
Arthur Langhaus, KLS Professional Advisors Group, Inc.

Picture Editors
J. David Ake, Associated Press
Caren Alpert, formerly *Health* magazine
Simon Barnett, *Newsweek*
Caroline Couig, *San Jose Mercury News*
Mike Davis, formerly *National Geographic*
Michel duCille, *Washington Post*
Deborah Dragon, *Rolling Stone*
Victor Fisher, formerly Associated Press
Frank Folwell, *USA Today*
MaryAnne Golon, *Time*
Liz Grady, formerly *National Geographic*
Randall Greenwell, *San Francisco Chronicle*
C. Thomas Hardin, formerly *Louisville Courier-Journal*
Kathleen Hennessy, *San Francisco Chronicle*
Scot Jahn, *U.S. News & World Report*
Steve Jessmore, *Flint Journal*
John Kaplan, University of Florida
Kim Komenich, *San Francisco Chronicle*
Eliane Laffont, *Hachette Filipacchi Media*
Jean-Pierre Laffont, *Hachette Filipacchi Media*
Andrew Locke, MSNBC
Jose Lopez, *The New York Times*
Maria Mann, formerly AFP
Bill Marr, formerly *National Geographic*
Michele McNally, *Fortune*
James Merithew, *San Francisco Chronicle*
Eric Meskauskas, *New York Daily News*
Maddy Miller, *People* magazine
Michelle Molloy, *Newsweek*
Dolores Morrison, *New York Daily News*
Karen Mullarkey, formerly *Newsweek, Rolling Stone, Sports Illustrated*
Larry Nighswander, Ohio University School of Visual Communication
Jim Preston, *Baltimore Sun*
Sarah Rozen, formerly *Entertainment Weekly*
Mike Smith, *The New York Times*
Neal Ulevich, formerly Associated Press

Website and Digital Systems
Jeff Burchell, Applications Engineer

Television Documentary
Sandy Smolan, Producer/Director
Rick King, Producer/Director
Bill Medsker, Producer

Video News Release
Mike Cerre, Producer/Director

Digital Pond
Peter Hogg
Kris Knight
Roger Graham
Philip Bond
Frank De Pace
Lisa Li

Senior Advisors
Jennifer Erwitt, Strategic Advisor
Tom Walker, Creative Advisor
Megan Smith, Technology Advisor
Jon Kamen, Media and Partnership Advisor
Mark Greenberg, Partnership Advisor
Patti Richards, Publicity Advisor
Cotton Coulson, Mission Control Advisor

Executive Advisors
Sonia Land
George Craig
Carole Bidnick

Advisors
Chris Anderson
Samir Arora
Russell Brown
Craig Cline
Gayle Cline
Harlan Felt
George Fisher
Phillip Moffitt
Clement Mok
Laureen Seeger
Richard Saul Wurman

DK Publishing
Bill Barry
Joanna Bull
Therese Burke
Sarah Coltman
Christopher Davis
Todd Fries
Dick Heffernan
Jay Henry
Stuart Jackman
Stephanie Jackson
Chuck Lang
Sharon Lucas
Cathy Melnicki
Nicola Munro
Eunice Paterson
Andrew Welham

Colourscan
Jimmy Tsao
Eddie Chia
Richard Law
Josephine Yam
Paul Koh
Chee Cheng Yeong
Dan Kang

Chief Morale Officer
Goose, the dog